INTERPRETING
the
TEXT

*A Critical Introduction to the Theory
and Practice of Literary Interpretation*

K. M. Newton

St. Martin's Press
New York

First published in the United States of America in 1990

Printed in Great Britain

ISBN 0-312-04757-6 cloth
ISBN 0-312-04758-4 paper

Library of Congress Cataloging-in-Publication Data

Newton, K. M.
    Interpreting the text: a critical introduction to the theory and
practice of literary interpretation / K. M. Newton.
        p.   cm.
    Includes bibliographical references.
    ISBN 0-312-04757-6.—ISBN 0-312-04758-4 (pkb.)
    1. Literature—History and criticism—Theory, etc.   2. Criticism.
I. Title.
PN441.N45   1990   90-8190
801'.95—dc20   CIP

Contents

Preface

A striking feature of literary criticism in the twentieth century, particularly in the English-speaking world, has been the emphasis on the interpretation of the text. This book charts the development of literary interpretation, in terms of both theory and practice, from its emergence in the 1930s in the work of the New Critics up to the interpretative practice of several of the most influential contemporary critical schools. During the 1950s and 1960s when New Critical interpretation was the dominant form of critical activity, especially in America, other forms of criticism tended to be judged by how far they could be a help to critics engaged in interpretation. But the very success of interpretative criticism created a crisis when it became clear that interpretations of what were regarded as the major works of the literary canon seemed to be accumulating uncontrollably. Opponents of interpretation who asserted that there were already enough readings of texts in existence and that criticism should develop alternatives to it began to be listened to seriously. As I try to show in this study, interpretation has survived such attacks. This can be seen from contemporary critical practice in which interpretation is still central, although the kind of interpretations produced by the most influential critics of the past twenty years are significantly different from those associated with the New Criticism.

What is clear from the current critical scene is that although interpretation continues to be practised, there is no consensus as to how literary texts should be interpreted. Thus several different and opposed modes of interpretation coexist at the present time. Many commentators on this situation have seen it as a recipe for relativism or anarchy in literary criticism. But a more positive response is possible. The reader has been liberated to a considerable extent, for more than at any stage in the past readers have a choice as to how they may read texts. Readers have available for their consideration several competing critical approaches which explicitly or implicitly seek to persuade them of their superiority as modes of interpretation.

This book offers a survey of the theory and practice of many of the most influential forms of twentieth-century critical interpretation but perhaps its more important aim is to try to help readers make a more informed choice as to which interpretative mode or modes they choose to favour. I also consider various attacks on or alternatives to interpretation since another possibility is rejecting interpretative criticism for some non- or anti-interpretative critical mode. I have attempted to give as clear and as fair an account of the interpretative approaches I discuss as possible but I have also commented critically on them because I believe that no mode of literary interpretation is invulnerable to criticism. These critical comments are not, however, intended to form part of a systematic critique derived from a committed position that I hold and in relation to which I judge alternative positions; rather, they attempt to call attention to certain problems or incoherences that anyone who identifies with or who is attracted by a particular position should be prepared to consider.

As will be clear from my final chapter, rather than being totally committed to one particular critical position I value the pluralism of contemporary interpretation even though this has created a power struggle between critical modes striving for dominance. Of course, if one engages in the practice of interpretation one will have to operate in a predominant mode but this does not entail the rejection of other approaches as invalid or mean that one cannot adopt a different interpretative mode on another occasion. But an awareness of the differences between critical positions and the issues that underlie conflict and debate encourages interpreters of literature at every level to think critically about their own practice. This seems to me to be healthy for criticism. Criticism also develops through argument and debate between different positions and through the need to confront objections or difficulties. I hope this book may make some contribution to this dialectical process.

I accept, however, that such a defence of pluralism is open to attack. It can be argued that change is created not by pluralists but by those who identify uncompromisingly with a given position.

Feminist critics, black critics, critics who are committed to a particular political persuasion clearly feel that pluralism is a luxury they cannot afford. Any changes that even a pluralism which encourages argument and debate may bring about are likely to seem insufficient to such critics: does it not lead to weak liberalism or finally create critical fragmentation? Perhaps three possible options suggest themselves most strongly to anyone interested in literature and criticism at the present time: that one should adopt a particular position because one believes it has greater validity or explanatory power than others; that in the present political climate it is necessary to give total commitment to a chosen position even if one accepts pluralism as theoretically valid; that one should accept pluralism positively and encourage continuing critical debate. Although I favour the last option I recognise that strong arguments could be put forward for the other two. I hope this book may help readers to decide where they stand on such questions.

Versions of two of the chapters have already appeared in print: Chapter 3 in *The British Journal of Aesthetics* and Chapter 5 in *English*; I am grateful to the Oxford University Press for permission to reprint. I should also like to thank my colleagues Stan Smith and R. J. C. Watt for critical comments and suggestions for improvement. I also have to thank Jackie Jones for giving me the idea of writing a book on this topic.

Ken Newton
Dundee 1989

CHAPTER 1

Introduction: interpretation and literary criticism

In a broad sense all literary criticism is concerned with inter-pretation. Critics have constantly had to make decisions that involve interpretative acts: what mode or genre does a text belong to? what function does its style serve? does it succeed in what it sets out to do? what criteria are appropriate in deciding questions of artistic success or failure? how should one relate a text to 'extrinsic' factors, such as biographical, historical, political, or religious con-siderations? Even critics hostile to interpretation as it has developed in the twentieth century admit that it is fundamental to literary criticism: 'Of course, in one sense all projects involve interpretation: selecting facts that require explanation is already an act of interpre-tation, as is positing descriptive categories and organizing them into theories.'[1]

In the twentieth century, however, the term 'interpretation' has tended to be used in the more restricted sense of a reading of a particular text which is concerned with such questions as the meaning and significance of the text as a whole, its thematic structure, the relation between the semantic and the linguistic or stylistic aspects of the text. As one modern literary theorist puts it: 'An interpretation . . . is a hypothesis about the most general organization and coherence of all the elements that form a literary text.'[2] It is this conception of interpretation that has tended to dominate twentieth-century literary criticism.

If one reads the work of pre-twentieth-century literary critics one finds little of this type of interpretation. The criticism of Dr Johnson or Matthew Arnold, for example - arguably the greatest English critics of the eighteenth and nineteenth centuries respectively -

seems hardly to be concerned with interpretation in the modern sense. Interpretation is scarcely present in the work of literary historians or literary scholars who tended to dominate criticism in the late nineteenth and early twentieth century, such as George Saintsbury or Herbert Grierson. Critics like Johnson or Arnold are mainly concerned with judging or evaluating how successful particular works or authors are in artistic terms. Johnson writes of Milton: 'The defects and faults of *Paradise Lost*, for faults and defects every work of man must have, it is the business of the impartial critic to discover.'[3] It would not have occurred to Johnson, I think, that interpreting the poem was necessary before considering the question of its faults and defects. It was enough merely to read and understand the poem. No distinction would have been made between reading and understanding and interpretation. And since one could judge a work only after one had read it and understood its meaning, there was no need to mention the subject explicitly in writing criticism.

A major difference, then, between modern literary criticism and literary criticism of earlier eras is that in most criticism of the past interpreting the text is not seen as being different from reading and understanding it. Merely by understanding the meaning of the language of a text, its cultural references, the literary mode it belongs to – such as lyric, dramatic, epic – one would be in a position to respond critically to that text; there is no need for interpretation beyond that. This view can still be found today both among critics antagonistic to developments in modern criticism and among general readers who often complain that critics are over-ingenious and 'read things into' texts.

The majority of modern critics, however, make a distinction between reading and understanding on the one hand and interpretation on the other: that is, they take the view that, given a certain linguistic competence and cultural awareness, anyone can 'read' *Paradise Lost* or any other literary text but interpretations of that work will differ. Of course, even the most literal reading of any text involves a minimal degree of interpretation, but in twentieth-century criticism interpretation has been seen as an activity in itself. Critics such as Johnson or Arnold would obviously have been aware that there could be disagreements about literary judgements but they would not, I think, have seen these as being rooted in different interpretations. Rather, they would see the text's meaning and significance as stable and would regard conflicting judgements as arising from different responses among critics as a result of their having, for instance, opposed philosophical or religious outlooks.

It would be absurd, of course, to argue that only twentieth-century critics have realised that literary texts are complex in meaning. Earlier critics were aware of such matters as allegory. Works such as Spenser's *The Faerie Queene* or Bunyan's *The Pilgrim's Progress* clearly had levels of meaning that underlay their surface narratives. Yet it could be argued that the decipherment of allegory is still not interpretation in the modern sense. Once it was clear that a work was meant to be read allegorically from certain signs within the text, then it was merely a matter of reading that work with the appropriate attention in order to discern and understand its various levels of meaning. Thus when one reads in *The Faerie Queene* of a knight who bears a bloody cross on his breast, who carries a battered shield, who serves Gloriana 'That greatest Glorious Queene of *Faerie* lond', and so on, any competent reader of literary texts will recognise that one is in the presence of allegory and read accordingly.

Yet a consideration of allegory reveals that interpretation is not merely a modern phenomenon but that it played a role in literary criticism even in the classical era. For example, a work attributed to 'Heraclitus', probably written in the first century AD, interprets Homer's works allegorically in order to defend them against Plato's claim that Homer depicted the Gods and his human characters in such a way as to promote impiety and immorality. 'Heraclitus' does not deny that Homer's works are, if read as straightforward narratives, open to this charge but argues that Homer intended his works to be read allegorically and not literally. However, Homer did not advertise this fact because he wished to protect the truths embodied in his works from the misunderstandings of an ignorant audience. His piety and adherence to moral principles are thus implicit in his narratives.[4]

This is an interpretation in the modern sense since it is distinct from merely reading and understanding Homer's text. It is the critic who takes the interpretative decision to read the text allegorically. Such critical practice is justifiable, for though some allegories draw attention to themselves in the manner of *The Faerie Queene* and *The Pilgrim's Progress* this is not necessarily the case with all allegories. Once the decision to read a text allegorically is taken it follows that it will be read differently and will take on a different meaning. The question of allegory is particularly central to literary interpretation because virtually any literary text can be read as an allegory even though it may display no explicit signs of allegory. Indeed, during the medieval period classical texts and books of the Old Testament were read allegorically as embodying Christian meanings even though their authors could not have intended them to be read in Christian terms. Another example of interpretation in the modern sense being practised in the classical period is Porphyry's essay, 'On the cave of the nymphs', in which he explicates in detail fourteen lines of Homer. This has been described by a modern critic as 'the first example of "new criticism", or at least the first serious attempt at *explication de texte*, in that Porphyry carefully examines every image in the passage as part of a deliberate fiction that needs to be interpreted.'[5]

Such examples of explicit literary interpretation before the modern era are comparatively rare. In most pre-twentieth-century criticism interpretation tends to be either indirect or undeveloped. But it is obvious that the cultural preoccupations of particular periods condition how literary works are read and this necessarily introduces an element of interpretation into the critical process. One of the most obvious instances of this is Blake's assertion that in *Paradise Lost* Milton was 'of the Devil's party without knowing it'. Blake, of course, does not go on to justify this opinion in an interpretation of the poem as a whole, but he provides the basis for an entirely different way of reading and understanding the work from that which assumes that it condemns Satan from a conventional Christian standpoint. A major difference between literary criticism before the twentieth century and modern criticism is not that the former does not undertake interpretation but that, with a few exceptions, it does not develop it. One of the most important facts about twentieth-century criticism is that it has created the technical means to develop interpretative comments such as Blake's into a detailed reading of the whole work.

Blake's view of *Paradise Lost* is a particularly extreme example of how a radical act of interpretation can fundamentally change the way in which a work is read and understood, but in most pre-twentieth-century criticism interpretation is much more indirect. Challenging interpretative statements, such as Blake's, are not to be found, for example, in the criticism of Matthew Arnold. It might be interest-

ing, therefore, to look at Arnold on *Paradise Lost* in order to discover
whether or not interpretative assumptions are nevertheless present.
At first glance Arnold's comments on the poem seem merely
descriptive and evaluative:

> Milton, from one end of *Paradise Lost* to the other, is in his diction and
> rhythm constantly a great artist in the great style. Whatever may be said
> as to the subject of his poem, as to the conditions under which he
> received his subject and treated it, that praise, at any rate, is assured to
> him.[6]

Indeed, Arnold avoids discussing the subject matter of the poem and
confines himself to what he regards as uncontroversial: the greatness
of Milton's style. Yet this view of the poem is not neutral but is
governed by assumptions which Arnold brings to the poem and
which reveal that his response to the poem cannot be separated from
interpretation.

At the beginning of his essay Arnold regrets the fact that the
Anglo-Saxon race tends to value the comparatively modest achievements of the majority of people more than the excellence of the
attainments of the few. Arnold fears this tendency of thought –
which he believes will promote ideas of equality, democracy, and as a
consequence vulgarity – since it will undermine civilisation and
culture as he understands them. He points out that 'In our race are
thousands of readers, presently there will be millions, who know not
a word of Greek and Latin, and will never learn these languages.'
The value of Milton's style is that it can provide such readers with
some awareness of the grand style of classical poets: 'All the Anglo-
Saxon contagion, all the flood of Anglo-Saxon commonness, beats
vainly against the great style but cannot shake it, and has to accept its
triumph.'[7] For Arnold the significance of Milton's style is that in a
culture threatened by commonness and vulgarity it is 'a leaven, and a
power' which may help to resist or ameliorate such vices. Milton's
style, therefore, is interpreted as embodying élitist values which are
alien to democratic forces. In the twentieth century, in the criticism
of T. S. Eliot and especially of F. R. Leavis, Milton's style was
interpreted in quite a different way: as a sign that Milton's work was
cut off from the sources of vitality within English as a spoken
language and thus constituted a symptom of what Eliot called
'dissociation of sensibility',[8] the breakdown of a more organic
culture.

From a philosophical point of view one can argue that interpretation is necessarily a part of all literary criticism, even the kind of criticism that appears only to be taking the words of the text at their face value, on the grounds that reading and interpretation cannot be separated in relation to literary discourse. With non-literary discourses certain constraints compel those discourses to be read in a particular way. They are so bound up with human purposes that one cannot, for example, 'allegorise' sets of instructions, scientific treatises, historical documents, without completely undermining these purposes. But literary discourse cannot be limited to a particular set of human purposes which places constraints upon how it must be read. It exists beyond any pragmatic context that could impose such constraints. Thus there is no reason, for example as I suggested above, why any literary text should not be interpreted as an allegory if a reader wishes to do so. In other words, how a literary text is read is always a matter of choice since there is no necessity that compels one to read it in a particular way. Logically this means that all forms of literary reading and understanding are interpretations, even if one takes the words in their most obviously literal sense, because other possibilities of reading always exist. Anyone who engages in reading literature and tries to communicate or discuss his or her response with someone else is inevitably involved in trying to justify a particular interpretation or to persuade the other of the validity of that interpretation.

The forms of literary criticism that seem to have least connection with interpretation are formalist criticism which ignores content and focuses on formal and stylistic matters, and especially textual criticism. It is fairly clear that there are interpretative consequences in formalist criticism. Aristotle's *Poetics* is probably the most influential piece of formalist criticism ever written. Although he intends to be descriptive when he asserts that 'mimesis' or imitation is the common principle of all the arts, this concept functions normatively to control how works of art are perceived and as a result interpreted. Different formalistic concepts, such as that art is not imitative but expressive of emotional states or the early Russian Formalist view that the function of art is to 'defamiliarise' one's habitual perception of the world, reveal the interpretative force underlying a formalist approach by demonstrating that other viewpoints are possible and that, for example, a tragic hero would be perceived very differently depending on which set of formalist views the reader held.

Modern textual criticism, with its aim of establishing what an author actually wrote by removing corruptions which may have entered the text during the process of its transmission, on the surface seems to be removed from interpretation. Editors of literary texts could claim that they need have no particular interpretation of a text in mind when they undertake an editorial task but of course interpretation in the broad sense must operate. For instance, the editor may have to decide on such matters as whether to use an earlier or later edition as the basis of the newly edited text and this cannot be done without having certain assumptions and principles in mind which will have interpretative consequences. Also, if one asks a textual critic why one should worry about textual or bibliographical matters, the critic would no doubt assert that a text that contains corruptions will not reflect fully an author's intentions and purposes and thus could mislead the reader. There would seem little point in textual criticism, at least as it is perceived by modern textual critics, if the critic did not regard authorial intention and the work as the product of its time, as having overriding importance. It could be argued, however, that the notion of a single authorial intention governing the production of texts is incoherent – for example, on the grounds that other people in addition to the author may influence the production of a text or that an author is not a single entity but multiple since in the course of writing and rewriting a text over time the authorial self will change – and one needs in consequence to question conventional editorial procedures. The fact that even textual critics cannot operate without certain preconceptions and that these can be challenged makes it clear that no form of literary criticism can escape interpretation. But although textual critics may be willing to admit that they cannot proceed without assumptions which will have interpretative consequences, nevertheless they could claim that their activities do not involve interpreting literary texts in the narrow sense.

Even this claim needs to be qualified. One of the major tasks of the textual critic is to decide which reading to prefer if variants exist or what emendations should be made in passages that appear to be corrupt. In taking such decisions the critic will need some conception of the total work, and interpretation will necessarily enter into that conception. One can illustrate this easily by looking briefly at one of the most famous textual cruces in Shakespeare. Many twentieth-century editors of *Hamlet* have emended the line

'O that this too too solid flesh would melt' (I, ii, 129) to read 'O that this too too sullied flesh would melt'. 'Solid' appears in the Folio text of the play, but the first and second Quartos have 'sallied' which, it is argued, is an older version of 'sullied'. It is clear that the reasons for editors' preference for 'sullied' were largely based on interpretative grounds. J. Dover Wilson, who was the first editor to print 'sullied' in a modern edition, favoured a psychological interpretation of the play. Hamlet, he declared, in this speech 'is thinking of the "kindless". . . incestuous marriage as a personal defilement'.[9] Fredson Bowers, one of the best known of textual critics, also prefers 'sullied' to 'solid' and this preference is likewise governed by interpretative considerations: 'In this particular case I fancy the choice is important on grounds of meaning, for the word *sullied* supports my contention that Hamlet feels his natural, or inherited, honour has been soiled by the taint of his mother's dishonourable blood.'[10] And for Harold Jenkins, editor of the Arden edition of the play, '*sullied* enlarges the meaning as *solid* does not. . . . The suggestion of contamination and self-disgust begins an important dramatic motif.'[11] Even modern editors who decide to accept the Folio reading and print 'solid' often justify this choice on interpretative grounds. Thus the editor of the recent Oxford edition of *Hamlet*, G. R. Hibbard, gives the following reasons for his preference of 'solid':

> It is the flesh, the solid earthy part of himself that Hamlet wants to shed, and in doing so he comes very close indeed to the poet of *Sonnets* 44 and 45, wishing 'the dull substance of [his] flesh . . . so much of earth and water wrought' were turned to thought, and lamenting that because two of the elements in his make-up, 'slight air and purging fire', are already with his friend, his life, dependent on earth and water alone, 'Sinks down to death, oppressed with melancholy'.[12]

One can go further and argue that textual scholarship is inseparable from interpretation at an even more fundamental level. The linguistic practice of a writer such as Shakespeare is highly figurative, characterised by word-play and numerous 'excesses' if judged by the standards of 'common sense'. Yet any textual critic must approach the text with expectations of some sort as to how it ought to make sense. In the case of earlier textual editors, such as Pope, these expectations created an over-prescriptive set of norms which led to Shakespeare's text being adapted to eighteenth-century taste. Even though modern editors reject such a prescriptive approach, they cannot avoid bringing certain assumptions or criteria to the text if they are to recognise corruptions and have any chance of restoring what they think the author originally wrote. Interpretation is therefore integral to the editorial process since there will never be complete congruence between the editor's concept of how the language of the text makes sense and the linguistic practice of its author. Indeed, editorial practice is likely to be particularly problematic if editors merely assume that a writer like Shakespeare shares their norms as to how language can and should make sense. As Christopher Norris, writing about Shakespeare from a post-structuralist position, has argued:

> Outside theological tradition, no body of writings has been subjected to more in the way of interpretative comment and textual scholarship. Yet the upshot of this activity . . . is to cast increasing doubt on the power of criticism to distinguish between the two.[13]

It seems clear from the above discussion that interpretation has always been an intrinsic part of criticism and it is not purely a modern critical development. What has changed in the modern period is that critics have regarded interpretation as much more central to literary criticism than previous critics had done and they have developed techniques of interpretation which enable them to write a kind of criticism that had rarely been attempted before the twentieth century. But the question remains as to whether it has been a good thing that interpretation has played such a major role in twentieth-century literary criticism. Before coming to any decision about this one needs first of all to consider why interpretation has become so dominant in the twentieth century.

CHAPTER 2

The New Criticism
and the rise of interpretation

The interpretation of texts is not, of course, confined to literature. A historian, for example, is also involved in the practice of interpreting texts with a view to deciding their historical meaning and significance. This has been particularly true since historiography adopted the viewpoint that texts should be related to the period which produced them rather than judged from the standpoint of the present. To use the terms of the first chapter: historians who viewed the past as essentially the same as the present and thus to be judged by the same standards merely 'read' and 'understood' historical documents, whereas historians who viewed a period of the past as intrinsically different from the present had to go beyond reading and understanding to interpretation. This distinction is implicit in Hugh Trevor-Roper's discussion of the differences between eighteenth-century historiography and the approach of later historians:

> The achievement of the great 18th-century historians was immense. . . . But their philosophy was essentially linear, and their weakness was a lack of sympathy with the past. . . . Their fundamental error was to measure the past by the present, as if the values of the present were absolute, and those of the past relative, so that the present was entitled to pass judgment on the past.

The major historians in the nineteenth century and later, in contrast, endeavoured to think themselves into the world of the past:

> To see the past in its own terms; to deduce it directly from its spontaneous records, widely defined – that is, from its literature, its traditions, its mythology, its portraiture, as well as from its public documents, to respect its autonomy, to sympathise with its coherent assumptions, and at the same time not to surrender to mere nostalgia or

lose one's position in the present – this requires a nice balance of imagination and realism.[1]

In other words, the historian must interpret the past. But once this change had taken place in historiography, there was considerable general agreement among historians concerning interpretative practice, and it is only comparatively recently that this has been questioned by writers such as Hayden White. In literary interpretation, however, there is little general agreement about what should be proper interpretative practice; debate about this is one of the dominant issues of twentieth-century criticism.

Perhaps the field that most resembles literature in this respect is the study of religious texts. Before the question of interpretation began to play such a prominent role in literary criticism, it was in the sphere of religion that the major debates concerning interpretation took place. Indeed, 'hermeneutics', the science or theory of interpretation, which I shall discuss in the next chapter, had its origins in the interpretation of religious texts. Looked at in broad terms, cultures are constituted by the triumph of particular interpretations of the world and cultures run into crisis when these interpretations (or belief systems or ideologies) are challenged by alternative interpretations. Until the eighteenth century Christianity formed the basis of the belief system of the West and the major questions of interpretation revolved round religious issues. It was clearly of central importance to Christianity as a belief system, for example, whether a religious text like the Bible should be interpreted in accordance with the doctrines of the Church, or should be directly understood as the word of God, or interpreted as a product of its times like any other historical text. Whichever interpretative decision was made clearly had crucial consequences for the culture at large.

In modern times the emergence of science and scientific rationalism as the dominant belief system of the West has relegated the question as to how religious texts are to be interpreted to comparatively minor significance since such texts no longer seem particularly relevant to a secularised society and thus their interpretation has come to be regarded as no longer of central cultural importance. But science itself, unlike religion in the past, has not been able to generate debate in the wider cultural sphere, with the result that the decline in the power of religion in Western society has created something of a cultural vacuum. This, perhaps, helps to account for the fact that in the twentieth century the major debates concerning interpretation have moved from the area of religion to that of literature. It is in this context that the work of I. A. Richards is crucial.

Richards has a strong claim to be regarded as the most important influence on the New Criticism which has been most responsible for the domination of interpretation in modern criticism. Although modern literary criticism is generally accepted as beginning with the Russian Formalists around the time of the Russian Revolution rather than with Richards in the 1920s, the Formalists' major concern was with literature as a unique use of language and not with questions of meaning or interpretation, as I shall discuss later. Richards's book *Practical Criticism*, published in 1929, was particularly significant since it persuaded many critics and readers of the need for a close reading of literary texts in which one considered how far their formal and semantic elements cohered as part of a unified structure. By presenting students with poems as pure texts without any indication as to who wrote them Richards endeavoured to show how inadequately poetry was read even by readers from whom one might expect reasonable competence, namely Cambridge students. The method Richards adopted clearly prepared the way for the New Critical approach to interpretation. Since he presented his poetry readers only with texts without extra-textual indicators as to how they should be interpreted, what readers were being implicitly asked to do was to justify a reading which could account for as much of the data of the text as possible. With no other interpretative pointers, that was the only way in which one reading of a poem could be judged as superior to another. What literary criticism should be doing, therefore, *Practical Criticism* appeared to be saying, was to show that those texts which deserved to be classified as literary could be comprehensively and coherently interpreted so that every element of form and meaning could be seen as an essential part of the text's structure; on the other hand, texts which did not possess literary merit would not survive such scrutiny.

But Richards had a 'more ambitious' aim[2] than merely promoting a more competent reading of poetry. He believed that in the modern era poetry was more central to the culture at large than ever before. Thus the interpretation of poetic texts was as important in the modern era as the interpretation of religious texts had been in the past. In one of his most influential essays, 'Poetry and beliefs', first published in *Science and Poetry* in 1926, Richards discusses the significance of literature in a world in which science is dominant and religion no longer has the power to direct the moral and social lives of human beings, at least in the West. He equates science with tests of verification which lead to the creation of truths about which there can be little or no dispute. But in what he calls the realm of 'emotive utterance',[3] which human beings inhabit most of the time, this kind of scientific truth hardly applies. Here one is in the presence of what Richards calls 'pseudo-statement'. In the past, of course, religious doctrine claimed that it embodied certain truths which (unlike scientific truth) were integrally connected with the realm of 'emotive utterance'. But Richards relegates religion, together with such domains as ethics and metaphysics – which it had supported and connected with the concept of truth – to the level of pseudo-statement.

Poetry or literature, in consequence, attains cultural centrality since it is pure pseudo-statement. It does not demand, unlike both science and religious doctrine, that one believe it to be true. What therefore is its relation to truth since, as Richards points out, poetry is constantly making statements? Because there are no tests that can be applied to establish either the truth or falsity of poetic statements in the manner of scientific experiments, they can only be categorised as pure pseudo-statements, by which Richards means, as he pointed out in a footnote added in 1935, that they are 'not necessarily false in any sense. It is merely a form of words whose scientific truth or falsity is irrelevant to the purpose in hand' ('Poetry and beliefs', hereafter cited as 'PB', 60). The 'pseudo-statements' of religion, in contrast, cannot be seen in the same way since, by demanding to be regarded as true, they reject 'pseudo-statement' as a categorisation. But clearly, for Richards, there is no going back to the sphere of religious truth and, by extension, to the interpretation of religious texts, unless read as literature: only literature can fill the gap created by the rise of science as the realm of truth in a verifiable sense and the loss of faith in religious truth:

> We need no [factual or verifiable] beliefs, and indeed we must have none, if we are to read *King Lear*. Pseudo-statements to which we attach no belief and statements proper, such as science provides, cannot conflict. It is only when we introduce inappropriate kinds of believing into poetry that danger arises. To do so is from this point of view a profanation of poetry. ('PB', 61-2)

Richards's use of the word 'profanation' in the above passage shows a clear link between his conception of poetry and religion. The literary text becomes, as the New Critic W. K. Wimsatt was to put it, a 'verbal icon',[4] with the advantage that its statements do not demand belief or aspire to 'truth' in an absolute sense as religious statements do.

The influence of Matthew Arnold on Richards is apparent, since in his essay 'The study of poetry' Arnold had asserted: 'Our religion has materialised itself in the fact, in the supposed fact; it has attached its emotion to the fact, and now the fact is failing it.' In contrast, 'Poetry attaches its emotion to the idea; the idea *is* the fact. . . . Without poetry, our science will appear incomplete; and most of what now passes with us for religion and philosophy will be replaced by poetry.'[5]

T. S. Eliot was also a major influence on Richards. In a passage strongly affected by Eliot's *The Waste Land*, Richards claims that in the modern world pervaded by

> A sense of desolation, of uncertainty, of futility . . . the only impulses which seem strong enough to continue unflagging are commonly so crude that, to more finely developed individuals, they hardly seem worth having. Such people cannot live by warmth, food, fighting, drink and sex alone. ('PB', 64)

Science has broken the 'Magical View' of a link between knowledge of the world and spiritual knowledge, 'that old dream of a perfect knowledge which would guarantee perfect life to retain its sanction' ('PB', 65). Yet human beings need a sense of *'raison d'être'* and this can come only from 'the imaginative life [which] is its own justification' ('PB', 66). And the greatest product of the imaginative life is poetry.

But if poetry cannot provide certain knowledge or beliefs which have the status of truth but only pseudo-statement, how can it fill this cultural vacuum? For Richards it is the psychological dimension of poetry that is important. A poem is a coherent ordering of impulses and when it is read by a competent reader, this coherence is transferred from poem to reader, enabling the reader to achieve a sense of wholeness of being. The New Critics, who emerged as a force in American criticism in the 1930s and have been dominant until fairly recently, although greatly influenced by Richards disapproved of his emphasis on psychology. They shifted the focus from psychology, either at the level of author or reader, to the poem as a structure of words which had an independent existence. Meaning is central but one does not read a poem to discover a paraphrasable meaning. In a poem, meaning, structure and form interact in such a way that the one cannot be separated from the other. A central doctrine of the New Critics was the inseparability of form and content.

Here one can see similarities between them and the Russian Formalists. Like the New Critics they insisted on the inseparability of form and content, and their interest was in the literary text as object, not in the intention of the author or the psychology of the reader. But whereas the New Critics saw form and meaning as one – that is, they viewed the literary text as an unparaphrasable pseudo-statement that possessed unique semantic functions – the Russian Formalists completely subordinated meaning to form. Their interest was in what makes certain texts have the unique status of being literary. As Roman Jakobson put it: 'the subject of literary science is not literature, but literariness, i.e. that which makes a given work a literary work.'[6]

Initially the Russian Formalists emphasised the concept of *ostranenie* or defamiliarisation, that is, how works of art create devices which undermine habitual modes of perception and allow the reader to see the world from a fresh perspective. Thus the 'content', even of a novelist in the realistic tradition, such as Tolstoy, is discussed solely in formal terms by Shklovsky in relation to its defamiliarisation of the reader's habitual perspectives. Works by such writers should not be understood as representing reality mimetically but as using formal means to renew the reader's perception of the world. Thus 'content' becomes form. As examples, Shklovsky cites how Tolstoy in one of his stories uses a horse as narrator and how in *War and Peace* he describes 'whole battles as if battles were something new'.[7] But given his emphasis on form as defamiliarisation it is not surprising that Shklovsky particularly valued Sterne's anti-novel, *Tristram Shandy*. As Russian Formalism developed, it became less interested in the device as a means of defamiliarising the reader's perception of reality; rather, the emphasis was on the work of literature as an assemblage of devices, some of which would take on a dominating role at the expense of others. Defamiliarisation thus functioned within the literary text and not between text and the reader's habitual mode of perceiving reality.

But whereas for the Russian Formalists the inseparability of form and content meant that meaning was subordinated to form, for the

New Critics form was subordinated to meaning. Thus although both forms of criticism have been called formalism, their concepts of form are very different. This can be seen clearly in an essay by one of the leading New Critics, Cleanth Brooks, entitled 'The formalist critic'. Brooks begins with some fundamental assertions to which he subscribes: 'That literary criticism is a description and an evaluation of its object'; 'That the primary concern of criticism is with the problem of unity – the kind of whole which the literary work forms or fails to form, and the relation of the various parts to each other in building up this whole'; 'That in a successful work, form and content cannot be separated'; 'That form is meaning'. He goes on to state that the critic 'attempts to find a central point of reference from which he can focus upon the structure of the poem or novel', and ends his essay with the following assertion: 'Literature has many "uses" – and critics propose new uses, some of them exciting and spectacular. But all the multiform uses to which literature can be put rest finally upon our knowing what a given work "means". That knowledge is basic.'[8]

The centrality of 'meaning' in New Critical theory created the foundation for the virtual identification of criticism with interpretation which has been a characteristic of the era in which the New Criticism has been dominant. For meaning was clearly not a matter merely of reading and understanding the paraphrasable content of a literary text. The fact that meaning could not be discussed independently of the form of a work made it virtually beyond paraphrase. What the New Critics understood by form was also not form in any traditional sense – that is, objective features like rhythm and metre, structural patterning, generic constraints – but an organic relation between all the elements of a work which fused them together. For the New Critics, therefore, form was seen in spatial terms in that every aspect of a work should cohere beyond the realm of the temporal, as it were, even though literature was a temporal medium that could be read only in time.[9]

But how could the critic interpret the 'meaning' of a text in the New Critical sense if that meaning was unique to that particular text? Since the meaning of a literary text could not be expressed directly, what the New Critic sought to demonstrate was how the formal and semantic elements of a work interacted to manifest the underlying structure of the work's meaning. That was as much as criticism could do. One of the main reasons that the critic could not directly reveal meaning was that the meaning of a text in New Critical terms could not be fully grasped by the rational intelligence; it could only be embodied concretely in the literary work. The influence of Eliot and Richards is crucial here.

Eliot's claim in an essay on the metaphysical poets that a 'dissociation of sensibility' had taken place in the middle of the seventeenth century, a disastrous cultural change that created a radical division in consciousness, was particularly influential on the New Critics. While for the important writers before the onset of the 'dissociation of sensibility' there was no sense of separation between feeling and intellect, for later writers this was no longer the case. Eliot referred to the ability of writers he admired, such as the Jacobean dramatists and the metaphysical poets, to think in terms of feeling: 'In Chapman especially there is a direct sensuous apprehension of thought, or a recreation of thought into feeling, which is exactly what we find in Donne.' Donne, he goes on, included in his poems elements which seemed radically opposed to each other or belonged to different categories of experience, yet he was able to incorporate them within one structure of meaning:

> A thought to Donne was an experience; it modified his sensibility. When a poet's mind is perfectly equipped for its work, it is constantly amalgamating disparate experience; the ordinary man's experience is chaotic, irregular, fragmentary. The latter falls in love, or reads Spinoza, and these two experiences have nothing to do with each other, or with the noise of the typewriter or the smell of cooking; in the mind of the poet these experiences are always forming new wholes.[10]

Clearly, then, the meaning of such a poem was beyond paraphrase and could not be expressed in words other than those of the poem. The poem must therefore be semantically autonomous. The New Critics accepted Eliot's version of literary history and most admired those writers unaffected by the 'dissociation of sensibility': that is, those who had written before it happened, and those modernists, such as Eliot himself, who were trying to overcome it. The task of criticism was to demonstrate the presence of this unity of sensibility, or the lack of it, in poetry.

Richards's distinction between major and minor poems reformulates the 'dissociation of sensibility' in psychological terms. In his *Principles of Literary Criticism* he compares poems which deal in an orderly and coherent way with limited experiences and emotions such as joy, sorrow, pride and love with poems superficially similar but in which one finds a greater diversity of elements. He regards poems in the first category, such as Tennyson's 'Break, break, break', as artistically inferior to poems in the second category, such as Keats's 'Ode to a Nightingale' or Donne's 'A Nocturnal upon St Lucy's Day'. He writes:

> A poem of the first group is built out of sets of impulses which run parallel, which have the same direction. In a poem of the second group the most obvious feature is the extraordinarily [*sic*] heterogeneity of the distinguishable impulses. But they are more than heterogeneous, they are opposed. They are such that in ordinary, non-poetic, non-imaginative experience, one or other set would be suppressed to give as it might appear freer development to the others.[11]

The New Critics projected this heterogeneity and opposition of impulses back into the poem itself. The structure of the poem fuses heterogeneous and opposed elements into unity. Discussing poetic structure in his essay 'The heresy of paraphrase', Brooks writes:

> The structure meant is certainly not 'form' in the conventional sense in which we think of form as a kind of envelope which 'contains' the 'content'. The structure obviously is everywhere conditioned by the nature of the material which goes into the poem. The nature of the material sets the problem to be solved, and the solution is the ordering of the material. . . .
> The structure meant is a structure of meanings, evaluations, and interpretations; and the principle of unity which informs it seems to be one of balancing and harmonizing connotations, attitudes, and meanings. . . . It unites the like with the unlike. It does not unite them, however, by the simple process of allowing one connotation to cancel out another nor does it reduce the contradictory attitudes to harmony by a process of subtraction. . . . It is a positive unity, not a negative; it represents not a residue but an achieved harmony.[12]

Brooks goes on to point out that it is this concept of structure as combining unity and diversity that leads to the habitual use in his criticism of such terms as 'ambiguity', 'paradox', 'complex of attitudes', and especially 'irony'. If we demand that the meaning of a poem should be paraphrasable

> we distort the relation of the poem to its 'truth', we raise the problem of belief in a vicious and crippling form, we split the poem between its 'form' and its 'content' – we bring the statement to be conveyed into an unreal competition with science or philosophy or theology. (*The Well Wrought Urn* (*WW*), 184)

Any attempt to formulate the meaning of a poem in simple

paraphrasable terms inevitably fails: 'whatever statement we may seize upon as incorporating the "meaning" of the poem, immediately the imagery and the rhythm seem to set up tensions with it, warping and twisting it, qualifying and revising it' (*WW*, 180). Here one can see a clear link between the early New Criticism and deconstruction as practised by the Yale critics.

What the New Critic has to do, therefore, is to display the form and structure of the work in such a way that the meaning does not emerge in paraphrasable form, but only indirectly through an awareness of how the heterogeneous or opposed elements of the poem are unified. In a sense the meaning of the work is not the major concern: the coexistence of opposed and diverse material within a unified form that one experiences as meaningful is the most important matter. And here perhaps one has an insight into the deeper motives underlying the New Criticism. Most of the American New Critics were strongly conservative in their political outlook and viewed with alarm developments in politics and history in the early twentieth century. Established structures seemed to be threatened with chaos and breakdown but the New Critics had no sympathy with Marxist solutions. This vision of a world in turmoil is strongly present in Modernist literature, most notably in Yeats's poem, 'The Second Coming':

> Things fall apart; the centre cannot hold;
> Mere anarchy is loosed upon the world,
> The blood-dimmed tide is loosed, and everywhere
> The ceremony of innocence is drowned . . .

Joyce also referred in *Ulysses* to history as a 'nightmare' and Eliot had presented a similar vision in *The Waste Land*. In a world in which 'the centre cannot hold', the value of literary works which could confront the contradictory and the disparate yet incorporate them without facile over-simplification in a structure in which the centre *did* hold was obvious. Poetry showed that the human imagination did not need to be reduced to despair by a chaotic reality but could triumph over it without the need to embrace religious belief or accept some philosophical system or political ideology. Poetry remained 'pseudo-statement'. Brooks writes towards the end of 'The heresy of paraphrase':

> If the poet, then, must perforce dramatize the oneness of the exper-
> ience, even though paying tribute to its diversity, then his use of

paradox and ambiguity is seen as necessary. He is not simply trying to spice up, with a superficially exciting or mysterious rhetoric, the old stale stockpot . . . . He is rather giving us an insight which preserves the unity of experience and which, at its higher and more serious levels, triumphs over the apparently contradictory and conflicting elements of experience by unifying them into a new pattern. (*WW*, 195)

This means that the critic as the interpreter of literary texts, in revealing the structure of the text as an 'achieved harmony' of disparate elements, must re-enact, even if at a lower level of intensity, the unifying process embodied within the literary text. Criticism like literature itself is trying to salvage order and coherence in an anarchic world. This gives a double edge to the best of the earlier New Critical interpretations: they are challenging and powerful as interpretations which seek to persuade but they are also cultural statements in themselves. I shall try to illustrate this by looking in some detail at Brooks's reading of *Macbeth*, 'The naked babe and the cloak of manliness'.

The New Criticism in practice

The literary ideal of the early New Critics was the metaphysical poem, especially Donne's lyrics in which apparent logical incoherences and contradictions were triumphantly overcome by poetic means. Metaphysical poetry, notoriously attacked by Dr Johnson because of its 'discovery of occult resemblances in things apparently unlike' so that the 'most heterogeneous ideas are yoked by violence together',[13] was defended by the New Critics as embodying their ideal of organic form. Doubts had been raised as to whether New Critical interpretative techniques could be applied successfully to longer literary forms. A lyric poem could be said to exist in the one plane in the sense that all the elements of it were related to each other and coexisted in a spatial rather than a temporal dimension. Longer works such as plays or novels obviously presented difficulties to a critical method adapted to shorter lyric forms. Brooks attempts to overcome these in his reading of *Macbeth*, published in *The Well Wrought Urn*.

His solution is to see the play as a poetic rather than a dramatic structure. Thus imagery rather than character dominates Brooks's analysis and plot in the Aristotelian sense is discounted in favour of the kind of poetic structure a New Critic would look for in a metaphysical poem. Brooks reveals the debt the New Critics owe to the Romantic concept of the imagination, despite their opposition to Romanticism in general and their low regard for most of the Romantic poets, when he makes use of Coleridge's distinction between fancy and imagination in discussing 'the nature of the dramatic poetry of Shakespeare's mature style': 'we shall expect to find the individual images, not mechanically linked together in the mode of Fancy, but organically related, modified by "a predominant passion", and mutually modifying each other' (*WW*, 26). He thus seeks to demonstrate that the images and metaphors of *Macbeth* are not local in their effect but form links which are an inseparable part of the play's meaning.

He seizes on two groups of recurrent images which on the surface have nothing in common with each other. First, there is imagery centred around babes, the most notable of which is the comparison Macbeth makes between the pity Duncan will arouse and 'a naked new-born babe,/Striding the blast'. This image itself seems to contain a contradiction since it is difficult to understand how a new-born babe could stride the blast. The other group of images Brooks is interested in is centred around clothes in relation to Macbeth, an image pattern first discussed by Caroline Spurgeon,[14] but modified by Brooks in the following way:

> The crucial point of the comparison, it seems to me, lies not in the smallness of the man and the largeness of the robes, but rather in the fact that – whether the man be large or small – they are not *his* garments; in Macbeth's case they are actually stolen garments. (*WW*, 32)

Brooks is also particularly interested in the clothes imagery's relation to a striking metaphor Macbeth uses when describing his discovery of Duncan's murder, perpetrated, Macbeth claims, by Duncan's guards: 'the murderers,/Steeped in the colors of their trade, their daggers/Unmannerly breech'd with gore'. This metaphor and that of the new-born babe striding the blast 'are far more than excrescences, mere extravagances of detail: each, it seems to me, contains a central symbol of the play, and symbols which we must understand if we are to understand either the detailed passage or the play as a whole' (*WW*, 29–30). He goes on to say: 'What is at stake is the whole matter of the relation of Shakespeare's imagery to the total structures of the plays themselves' (*WW*, 30). What is also at stake is whether or not the New Critical approach can be convincingly applied to one of the major works of a writer almost universally regarded as the greatest in the English language.

The key for Brooks in unifying the images and metaphors of the play lies in Macbeth's tragic situation. He places the tragic emphasis in the play not on the murder of Duncan but on Macbeth's need to go on killing in an effort to find security. This Brooks characterises as 'his attempt to conquer the future, an attempt involving him, like Oedipus, in a desperate struggle with fate itself' (*WW*, 38). Thus he interprets the killing of Banquo as arising not out of any fear that Macbeth may have that Banquo may use violence on him as he has on Duncan, but on his need to counter the prophecy that Banquo's line will eventually inherit the throne.

Given this view of the tragedy as being concerned with an attempt to master the future, Brooks can accommodate the apparent contradictions or extravagances of the imagery by seeing them as intrinsic to the play's structure: 'For the babe signifies the future which Macbeth would control but cannot control' (*WW*, 42). Macbeth claimed that he would be willing 'to jump the life to come' if the killing of Duncan could succeed in establishing him as king, but Brooks argues that this contradicts his desire to found a line of kings: 'The logic of Macbeth's distraught mind, thus, forces him to make war on children', and Brooks points to a link between this and the murder of Macduff's wife and children. Yet the child, as in the image of the babe striding the blast, proves far from helpless, as Macduff's child defies the murderers: 'Its defiance testifies to the force which threatens Macbeth and which Macbeth cannot destroy' (*WW*, 42).

Aware that he might be accused of allegorising away the human power of the play, Brooks goes on to say that the babe does not only signify the future: 'it symbolizes all those enlarging purposes which make life meaningful, and it symbolizes, furthermore, all those emotional and – to Lady Macbeth – irrational ties which make man more than a machine – which render him human' (*WW*, 42–3). He goes on to suggest its links with the babe whose brains Lady Macbeth claims she would willingly dash out if it stood in her way and with Macduff's being from his 'mother's womb/Untimely ripp'd'. The power of the babe in that last instance lies in the fact that it 'has defied even the thing which one feels may reasonably be predicted of him – his time of birth' (*WW*, 44). We can see, then, the apparent contradiction between the weakness of a new-born babe and the strength needed to 'stride the blast' being overcome in Brooks's reading. The 'naked new-born babe' creates pity which becomes a power that can undo the work of a murderer; this paradox 'will destroy the overbrittle rationalism on which Macbeth founds his career' (*WW*, 45).

In a final attempt at synthesis Brooks argues that what for him are the two dominant images of the play – the naked babe and the daggers clothed in blood – 'are facets of two of the great symbols which run throughout the play' (*WW*, 45). The daggers and the babe are diametrical opposites: mechanism and life, instrument and end, death and birth. As the one should be left bare and clean the other should be clothed and warmed:

> with a flexibility which must amaze the reader, the image of the garment and the image of the babe are so used as to encompass an astonishingly large area of the total situation. And between them . . . they furnish Shakespeare with his most subtle and ironically telling instruments. (*WW*, 45–6)

Brooks's interpretation is open to attack on several grounds. Most obviously, it can be criticised for ignoring the fact that *Macbeth* is a play. This is the basis for a critique by Oscar James Campbell, a critic who sees Shakespeare's plays in a traditional scholarly, historical and dramatic context. He picks out certain details in Brooks's reading and judges them to be 'strained beyond the limits of credulity'. In discussing the 'unmannerly breech'd with gore' image he claims that Brooks 'ignores the value of the metaphor for the speech in which it occurs', which is to reveal Macbeth's state of mind at the time, that is, his 'neurotic embarrassment'. Campbell also dismisses Brooks's claim that the centre of the tragedy is Macbeth's attempt to impose his will upon the future: Macbeth's

> tragedy lies not in a failure of his efforts to impose his will upon the future but in the multitudinous fears and superstitions that form the psychological punishment for his crime. Whatever the value of imagery as an objective correlative of emotion, it obviously must not be interpreted in such a way as to contradict directly the clear meaning of the plot.

Campbell goes on to suggest that Brooks's interpretation goes wrong because his critical method endeavours 'to force all the references to babes into one connected system of imagery to form a structural principle for the drama'. Campbell sees Macbeth's situation as typical of murderers in Elizabethan drama: his fear is not of an inability to control the future 'but of the knife in the hands of a human avenger'. His conclusion is that the play cannot be legitimately interpreted as if it is constructed on poetic and not dramatic principles; although there may be recurrent imagery in the play, each time a particular image is used it is 'for an immediate imaginative purpose relevant only to a specific situation'.[15]

The leading theoretical opponents of the early New Critics were a group of critics based at the University of Chicago, the Chicago Aristotelians, the most important of whom was R. S. Crane. Their prime criticism of the New Critics was that they ignored traditional poetics. For these neo-Aristotelian critics it was necessary to distinguish between different types of literary discourse, whereas the New Criticism, they claimed, tended to treat all literary texts as if they were essentially similar in structure. For Crane this leads the New Critics into 'a priori' reasoning and creates a critical method that is irreconcilable with the spirit of inquiry. The New Critics already know what they are looking for when they read a literary text, and thus tend to find it: 'You know that there will almost certainly be "ambiguity" in the next poem you look at, or that its structure will probably be "some kind of paradoxical tension".' This results in what Crane calls the 'dialectical fallacy':

> the tacit assumption that what is true in your theory as a dialectical consequence must also be, or tend to be, true in actuality – that if you can so read a literary work as to reveal in it the particular kind of meaning or structure that is entailed by your definition of literature, poetry, poetic language, or the like . . . you have sufficiently demonstrated that it has that kind of meaning or structure. The fallacy lies in the circumstance that, with a little interpretative ingenuity, these conditions can almost always be fulfilled.[16]

Thus Brooks and the New Criticism generally are guilty of what Crane in another essay calls 'critical monism'.[17]

There is no reason, however, why a critic should not read a play as if it were constructed on the same principles as a particular kind of lyric poetry. According to Stanley Fish, not only the New Critics but every school of criticism inevitably succumbs to the 'dialectical fallacy'. He argues that a literary work cannot be objectively described: it is the creation of the critic's interpretative strategies and principles. There is no way one can read without having such strategies and principles, therefore one cannot have access to a text independent of them. As Fish puts it in relation to a discussion of Milton's *Lycidas*: 'in the analysis of these lines from *Lycidas* I did what critics always do: I "saw" what my interpretive principles permitted or directed me to see, and then I turned around and attributed what I had "seen" to a text and an intention.'[18] Critics' possession, then, of different interpretative strategies and principles leads to the existence of what Fish calls 'interpretive communities', groups of critics who share a set of strategies and principles. Brooks and the New Critics belong to one such community of interpreters and Campbell and Crane to another, and there is no possibility that they are going to agree about *Macbeth*.

It is doubtful whether Brooks would welcome this defence of his reading of *Macbeth* since almost certainly he would see it as entailing critical relativism, although Fish rejects the concept of relativism. The New Critics believed that their critical approach was objective and that it led to true knowledge of literary texts. It was the text as object that for them was central and they rejected or downgraded critical criteria based on such factors as authorial intention, historical context, or audience response as directing attention away from the text as object. They believed that one could have a tenable objective criterion for deciding between critical interpretations: the interpretation which could include as much as possible of the material of a text in a consistent and coherent interpretation of it was to be preferred. It could thus be objectively demonstrated that certain interpretations were superior to others.

But what strikes one about Brooks's reading of *Macbeth* is not how much of the detail of the play he can incorporate in his interpretation but how he takes apparently dissimilar or diverse features and attempts to show how they can be coherently related to each other. The emphasis in the early New Criticism is thus less on comprehensiveness as such than on the bringing together of what appear to be unrelated or dissimilar features of a text. This is a difference between the earlier New Criticism and its later developments, as I shall discuss later. Brooks's critical model, as I suggested above, is the metaphysical poem. By implication he believes that criticism, like the poetry the New Critics most admired, could impose coherence on a reality that seemed divided or fragmented. Although the New Critics, in contrast to critics influenced by deconstruction, such as Geoffrey Hartman, made a clear separation between the literary text and the critical text, the latter being subordinate to the former, in practice much of the work of the early New Critics resembles the literature they most admired in its structure though not in its texture. Critics like Hartman who support the view that criticism should regard itself as the equal of literature would argue that criticism should also seek to emulate literary texts at the level of texture by making use of rhetorical devices associated with literature.[19] A possible objection to Brooks's reading of *Macbeth* is that it is like a paraphrase of a metaphysical poem: that is, one sees apparent dissimilarities and contradictions being incorporated in a unified structure but the rhetorical power of the metaphysical poem which supported that structure through its aesthetic or imaginative appeal is lacking.

The early New Criticism is in a sense trying to have it both ways. It imitates the literary texts it admires at the level of structure but it wishes its interpretations to be seen as objective in a scientific sense and so adopts the plain or neutral style which one associates with discourses that aspire to scientific objectivity. By attempting to combine the bringing together of apparently contrary or dissimilar elements in a literary work with criteria based fundamentally on quantity – that is, the amount of detail an interpretation could account for – there is a danger of falling between two stools. But although the work of the early New Critics may be vulnerable to these criticisms, at its best, as in the work of Brooks, it has sufficient imaginative power to be worth reading for its own sake even by those who do not accept New Critical assumptions. The more serious problems of the New Criticism were to emerge later.

The later New Criticism

As the New Criticism became the major critical force in American universities it gradually changed. On the face of it these changes removed some of the contradictions I have discussed above, between, for example, the concentration on ambiguity and paradox and the aspiration towards scientific objectivity. In the New Criticism as it developed in the 1950s and 1960s one finds little emphasis on ambiguity, paradox, or irony as integral to the structure of literary texts. The aim of these later New Critics is to accommodate as much of the material of a text as possible in an interpretation which is as coherent, consistent and comprehensive as it can be.

Interpretations by later New Critics appear to be less forced or strained than, for example, Brooks's reading of *Macbeth* for these later critics are not actively seeking out ambiguous or paradoxical elements and trying to unify them by incorporating them within a structure based on the metaphysical poem. The later New Critic tends to look for a theme that will be seen as the common denominator of every other element in a text. As much detail as possible, theoretically all of it, should be part of the text's thematic unity. John M. Ellis and Stein Haugom Olsen are two theorists who defend this position. Ellis writes:

> The object of literary criticism, then, is an interpretative hypothesis as to the most general principle of structure which can be abstracted from the combination of linguistic elements in a literary text. The term 'structure' is often used in literary criticism in a more superficial sense, to refer to one particular aspect of a text, for example, its natural breaks, its plot outline, and so on. I should propose to reserve the use of this term to designate the most general principle of organization which binds together and makes sense of all the detail of a text in combination. The most general statement of structure, in this sense, is equally a statement of thematic structure and therefore of the meaning of the text. The test of statements of this kind is simply comprehensiveness – they must synthesize and thus make sense of as much as possible of the text.[20]

Ellis goes on to argue that style has no existence separate from thematic structure or meaning since any linguistic element of a text must affect meaning. Thus all formal or stylistic aspects of literary texts must ultimately be incorporated in their thematic structure.

Olsen declares that five interpretative criteria need to be satisfied if a text is to possess the coherence required to qualify as a work of literature: completeness, correctness, comprehensiveness, consistency and discrimination. He writes of comprehensiveness:

> Comprehensiveness is a criterion for the acceptability of an interpretation because the principle of functionality, i.e. the convention that all the identifiable parts of a literary work should be artistically relevant, is a part of the literary institution. Ideally, a text which is construed as a literary work can be segmented completely so that no part of the text is resistant to interpretation.[21]

Ellis's and Olsen's arguments are vulnerable to the objection that they are based on a textual idealism which cannot easily accommodate the fact that in many cases it is impossible to establish definitive texts. For example, Shakespeare scholars have recently claimed that such seminal literary works as *Hamlet* and *King Lear* exist in two versions and we should therefore accept that there are two *Hamlets* and two *Lears*.

The redirection of the New Criticism towards thematic unity and coherence with little or no requirement that irony, ambiguity and paradox should be an integral part of that coherence made it possible for the New Criticism to be applied to virtually any literary text. The earlier New Critics had fairly narrow literary sympathies as only those works in which irony, ambiguity, or paradox seemed central to the structure tended to gain their approval. This led to their emphasis on a narrow range of lyric poetry or on works, such as *Macbeth*, which could be interpreted in similar terms. But in general, longer literary genres, especially the novel, were difficult to reconcile with the criteria that the early New Critics applied. The later form of the New Criticism, however, could be applied easily to fiction. A great deal of later New Critical interpretation also adopts a more compromising position towards authorial intention and historical context than earlier New Criticism, which rejected what Wimsatt and Beardsley called the 'intentional fallacy': the idea that authors' intentions were no secure guide in interpreting their works.[22] Although the text as an objective structure remained central for the later New Critics, it was permissible to make use of authorial or historical material if this was a help in understanding a work's structure. One of the major results of these modifications to the New Criticism was an explosion in interpretative criticism.

It is this very profusion of interpretations which raises doubts about the later New Criticism as a critical method. It is clear from consulting the bibliographies on writers regarded as central to the literary canon that their works have generated so many interpretations that it is difficult often even for specialists to keep up with them. Although in theory the criterion of comprehensiveness should allow one to judge whether one interpretation is better than another, in practice it is difficult to decide whether one interpretation is more comprehensive than another. Total comprehensiveness in interpretation being impossible, comprehensiveness becomes, therefore, a relative concept. One needs only to glance at any critical bibliography on a canonic text, such as a play by Shakespeare, to see that it has been possible to interpret such a work from almost every conceivable angle, and critics of reasonable competence are able to produce interpretations that have some degree of comprehensiveness. Nor is there any evidence of interpretations combining cumulatively to produce the ideal of a totalising interpretation that will account for all the detail of a text; rather, one forms the impression of critical fragmentation.

If one investigates how interpretations are actually created, then it becomes clear that critics are able to produce new readings by bringing their particular interests into relation with a text in order to create an interpretative hypothesis which they then apply to that text. The validity of the hypothesis is judged by its success in accounting for as much of the data of the text as possible. But the New Criticism neglected to face the difficulty that in regarding a literary text as a structure of words which has an independent existence – that is, not subject to authorial or historical constraints – then there is no theoretical limit to its meanings and it becomes open to a multitude of interpretations. Since comprehensiveness in practice is a relative concept, the real New Critical criterion for justifying a new interpretation is whether it is sufficiently novel and is able to justify itself by accounting for details of the text that previous interpretations have either failed to account for or have accounted for differently.

Although the New Criticism still remains powerful in America, it is being increasingly challenged by alternative approaches which regard theory as at least as important as practice in literary criticism. The main tradition of the New Criticism has neglected theory in favour of practice since its main concern has been the interpretation of individual texts. An implicit assumption was that some kind of interpretative absolute would eventually be reached in which all interpretations would be harmoniously accommodated. Thus there was no real need to concern oneself much with previous readings as long as one's own reading was sufficiently different. But with the indefinite postponement of any interpretative absolute what emerged was an accumulation of essentially self-contained interpretations which aimed at internal coherence and which entered into debate or dialogue with other interpretations only to a very limited degree. With the realisation that this accumulation of interpretations could continue indefinitely there was a loss of confidence in the New Criticism, at least among certain influential critics. Perhaps it is only a matter of time before its standing in the literary critical community as a whole, and not merely in certain élite institutions, is seriously threatened.

One important factor, however, that may make it difficult for any alternative critical approach to displace the New Criticism is its pedagogical power. Before the New Critics, when literary scholarship reigned in universities, it was not easy to engage the interest of ordinary students in literary study as it was assumed they had little or nothing to contribute because they did not know enough or had not read enough. The relation between students and their teachers was thus a predominantly passive one in which students for the most part listened to lectures. But with the emergence of the idea that it is the text in itself that is important and the criterion for an authentic reading is a coherent interpretation of the text, students had a more active role to play and teaching, at least in theory, could be more of a dialogue between teacher and student and less of a monologue. In practice, of course, this ideal may have been less easy to achieve. F. R. Leavis claimed that criticism should have the form of claim and response: 'This is so, isn't it' followed by 'Yes, but'. A problem was created, however, if instead of 'Yes, but' the response was 'No, it's not'. Further, critics like Leavis tended to create disciples rather than sharers in dialogue. Even with less charismatic teachers than Leavis, the teacher would almost invariably know more than the student even if this knowledge was not openly displayed. The teacher's power was thus seldom threatened. Despite these points, the pedagogical advantages of the New Criticism are likely to prevent it being easily superseded.

Leavis, Empson, Burke

In the previous discussion I have concentrated on American New Criticism because it was primarily responsible for interpretation becoming central to modern literary criticism. The situation in Britain, however, has been somewhat different, although one could point to many British critics whose critical practice may be described as New Critical in its nature. But traditional historical and scholarly criticism retained greater power in British academic criticism than it did in America during the ascendancy of the New Criticism, and even more important, the influence of F. R. Leavis and the *Scrutiny* group of critics tended to lessen the impact of the New Criticism in Britain.

In several important respects Leavisian criticism is similar to the earlier form of the New Criticism. Like the American New Critics, Leavis and his followers were influenced by Eliot's critical preferences, Richards's critical theory and (to some extent) William Empson's methods of close reading. Both the New Critics and Leavis also valued particularly metaphysical poetry and discussed longer literary forms such as drama and the novel in terms of poetic structure. But interpretation is not central to Leavis's criticism as it is to that of the New Critics. The aim of close reading for Leavis is not to construct an interpretation which will account for as much of the detail of a work as possible but, in brief, to show how in the greatest works meaning and expression cannot be separated.

Like the early New Critics, Leavis and his followers were much affected by Eliot's doctrine of the 'dissociation of sensibility'. But whereas the New Critics were interested in how poets like Donne were free from its effect by their ability to incorporate diversity and apparent logical contradiction in a poetic structure in which irony and ambiguity were an integral part, Leavis emphasises the wholeness of literary works in which the meaning is achieved through 'concrete realisation' and 'sensuous particularity' in such a way that there can be no split between feeling and intellect. Leavis's criticism seldom explores complexities of meaning or attempts to construct a complete reading of a text in the manner of the New Critics. Indeed, it would not be going too far to describe his critical approach as anti-interpretative. Thus comparing Keats's 'Ode to a Nightingale' with Shelley's 'To a Skylark' he writes:

> Now, if intellectual structure is what Shelley characteristically exhibits, the *Ode to a Nightingale* may freely be allowed to lack it. But the superiority of the *Ode* over *To a Skylark*, which beside it appears a nullity, is not merely a superiority of details. . . . The rich local concreteness is the local manifestation of an inclusive sureness of grasp in the whole. What the detail exhibits is not merely an extraordinary intensity of realization, but also an extraordinary rightness and delicacy of touch; a sureness of touch that is the working of a fine organization. The *Ode*, that is, has the structure of a fine and complex organism; whereas *To a Skylark* is a mere poetical outpouring, its ecstatic 'intensity' being a substitute for realization in the parts and for a realized whole to which the parts might be related.[23]

Leavis's interest is in considering how far a work achieves this wholeness of realization, which for him is an intrinsic quality of the literature he values. A certain minimum degree of interpretation may be unavoidable but it is pursued only to the point where he can demonstrate that what is expressed and how it is expressed are inseparable, and that one cannot judge the one without judging the other. The reason that he holds such critical principles could perhaps be related to my account of why the early New Critics valued an organic unity in poetry that could accommodate irony and ambiguity. The question of literary value was crucial for both the New Critics and Leavis but perhaps Leavis was more aware that interpretation could be a threat to the concept of value if it were pushed too far. This potential threat is clearly seen in the work of two critics who are associated with the New Criticism but who have tended to be regarded as somewhat marginal figures. Both have neglected the question of value and have practised a form of interpretation subject to few of the constraints that one observes in mainstream New Criticism. Until recently their work has tended to be viewed as over-ingenious, eccentric, or perverse, but with the emergence of post-structuralism as a powerful force in contemporary criticism this judgement is being revised. These critics are William Empson and Kenneth Burke.

Empson has a strong claim to be the first interpreter of literature in the modern sense: that is, the first critic to look in detail at the language of a text and subject its meaning to relentless analysis, although Empson acknowledged the influence of Robert Graves's and Laura Riding's book, *A Survey of Modernist Poetry*, first published in 1927. His achievement was fully acknowledged by the early New Critics and, initially at least, by Leavis. John Crowe Ransom wrote that Empson's first book, *Seven Types of Ambiguity*, published in 1930, was 'the most imaginative account of readings ever printed, and Empson the closest and most resourceful reader that poetry has yet publicly had.'[24] For Cleanth Brooks Empson's 'criticism is an attempt to deal with what the poem "means" in terms of its structure *as a poem*'. Whereas previous critics had tended to concentrate either on the paraphrasable prose argument of a poem or on 'decorative' features such as imagery or metrical patterning, 'Empson fights throughout the *Seven Types* against this crippling division by showing how poem after poem actually "works" as a complex of meanings'.[25]

Yet it is clear that both the New Critics and Leavis and the

Scrutiny group were worried by the Empsonian method and approach. While for the New Critics and for Leavis interpretation is inextricably related to their wider critical and cultural concerns, Empson's aim, they suggest, is only to tease out the layers of meaning of a poem. He has no interest in the New Critical conception of the poem as a 'verbal icon' in which irony, paradox, or contradiction are embodied in a unified structure of meaning or in the Leavis ideal of total integration between what is expressed and how it is expressed. For Ransom, Empson's criticism was weakened by the fact that it was concerned with 'texture' and not 'structure'. In other words, his detailed readings do not cohere into a total structure of meaning. Discussing Empson's second book, *Some Versions of Pastoral*, Ransom refers to his 'almost inveterate habit of over-reading poetry', and goes on to say more generally: 'The "ambiguity" which he has hallmarked as the object of his criticism is generally multiplicity. And the multiple meanings have no special unity except the loose psychological one of being tied up in the same moment of thought.'[26] Brooks is more sympathetic to Empson, but he also is worried about the dangers of the pursuit of ambiguity for its own sake, since 'one can make out a case for richness and complexity in almost any poem – in the poem that has not earned it as well as the poem that has; and that the mere process of spinning out a web of complexities and ambiguities is not sufficient to validate a poem. There must be a further criterion.' For Brooks, an ambiguity is justified only if it 'is functional in developing the poem's total effect'.[27] Contributors to *Scrutiny* continually accuse Empson of over-ingenuity and strained readings, and Leavis himself wrote of *Seven Types of Ambiguity*:

> Empson's extremely mixed and uneven book, offering as it does a good deal of valuable stimulus, serves the better as a warning – a warning against temptations that the analyst whose practice is to be a discipline must resist. It abounds in instances of ingenuity that has taken the bit between its teeth. Valid analytic practice is a strengthening of the sense of relevance . . . and all appropriate play of intelligence, being also an exercise of the sense of value, is controlled by an implicit concern for a total value-judgment.[28]

These objections to Empson, which undermined his influence during the period when the New Critics and Leavis were most powerful, seem less persuasive in a contemporary critical context in which such concepts as 'freeplay' and 'dissemination', associated

with Derridean deconstruction, have had wide currency. Much
contemporary criticism has been concerned to show how the play of
meaning in a literary text disrupts forces which claim to control it –
authorial, generic, historical – as I shall discuss in more detail later.
Empson's concentration on texture rather than structure, to use
Ransom's terms, has an obvious connection with the emphasis in
much contemporary criticism on 'textuality'. Further, by showing
that ambiguity can be divided into various distinct types and by
claiming that a literary mode such as pastoral should not be
understood in traditional terms but as, in the words of one writer on
Empson, 'at once a philosophy, a social attitude or feeling, an ironic
ambiguity, a propaganda subject, and a stylistic device, and . . .
must be all those things together or it is nothing',[29] Empson's
criticism displays some similarities to that of Roland Barthes. In
S/Z, Barthes analyses a text of Balzac in terms of a number of codes
that reveal layers of meaning but he makes no attempt to integrate
these meanings within a coherent structure. Indeed, the dissemination of these meanings is what he is concerned with.

Kenneth Burke is perhaps even more of a maverick figure among
the New Critics but one who, from the standpoint of contemporary
criticism, anticipates much current theory and practice. He has some
important resemblances to Empson. Both were strongly influenced
by Freud and were sympathetic towards Marxism, in contrast to the
more right-wing sympathies of the New Critics. Clearly, a text like
Freud's *The Interpretation of Dreams* must have had considerable
impact either directly or indirectly on literary interpretation because
the methods it used in teasing out hidden or suppressed meanings in
dreams had an obvious literary application. But Empson and Burke,
unlike most of the New Critics, were prepared to take seriously
Freudianism as a system. For both, analysis came before the
question of literary value. Indeed, the emphasis in their work is on
demystifying the literary text rather than on seeing it as a source of
unique value in a chaotic or vulgar world. Burke, however, is
primarily a cultural theorist, with literary theory a central part of his
wider concerns, and comparatively little of his output is devoted to
the practice of interpretation, whereas Empson's criticism is
predominantly directed at the analysis of particular texts.

Burke is prepared to go part of the way with the New Critics. In a
response to Brooks's essays 'The formalist critic' and 'The heresy of
paraphrase' he asserts that 'the Formalist critic fulfills his "proper"

task by imputing to the work whatever design, or intention, he thinks is best able to account for the nature of the work' and a critic substantiates this 'by showing in detail how much the imputed design might account for'. A critic who disagrees must 'offer a different postulate, and . . . demonstrate pragmatically how much can be accounted for on the basis of his thesis'.[30] But unlike the New Critics he rejects confining critical discussion purely to the internal dimensions of texts and ignoring intentional and sociological factors. For Burke, literature is 'symbolic action':

> Critical and imaginative works are answers to questions posed by the situation in which they arose. They are not merely answers, they are *strategic* answers, *stylized* answers. . . . So I should propose an initial working distinction between 'strategies' and 'situations', whereby we think of poetry (I here use the term to include any work of critical or imaginative cast) as the adopting of various strategies for the encompassing of situations. These strategies size up the situations, name their structure and outstanding ingredients, and name them in a way that contains an attitude towards them.[31]

Thus Burke does not confine himself to the text itself in the manner of the New Critics but continually seeks to enlarge its significance by finding connections with wider issues: psychological, sociological, cultural: 'The main ideal of criticism, as I conceive it, is to use all that is there to use.' For his critics this leads to uncontrolled allegorising and sheer associationism. An aspect of his theory that particularly connects him with deconstructionist criticism is the importance he attaches to rhetorical figures. Thus he writes of synecdoche, in which the part can stand for the whole, and the whole for the part: 'The more I examine both the structure of poetry and the structure of human relations outside of poetry, the more I become convinced that this is the "basic" figure of speech, and that it occurs in many modes besides that of the formal trope.'[32]

Burke's reading of Keats's 'Ode on a Grecian Urn' illustrates his approach. This poem has also been analysed by Brooks in *The Well Wrought Urn*, and although Brooks praises Burke's interpretation and suggests that his reading has much in common with Burke's, the differences seem more striking than the similarities. Whereas Brooks's reading is typically New Critical in concentrating on the poem itself as a structure, ignoring authorial intention and wider cultural issues, Burke is concerned to discuss the poem in a much broader context of meaning. He begins by interpreting the line

'Beauty is truth, truth beauty' in the following way: '"Truth" being
the essential word of knowledge (science) and "beauty" being the
essential word of art or poetry, we might substitute accordingly.'[33]
Burke claims that the poem, therefore, is denying 'the dialectical
opposition between the "aesthetic" and the "practical" ' ('*A
Grammar of Motives*' and '*A Rhetoric of Motives*' (*GM*), 447). The
figure which dominates the poem is that of the 'mystic oxymoron'
(*GM*, 449). Burke does not indicate any sympathy towards the
poem's attempt to unify truth and beauty; his interest is in
explaining how this effect is created through language. He proceeds
then to introduce a further level of explanation by relating the poem
to a wider nineteenth-century context. He sees in the second stanza
'a variant of the identification between death and sexual love that
was so typical of 19th-century romanticism' (*GM*, 450). He pursues
the significance of this further into nineteenth-century culture:
'Adding historical factors, one can note the part that capitalist
individualism plays in sharpening this consummation' and goes on to
discuss 'the relation between private property and the love–death
equation' (*GM*, 450).

Following his conviction that the critic 'should use whatever
knowledge is available' (*GM*, 451), Burke does not hesitate to draw on
Keats's biography, particularly his illness and his relationship with
Fanny Brawne, although he accepts, alluding to the anti-intention-
alism of the New Critics, 'that such speculations interfere with the
symmetry of criticism as a game' (*GM*, 451). This is another link
between Burke and Empson, who also rejected the New Critics' anti-
intentionalism. Keats's 'phthisic fever' (*GM*, 452) is seen as central to
the state of agitation in the poem but this is used by the poet to create a
division between a malign passion and a spiritual activity that has
broken free from it. This raises theological issues concerning the
relation between God's will and the good. Whereas Brooks in his
analysis restricts himself to the poem as an integrated structure of
meaning, Burke continually endeavours to reveal layers of meaning
that relate to the poem's situation in his sense of the word. He is
prepared to use anything that will help in this endeavour, such as
biographical knowledge or word-play. It is interesting that Brooks
chose not to see a pun in 'brede' – in 'brede of marble men and
maidens overwrought' – although he says he considered it. Burke,
however, does not hesitate to see a pun here and to interpret 'overwrought' as suggesting 'excited', and concludes: 'Both expressions

would thus merge notions of sexuality and craftsmanship, the erotic and the poetic' (*GM*, 459).

Thus while Brooks and Burke are both concerned with the opposition between 'beauty' and 'truth' and the poem's attempt to overcome it, their critical aims are quite different. Brooks's main concern is to find a poetic justification for the claim in the poem that beauty and truth are one by showing that it is integral to the poem's poetic structure, not an extraneous philosophical statement. Burke likewise sees it as integral to the poem but he wants to go beyond a merely aesthetic appreciation to an analytic understanding of its role in the poem. This requires reading the poem in a much wider context of meaning. It is here that Burke, with his concept of the poem as a strategy for encompassing situations, anticipates deconstructive analysis. The order and coherence of the poem are constructed as a response to a situation with which the poet is grappling. Burke reveals both the nature of this situation and the strategies in the poem which seek to encompass it. In other words, Burke is concerned not with an aesthetic appreciation of the poem's unity but with promoting analytic awareness of the problematic that underlies the poem's existence, as is shown by his conclusion: 'it was gratifying to have the oracle proclaim the unity of poetry and science because the values of technology and business were causing them to be at odds' (*GM*, 462).

Another aspect of Burke's anti-aesthetic approach to the poem can be found in some further comments on it in *A Rhetoric of Motives*. Here he favours a more Joycean reading of the line 'Beauty is truth, truth beauty': that is, 'experimentally modifying both "truth" and "beauty" punwise until one found some tonal cognates that made sense, preferably obscene sense' (*GM*, 728). Although Burke is too polite to spell out his reading, it is clear that this leads to Keats's line being rendered as 'Body is turd, turd body'.

One of Burke's severest critics is René Wellek, a critic whose strongest sympathies are with the main tradition of the New Criticism. He complains that Burke 'has little aesthetic sense' and 'does not or does not want to discriminate between great art and ephemeral writing'.[34] He contrasts him with the more orthodox New Critics:

> Nowhere in Burke is there an awareness of the normative nature of the criteria proposed by the New Criticism, nor is there any attempt to grasp the coherence and integrity of an individual work of art or to see

the unity of form and content. (*A History of Modern Criticism, 1750–1950: American Criticism, 1900–50 (HMA)*, 246)

Burke's method, Wellek believes, is rather to adapt Freud's free association method in discussing literary texts and then to go on to align Freud with Marx. For Wellek this leads to 'a forcing both of phonemic resemblances (truth and turd are far apart) and of conceptual analogies which strains all credulity' (*HMA*, 248). Burke's method as applied to 'Ode on a Grecian Urn' 'compounds arbitrary allegorizing with misconstrued psychoanalysis and far-fetched Marxist analogizing' (*HMA*, 250). This 'leads to his denial of any sense of the correctness of interpretation, to his advocacy of complete liberty of interpretation' (*HMA*, 255). Wellek's final judgement is damning:

> In his theory, literature becomes absorbed into a scheme of linguistic action or rhetoric so all-embracing and all-absorbing that poetry as an art is lost sight of and the work of art is spun into a network of allusions, puns, and clusters of images without any regard for its wholeness or unity. . . . The laws of evidence have ceased to function. He moves in a self-created verbal universe where everything may mean everything else (*HMA*, 255–6)

This is very reminiscent of contemporary attacks on Derrida and deconstruction.

Wellek is also a harsh critic of Richards and Empson, in similar if less severe terms. Empson is 'steeped in Richards's value theory, in his psychology of literary criticism, and his theory of meaning which allows and encourages multiple definitions as language is conceived as fluid and poetic language appreciated for being fluid'.[35] Like Burke, Empson in *Seven Types of Ambiguity* operates 'by a method which could be called "loose association", somewhat similar to the Freudian technique to elicit associations from a patient on the couch' (*A History of Modern Criticism: 1750–1950: English Criticism, 1900–50 (HME)*, 276). This leads to 'chaotic enumerations of all possible (and many impossible) associations which might be evoked in the mind of a reader' (*HME*, 276). Wellek finds Empson's criticism, like Burke's, at odds with New Critical concepts of unity and aesthetic value: 'While Empson has done much to exalt verbal analysis he has, I think, done damage to criticism by his neglect of the form of a play, or a poem, of its overall structure, its totality' (*HME*, 285). Wellek concludes: 'he rarely discusses a work of art as a whole or judges as a literary critic with some aesthetic values in mind' (*HME*, 292).

Richards's psychologism similarly 'denies the objective structure of a work of art'; 'Words in poetry are "free to mean as they please", "free to waltz about with one another as much as they please" ' (*HME*, 225). For Wellek this opens the door to 'complete anarchy in criticism' (*HME*, 226). The fact that Richards's work influenced the New Criticism by stimulating 'the analysis of poetic texts in terms of the interaction of words and the functions of imagery' was an effect of Richards's criticism that went against its general thrust, which Wellek summarises in the following terms:

> the radical rejection of aesthetics, the resolute reduction of the work of art to a mental state, the denial of truth value to poetry, and the defense of poetry as emotive language ordering our mind and giving us equilibrium and mental health. (*HME*, 237)

What emerges from this is that many of the divisions in more recent criticism between, for example, deconstructionist or reader-response criticism and more orthodox critical approaches are to be found within the early New Criticism if one includes Richards, Empson and Burke as part of it. The fact that the work of Ransom, Brooks, Allen Tate, Robert Penn Warren, W. K. Wimsatt and Leavis and the *Scrutiny* group proved to be the most influential in Anglo-American criticism and made Empson, Burke and even Richards appear to be marginal in comparison may turn out to have been a temporary phenomenon. Certainly, from a contemporary critical viewpoint the work of Empson and Burke seems highly relevant to current deconstructionist criticism while Richards's elevation of the reader's response over the structure of the object which stimulates that response has an obvious relation with reader-response criticism. The work of the main tradition of the New Criticism, in contrast, has been widely attacked by many contemporary critics at the level of both theory and practice. Although it seems certain to survive such attacks – some significant theorists are still prepared to defend it[36] – it is unlikely to regain its former dominance if it merely ignores them. Perhaps the way forward would be for it to attempt to come to terms with those forces within its own tradition that it has tended to marginalise.

CHAPTER 3

Hermeneutics

Although the centrality of interpretation to literary criticism was established when the New Criticism became a major force in the 1940s, there was relatively little interest in the theory of interpretation among Anglo-American critics during the period in which the New Criticism was most dominant. An indication of this is the fact that the word 'hermeneutics' is to be found only relatively recently as a common term in Anglo-American criticism. The first important work of American criticism to give it prominence was *Validity in Interpretation*, by E. D. Hirsch, a critic with a strong interest in German Romanticism and thus well aware of the significance of hermeneutics in the German tradition. Hirsch is an opponent both of the approach to interpretation associated with the New Criticism and of the Heidegger-influenced hermeneutics of Hans-Georg Gadamer, the leading contributor to hermeneutic theory of the past thirty years or so. Indeed, Hirsch's book suggests that there are strong links between the two even though few of the New Critics would have been aware of this. In supporting the traditional form of hermeneutics, most closely associated with the work of Friedrich Schleiermacher and Wilhelm Dilthey, and attacking the opposed interpretative theory of both the New Critical tradition and Gadamer, Hirsch's book was probably more influential than any other in making Anglo-American criticism aware of the relevance of hermeneutic theory to literary interpretation.

Hermeneutics, or the science or theory of interpretation, can be traced back to the classical and Judaic origins of Western civilisation, although modern interest in it tends to start with the work of Schleiermacher, one of the leading German Romantics. The central concern of hermeneutics as it relates to the study of literature is the problem created by the fact that texts written in the past continue to exist and to be read while their authors and the historical context which produced them have passed away in time. Reading such texts, therefore, becomes inseparable from the question of interpretation. Before the modern period hermeneutics was concerned primarily with how scriptural texts such as the Bible should be read. Should the Bible, for example, be seen as a text which exists in its own terms and read accordingly or should any understanding of it be mediated by an acceptance of the doctrines of the church? Schleiermacher is considered to be the founder of modern hermeneutics because, although interested in Biblical interpretation, he extended hermeneutics beyond the sphere of religion with the result that it could be applied to the interpretation of texts in a more general sense.

Schleiermacher's major contribution was to make 'understanding' (*Verstehen*) central to hermeneutic theory. He shifted the focus away from the difficulties of reading texts created by the fact that they might contain corruptions or contradictions and directed attention to the question of the conditions necessary before it was possible to understand such texts. Interpretation thus took a theoretical turn. Understanding, he argued, had two essential aspects: the grammatical and the psychological, or, as he called it, the technical. Any utterance, spoken or written, must form part of a linguistic system and it could not be understood unless one had knowledge of the structure of that system. But such an utterance was also a human product and had to be understood in relation to the life of the person uttering it. Both of these aspects must be kept in mind in interpretation. The 'First canon' of 'Grammatical Interpretation' is the following: 'A more precise determination of any point in a given text must be decided on the basis of the use of language common to the author and his original public.' The 'Second canon' states: 'The meaning of each word of a passage must be determined by the context in which it occurs.' Discussing 'Technical Interpretation' he writes: 'Before technical interpretation can begin, one must learn the way the author received his subject matter and the language, and whatever else can be known about the author's distinctive manner [*Art und Weise*] of writing.' Technical interpretation consists of two methods, which he calls the 'divinatory' and the 'comparative':

> By leading the interpreter to transform himself, so to speak, into the author, the divinatory method seeks to gain an immediate com-

prehension of the author as an individual. The comparative method
proceeds by subsuming the author under a general type. It then tries to
find his distinctive traits by comparing him with the others of the same
general type. Divinatory knowledge is the feminine strength in knowing
people; comparative knowledge the masculine.[1]

Schleiermacher's approach to hermeneutics was developed further
later in the nineteenth century by Wilhelm Dilthey. He made a
distinction between the human sciences, that is, the humanities and
the social sciences, and the natural sciences. Because the natural
sciences directed their attention to data which had no connection
with human consciousness interpretation took the form of 'explanation' (*Erklären*). He restricted 'understanding' to the human sciences
since in that sphere interpretation was concerned with what had
been produced by human agency. Dilthey's hermeneutics attempted
to give a philosophical basis and a secure methodology to the study
of the human sciences. He departed from Schleiermacher's view that
understanding could be confined to a knowledge of the language and
context of a text and of the subjectivity of its creator. Rather he saw
understanding as intrinsic to the process of human life: it was what
he called a 'category of life'. That is to say, people continuously
found themselves in situations in which they had to understand what
was happening around them in order to act or take decisions.
Understanding, therefore, cannot be separated from our sense of
being human: an act of understanding constitutes what he called a
'lived experience'. Although these ideas had a much wider application than merely the interpretation of written texts, Dilthey
considered that the highest form of interpretation:

> The methodological understanding of permanently fixed life-
> expressions we call explication. As the life of the mind only finds its
> complete, exhaustive and therefore, objectively comprehensible
> expression in language, explication culminates in the interpretation of
> the written records of human existence. This art is the basis of
> philology. The science of this art is hermeneutics.

The major task of hermeneutics, Dilthey believed, was to analyse in
philosophical terms understanding and interpretation as they had
evolved in the various human sciences:

> Today hermeneutics enters a context in which the human studies acquire
> a new, important task. It has always defended the certainty of
> understanding against historical scepticism and wilful subjectivity . . . .
> Now we must relate hermeneutics to the epistemological task of

showing the possibility of historical knowledge and finding the means of acquiring it. The basic significance of understanding has been explained; we must now, starting from the logical forms of understanding, ascertain to what degree it can achieve validity.[2]

It is with the Schleiermacher–Dilthey tradition of hermeneutics, particularly Schleiermacher, that E. D. Hirsch identifies and from which both the New Criticism and Gadamer's hermeneutics depart. Hirsch quotes approvingly the following assertion by Schleiermacher: 'Everything in a given text which requires fuller interpretation must be explained and determined exclusively from the linguistic domain common to the author and his original public.'[3] This sums up Hirsch's position. He accuses the New Critics and Heidegger and Gadamer of accepting a doctrine of 'semantic autonomy': that is, that all written language remains independent of 'the subjective realm of the author's personal thoughts and feelings'.[4] Rather than discussing Gadamer's hermeneutics in its own terms, it will be more useful to discuss it primarily in the context of Hirsch and the New Criticism by looking at Hirsch's criticism of Gadamer's major work, *Truth and Method*.

It should be emphasised first of all that Gadamer is concerned with hermeneutics in the wider sense rather than with literary interpretation. However, his view of the nature of the literary text – what he calls the 'eminent text' – has strong similarities to that of the New Critics:

> A poetical work is encountered within a literary tradition or at least it merges into one. And it is in an essential and demanding sense a text, namely the kind of text that does not refer back to inner speech or spoken utterances as their fixation but, released from its provenance, postulates its own validity as a last court of appeal for reader and interpreter alike. . . . What precisely does not exist in such a text is something that elsewhere justifies the truth claim of assertions, namely the kind of relationship to 'reality' which one is used to call 'reference'. A text is poetic when it does not admit such a relation to truth at all or at best allows it only a secondary sense. This is the case with all texts which we classify as 'literature'. The literary work of art possesses its own autonomy, and this means its explicit freedom from that question of truth which qualifies assertions, be they spoken or written, as true or false.

Like the New Critics, he attaches great importance to interpretation but he sees the literary text as not possessing meaning in the ordinary sense:

My thesis is that explication is essentially and inseparably bound to the poetic text itself, precisely because it is never to be exhausted through explication. No one can read a poem without penetrating ever more into understanding and this includes explication. Reading is explication, and explication is nothing but the articulated fulfillment of reading. . . . Just as the word 'text' really means an inter-wovenness of threads that does not ever again allow the individual threads to emerge, so, too, the poetic text is a text in the sense that its elements have merged into a unified series of words and sounds.[5]

Here one can see clear links with the central New Critical doctrine that poetry is 'pseudo-statement' in which form and content are unified and which has its own special claim to truth.

Hirsch attacks Gadamer's hermeneutics because like the New Criticism it rejects authorial intention:

To suppose that a text means what its author meant is to Gadamer pure romantic *Psychologismus*, for a text's meaning does not lie in mental processes, which are in any case inaccessible, but in the subject matter or thing meant, the *Sache*, which, while independent of author and reader, is shared by both. (*Validity in Interpretation (VI)*, 247)

Thus for Gadamer, in contrast to Schleiermacher and Dilthey, 'textual meaning can somehow exist independently of individual consciousness' (*VI*, 248). Hirsch quotes Gadamer: 'The meaning of a text goes beyond its author not just sometimes but always. Understanding is not a reproductive but always a productive activity' (*VI*, 249). For Hirsch the clear consequence of this is that all textual meaning is indeterminate and interpretation becomes pointless, 'for it is only when a text does mean something and not just anything that interpretation is a plausible enterprise' (*VI*, 249).

Hirsch recognises that Gadamer's concept of tradition is designed to exercise control over indeterminacy and quotes the following passages from *Truth and Method*:

The substance of literature is not the dead persistence of an alien being that exists simultaneously with the experienced reality of a later time. Literature is rather a function of spiritual conservation and tradition, and therefore carries into every present its hidden history.

In truth, the important thing is to recognize distance in time as a positive and productive possibility of understanding. It is not a yawning abyss, but is filled out through the continuity of its coming hither and by that tradition in whose light shines everything that comes down to us. (*VI*, 250)

But for Hirsch:

> tradition cannot really function as a stable, normative concept, since it is in fact a changing, descriptive concept. . . . Without a genuinely stable norm we cannot even in principle make a valid choice between two differing interpretations, and we are left with the consequence that a text means nothing in particular at all. (*VI*, 250-1)

He is similarly critical of the key Gadamerian idea of 'fusion of horizons' by which an identification takes place between the perspective of the reader in the present and the historical perspective of the text, creating a unique perspective which is neither wholly one nor the other. Whereas in the traditional hermeneutics of Schleiermacher and Dilthey the interpreter of a text should attempt to avoid allowing his own anachronistic perspective to influence his interpretation, for Gadamer not only is this impossible but it is undesirable even to attempt to do so. Following Heidegger, Gadamer believes that an interpreter should accept the fact that there is no way of breaking free of the hermeneutic circle – a concept based on the contradiction that in order to understand a part of a text one needs to have knowledge of the whole, while understanding the whole text depends on understanding every part. Dilthey thought this could be overcome by a constant feedback between part and whole but Heidegger rejected this and extended the concept of the hermeneutic circle to embrace the existential situation of the individual. As Hirsch summarises it:

> The prior sense of the whole which ultimately lends meaning to any person's experience is his spiritual cosmos or *Welt*. But, since a person's *Welt* is always constitutively historical, it follows that any meaning we experience must have been pre-accommodated to our historical world.

Thus 'It is futile to project ourselves into the historical past where our texts arose, since our own present world is already pre-given in our attempted projection.'[6] For Heidegger and Gadamer, any attempt to break out of this hermeneutic circle is a denial of one's own intrinsically historical being. Hirsch argues that such concepts as fusion of horizons and the hermeneutic circle are irreconcilable with traditional historical criticism which seeks to discover the original meaning of texts. Gadamer's hermeneutics, however, has been a major influence on the historical criticism of Hans Robert Jauss which focuses on the reception of literary works and which I shall discuss in Chapter 7.

Hirsch's historicism and intentionalism, however, coexist with a view of the nature of language and meaning that on the surface places him closer to the New Critics and Gadamer than to most traditional historical critics. One of the key ideas he puts forward in *Validity in Interpretation* is that language cannot be pinned down to a single meaning. If one looks at a text as an independent piece of language it is open to a plurality of meanings. He contends that the various possible meanings which inhere in the language of the text itself can be reduced to one meaning only by recognising that the author intended a particular meaning. He illustrates this point by taking two opposed interpretations of Wordsworth's poem 'A Slumber Did My Spirit Seal', by Cleanth Brooks and F. W. Bateson, and arguing that both are equally likely if one considers the poem only in terms of its language. The only way of deciding that one interpretation is to be preferred over the other is by deciding which is likely to be closer to the author's intention. Hirsch implicitly rejects the New Critical criterion of comprehensiveness as being sufficient to decide among interpretations on the grounds that opposed interpretations may exhibit a similar degree of comprehensiveness.

He also believes, however, that readers of literature have a basic desire to feel that a text has some relation to the preoccupations of their own time. Here he is closer to Gadamer than to traditional hermeneutics or to orthodox historical criticism since, like Gadamer, he emphasises that the modern reader cannot and should not deny his or her own modernity. But he differs from Gadamer in arguing that a text's modern significance should not be confused with its meaning. In contrast to Gadamer's fusion of horizons, Hirsch argues that it is possible for a modern reader to separate the 'meaning' of a text, its meaning in relation to its own time, from its 'significance': that is, what it may mean in the context of the time of later readers:

> The fundamental distinction overlooked by Gadamer is that between the meaning of a text and the significance of that meaning to a present situation. . . . There is a difference between the meaning of a text (which does not change) and the meaning of a text to us today (which changes). The meaning of a text is that which the author meant by his use of particular linguistic symbols. . . . However, each time this meaning is construed, its meaning to the construer (its significance) is different. (*VI*, 10)

Hirsch contends that Gadamer has confused these two processes.

The crucial difference between Hirsch's and Gadamer's approach to hermeneutics is a philosophical one. Hirsch is aware that the logic of his position that a text is open to any number of meanings if it is considered purely as a text entails that from the reader's point of view an anachronistic meaning may for some reason or other be preferable to the authorial meaning. But such a meaning must be consigned to the category of 'significance' on ethical grounds:

> let me state what I consider to be a fundamental ethical maxim for interpretation, a maxim that claims no privileged sanction from metaphysics or analysis, but only from general ethical tenets, generally shared. *Unless there is a powerful overriding value in disregarding an author's intention (i.e. original meaning), we who interpret as a vocation should not disregard it.*[7]

He goes on to say that this maxim also holds good for literature as well as for non-literary discourses. Hirsch, unlike both the New Critics and Gadamer, denies literature special status and it is significant that he does not call his book *Validity in Literary Interpretation* although it is concerned almost entirely with literary interpretation.

Gadamer would reject Hirsch's distinction between meaning and significance since for him we can understand a text only in relation to our own situation. Thus there is no fundamental difference between meaning and significance. One of his major preoccupations in *Truth and Method* is to rehabilitate the concept of 'prejudice' from attacks upon it by the Enlightenment tradition of thinking. Perception and cognition are always 'prejudiced' and this should be accepted. The Enlightenment belief that interpretation should aspire to complete neutrality fails to recognise that consciousness is always governed by what Gadamer calls a 'fore-structure of understanding'. One might argue, however, that one should nevertheless try to eliminate 'prejudice' as far as possible even if one adopts Gadamer's position that total elimination is impossible. But Gadamer argues that one should accept with equanimity the inevitability of 'prejudice' and here it is clear that he has a different view of the ethics of interpretation from Hirsch. What understanding is for him is quite different from the Schleiermacher–Dilthey tradition. It involves participation in the meaning of a text through confronting the text as object from one's own situation. If a text is to live, then the reader must discover its meaning and truth by an existential engagement with it. To regard the meaning of a text as being entirely under the

control of the author is to identify meaning with the author's
intentions and thus to avoid confronting and sharing in the meaning
embodied in the text itself.

The problem of intention

Although there has been wide support among traditional historical
critics for Hirsch's attempt to rescue intentionality and historical
meaning from the New Critical view of the text as an independently
existing structure and from Gadamer's position that interpreters are
trapped in the hermeneutic circle, some of these critics have been
worried by Hirsch's admission that texts considered purely in terms
of language do in fact possess semantic autonomy and that the
meaning the author intended has only an ethical priority. Such
critics are right to be worried, I believe, for the concept of semantic
autonomy together with the meaning–significance distinction creates
the difficulty that Hirsch's intentionalist theory of meaning is not
different in kind from that of the New Critics or Gadamerian
hermeneutics. Indeed, I shall argue that the differences between
Hirsch and traditional hermeneutics on the one side and the New
Critics and Gadamer on the other are less fundamental both at the
level of theory and practice than they seem.

It is almost certain, for example, that the great majority of the
New Critics would be quite happy to accept Hirsch's intentionalist
concept of meaning at the semantic level. Such critics, coming across
the word 'gales' in Collins's poem 'Ode to Evening', would not raise
any objection to the view that what Collins meant by 'gales' was not
high winds but gentle breezes. The New Critics were well aware that
language is not static and that any understanding of the language of a
poem has to take this into account in reading and interpreting poems
written in the past. But although one might be able to reach general
agreement about what the language of a poem means in semantic
terms sentence by sentence – and it should be stressed that a minimal
degree of interpretation is required even at the level of basic
semantics as meaning is never context-free – the meaning of the
poem as a whole is something quite different. This difference seems
to be blurred in Hirsch's theory of meaning, and of course what
literary critics are predominantly concerned with is meaning in
relation to a whole work. Even when they concentrate on the

meaning of a phrase or sentence, they are seldom concerned with meaning in a basic semantic sense but rather with how certain connotations of the meaning of that phrase or sentence relate to the text as a whole.

The main difficulty of Hirsch's theory is how authorial intention relates to the meaning of a work as a whole. Traditional historical critics, the New Critics and Gadamer, I suggest, would all accept the power of authorial intention as it relates to the meaning of texts in a semantic sense. But what does *King Lear* as a whole mean? Even if one were able to resurrect Shakespeare and ask him, it seems probable that he would not be able to provide a useful answer, for there does not seem to be any way of distinguishing the meaning of a text as a whole from an interpretation of it and writers are not necessarily skilled at literary interpretation. The best that an author could do would be to provide some guidelines which the literary critic might be able to elaborate, and of course the critic could not necessarily take the author's views on trust since one has to recognise that authors sometimes are liars or have bad memories. What the meaning of a whole work is in Hirschian terms, therefore, is an interpretation which could have been intended by an author – but there is no direct connection between the interpretation and the author, whereas at the semantic level such a direct connection can usually be clearly established. All that Hirsch can claim is that in interpreting a whole work the essential criterion is that the interpretation should not be irreconcilable with what is known of the author and his or her historical context.

How does this relate to the meaning–significance distinction? This distinction must operate in relation both to semantic meaning and to the meaning of whole works. Hirsch cannot coherently argue that a reader who prefers to interpret 'gales' in 'Ode to Evening' as high winds is wrong, given his view that language is semantically autonomous; he must therefore categorise a historical interpretation of the word as 'meaning' and a non-historical interpretation as 'significance'. But the same distinction cannot be as plainly established at the level of the interpretation of whole works. Clearly, blatantly anachronistic interpretations would possess significance and not meaning. It is not uncommon, however, for several opposed interpretations of the same literary text to exist, all of which seek to take account of authorial and historical data, but because of the fact that such data are ambiguous, different interpretations are produced.

In Hirschian terms only one interpretation can have 'meaning', even if it may be impossible to decide which one that is. Since Hirsch is committed to semantic autonomy he cannot say that the other interpretations are merely examples of mistaken meaning. The concept of semantic autonomy cannot be reconciled with mistaken meaning unless that meaning is unsustainable at a grammatical and semantic level. There thus seems no alternative but to place 'wrong interpretations' which adhere to authorial and historical criteria in the category of significance. This clearly creates a contradiction in Hirsch's theory, for the meaning–significance distinction was designed to separate intentionalist from non-intentionalist interpretation but, as I have tried to show, intentionalist interpretations which happen to be wrong must also have significance according to Hirsch's theory. In fact, where authorial and historical data are ambiguous, it may be impossible to decide whether intentionalist interpretations belong to the category of meaning or the category of significance. Given these difficulties Hirsch cannot use the meaning–significance distinction for differentiating intentionalist interpretation from text-based interpretation unless the latter is wilfully anachronistic, which is seldom the case.

What leads Hirsch's theory into these difficulties is his adherence to the concept of semantic autonomy. It is this which makes it necessary to distinguish between meaning and significance since he cannot assert that any meaning which is semantically possible is wrong, even though he is committed to an intentionalist position. It is not surprising therefore that recent developments in intentionalist theory have attacked the notion of semantic autonomy. These have the advantage from the intentionalist point of view of avoiding the complications of Hirsch's concept of significance since intentionalist interpretations which may be wrong are merely mistaken, and it seems possible then that a fundamental distinction between intentionalist and text-based interpretation may be established.

One of the leading advocates of such an intentionalist position is P. D. Juhl. He argues that the concept of semantic autonomy does not make any logical sense. He thus seeks to undermine the theoretical basis of text-based approaches which ignore the question of authorial intention, such as the New Criticism and Gadamerian hermeneutics. In his book *Interpretation* he discusses Wordsworth's 'A Slumber Did My Spirit Seal', as Hirsch had done in *Validity in Interpretation*, and agrees with him that the language of the poem is open to more than one interpretation. But whereas Hirsch goes on to argue that the only coherent way to avoid a situation in which there is no means of deciding between one interpretation and another is by choosing the interpretation that can be reconciled with the author's intention, Juhl argues that one must choose the meaning that the author intended since meaning is the product of a speech act and therefore inseparable from the concept of intention. To believe that language can have meaning that is independent of human intention, he argues, has no logical basis, since language has meaning only when it is a speech act perpetrated by a human being. Discussing whether a phrase in the poem, 'in earth's diurnal course', suggests that the motion of the woman in the poem is orderly or violent, Juhl writes:

> Now suppose that the poem I have quoted above is not in fact by Wordsworth but has been accidentally typed out by a monkey randomly depressing keys on a typewriter. (Or suppose that we found the lines as marks – on, say, a large rock – produced by water erosion.) It is immediately obvious that we can no longer say that the words 'in earth's diurnal course' – rather than some other words which suggest violent motion – qualify 'rolled round' *because* they are an appropriate means to suggest gentle motion (or because they suggest gentle motion). . . . All we can now say is: The words 'in earth's diurnal course', rather than some other words, qualify 'rolled round' because the monkey just happened to hit that series of keys there (or because the water just happened to erode the rock in such a way that those marks, rather than some others, were produced there).[8]

Juhl concludes that one can give a reason why 'in earth's diurnal course' qualifies 'rolled round' only if one assumes that the poem had an author who had certain intentions when he wrote the poem. If one treats the poem as pure text, without considering intention, discussing such matters would make no more sense than trying to decide whether or not a piece of language produced by a random process was better interpreted in one way rather than another. Such random language could not be a speech act.

For Juhl, therefore, interpretation has no logical justification if it is not an effort to discover the intention of the author of a text. The concept of semantic autonomy makes no sense in discussing interpretation because there is no point in considering whether a text has a particular meaning unless that meaning was intended by the writer of the text. Juhl accepts that the author's intention cannot be directly inferred from the text itself. The interpreter must construct a hypothesis as to what meaning an author intended and support such a hypothesis by whatever evidence is available. Opposed interpretations might emerge, but only one would be right; the others would be mistaken.

Juhl's argument has been supported and extended from a radical pragmatist perspective by Walter Benn Michaels and Steven Knapp in an article entitled 'Against theory'. Like Hirsch and Juhl they use 'A Slumber Did My Spirit Seal' as their example and envisage someone coming across the first verse of this poem written in the sand. While gazing at this a wave comes and retreats leaving the second verse, so that there is no doubt that this 'poem' has been produced not by human agency but by accident. Knapp and Michaels argue that 'As long as you thought the marks were poetry, you were assuming their intentional character', but when it becomes clear they are authorless, they cease to be words at all: 'to deprive them of an author is to convert them into accidental likenesses of language. They are not, after all, an example of intentionless meaning; as soon as they become intentionless they become meaningless as well'.[9]

Knapp and Michaels criticise Juhl for continuing to believe that the poem would still function semantically even if it were produced by a random process: 'Our point is that marks produced by chance are not words at all but only resemble them. For Juhl, the marks remain words, but words detached from the intentions that would make them utterances.'[10] Knapp and Michaels claim that the marks are not only not speech acts; they are not language at all. They go on to argue that since meaning is always intentional, all debate about interpretative theory is rendered futile. One has no choice but to assume that language has an intentional character and anyone who chooses to interpret language as if it is authorless or who prefers an interpretation that has no relation to the intention of the author is merely behaving irrationally. Thus such a person's behaviour can find no justification at the level of theory.

Although both Juhl and Knapp and Michaels reject semantic autonomy, different consequences follow from the positions they adopt. Juhl implies that text-based criticism interprets literary works as if they are language divorced from speech acts. Its interpretations therefore can have no theoretical justification. Knapp and Michaels, however, suggest that all interpretation assumes that language is intentional even if it adopts an apparently anti-intentionalist stance. One cannot discuss meaning without discussing intention because meaning is inextricably linked with intention. It seems to me that Knapp and Michaels are right and that it is virtually impossible to find any literary interpretation that does not, at least implicitly, assume intentionality in some form or other. However, intentionality cannot be confined only to the author's conscious intention – a point Knapp and Michaels do not discuss – as the author can be seen as the product of such supra-personal forces as culture, language, history, ideology, the unconscious. Knapp and Michael's argument, as they admit, has no consequencs for interpretative practice, for although interpretation cannot be separated from the question of intentionality, this makes it no easier to decide what an author's intention was and therefore what a work's meaning is. This leads me back to the point I made earlier that the differences at the level of theory or practice between traditional hermeneutics supported by intentionalists like Hirsch and Juhl and the text-based interpretation associated with the New Criticism and Gadamerian hermeneutics are less fundamental than they seem at first sight.

This can be illustrated by looking again at the New Criticism which is widely held to be anti-intentionalist. Wimsatt and Beardsley's essay, 'The intentional fallacy', is generally regarded as a classic New Critical text.[11] Yet in practice there is no rejection of intentionalism. As I suggested above, the New Critics accept historical semantics and implicitly they treat literary texts as speech acts. Even though they concentrate on the text itself and do not explicitly discuss intentional matters, their interpretations are almost never blatantly anachronistic. It seems likely, for example, that a New Critic like Cleanth Brooks would argue that although he might use critical terminology that writers of the past would not have been familiar with and although he directs his attention to the work itself, nevertheless he does not impose meanings which could not have been possible at the time the work was written. Hirsch, in discussing Brooks's reading of Wordsworth's 'A Slumber Did My Spirit Seal' implies that Brooks takes no account of historical criteria, but this is a gross simplification of Brooks's position. Brooks may concentrate on the text itself but a reading of his criticism as a whole reveals an underlying awareness of authorial and historical considerations. The same is true of the New Criticism in general. Similarly, even though Gadamerian hermeneutics may emphasise a fusion of horizons, this does not lead to a wilfully anachronistic approach to interpretation but to the discovery of meanings in the original text which seize the interest of modern readers. But, Gadamer would argue, these meanings are part of the historical reality of the text and not merely projected on to it. One should also point out that Eliot's essay, 'Tradition and the individual talent' which had a major influence on Anglo-American criticism, has important similarities with Gadamer's idea of tradition and his concept of a fusion of horizons. Eliot emphasises the importance of a historical sense but asserts that it 'involves a perception, not only of the pastness of the past, but of its presence'. Similarly, the significant new work of art does not exist in its own terms but fits into an existing tradition and alters it in the process, creating 'conformity between the old and the new'.[12]

The Hirschian position that an interpretation must be one that would have been possible and acceptable within the original authorial and historical context of the work fails to create a fundamental difference between intentionalist criticism and either the New Criticism or Gadamerian hermeneutics. These apparently opposed forms of interpretation are thus less irreconcilable than they seem. Hirsch and Juhl, of course, would disagree with the New Critics and Gadamer on how the historical situation and beliefs and the modern critic should affect the interpretative process. But this disagreement need not lead to major differences at the level of interpretative practice. As I argued above, literary interpretation is primarily concerned with the interpretation of whole works and the meaning of a whole work cannot be differentiated from an interpretation of it. Even if an author has left some record of his or her intention regarding the meaning of the whole work, at the very least this will have to be supplemented and elaborated by the critic. The critic has to interpret what the author intended, and develop and apply it to the text concerned. The intentionalist critic is therefore as much an interpreter as a critic in the New Critical tradition and their interpretative methods and approaches are not, I think, different in kind, although there will almost certainly be differences in critical rhetoric.

This point can be illustrated by looking at the interpretative method Juhl advocates. He argues that other texts by the same author should be consulted in trying to decide what the author meant in a particular text, although this creates the logical problem that these other texts would also have to be interpreted in the same way as the original text, thus creating a circularity that is unsatisfactory in theoretical terms. But Juhl's major point is that in considering how a text should be interpreted 'we do not appeal to the *meaning* of the text, but to certain *textual features* which . . . constitute evidence for the meaning of the text if and only if they are evidence of the author's intention'.[13] Juhl fails to prove, however, that there is a fundamental division between the kind of intentionalist interpretations that would be produced by the method he advocates and the majority of New Critical interpretations which, although apparently concentrating only on the text itself, in fact virtually always take into account historical semantics and what is known of an author and his or her historical and literary context even if they do not discuss these matters directly.

Where one would find a significant difference between the traditional hermeneutics of Juhl and Hirsch and Gadamerian hermeneutics is in relation to Gadamer's contention that the interpreter cannot escape his or her own historical context, since Juhl and Hirsch would deny that one is trapped in the hermeneutic circle. But, again, this theoretical difference is unlikely to have much practical effect, for if Gadamer is right, even if supporters of traditional hermeneutics think they are reconstructing an author's original intention in its own terms, in fact they cannot avoid allowing their own historical perspective to condition how they interpret works written in the past. The difference, then, is only in how the critic perceives his or her interpretative situation, but from a Gadamerian point of view this need have no effect on practice. Although a supporter of traditional hermeneutics would not aim at achieving a 'fusion of horizons', if Gadamer is right it will happen whether the critic believes in it or not, and in any case it would seem difficult for the intentionalist critic to argue that his or her preconceptions and interests, 'prejudices' in Gadamer's terms, can be completely transcended.

Traditional hermeneutics, the New Criticism and Gadamer also agree in one particular respect regarding interpretation, and this is more significant, in my view, than their differences. There is explicit agreement among them on the subject of textual coherence. Hirsch writes in *Validity in Interpretation*: 'Faced with alternatives, the interpreter chooses the reading which best meets the criterion of coherence. Indeed, even when the text is not problematical, coherence remains the decisive criterion, since the meaning is "obvious" only because it "makes sense" ' (*VI*, 236). Hirsch of course believes that such coherence should take into account the author's intention and Juhl would go further and argue that coherence makes no logical sense unless one relates it to intention. The belief that interpretation should aim at revealing or discovering textual coherence is also held by the New Critics and Gadamer. I have discussed the New Critics' emphasis on coherence of interpretation in the previous chapter and Gadamer's view of interpretation as a search for 'truth' directed at an object, '*die Sache*' implies that the text must be assumed to possess an internal coherence and consistency which the interpreter seeks to demonstrate. This commitment to coherence aligns traditional hermeneutics, the New Criticism and Gadamer together against developments in interpretation in contemporary critical theory – what has been called 'negative hemeneutics' – for the major difference in the theory of interpretation today is not so much between traditional and Gadamerian hermeneutics but between those who believe that the aim of interpretation is to demonstrate unity and coherence and those who argue that its aim is to reveal that texts are contradictory and incoherent. This difference reflects the situation in Anglo-American criticism in which the New Criticism has been identified with such concepts as organic unity and spatial form, whereas post-structuralist-influenced criticism has attacked such concepts and emphasised the gaps, disruptions and impasses within texts, as I shall discuss later.

Paul Ricoeur, one of the leading figures in contemporary hermeneutics, sees hermeneutics as being fundamentally divided in the following way:

> According to the one pole, hermeneutics is understood as the manifestation and restoration of a meaning addressed to me in the manner of a message, a proclamation, or as is sometimes said, a kerygma; according to the other pole, it is understood as a demystification, as a reduction of illustration.

As against 'interpretation as restoration of meaning' there is 'interpretation according to what I call collectively the school of suspicion' which is concerned with the 'reduction of the lies and illusions of consciousness'.[11] The founding fathers of the hermeneutics of suspicion, Ricoeur claims, are Marx, Nietzsche and Freud. While Gadamer sets out to discover 'truth' in a text, the hermeneutics of suspicion seeks to reveal 'truth as lying'. What links Marx, Nietzsche and Freud as advocates of a hermeneutics of suspicion, Ricoeur aruges, is that they 'present the most radically contrary stance to the phenomenology of the sacred and to any hermeneutics understood as the recollection of meaning and as the reminiscence of being'.[15]

This negative form of hermeneutics can be connected with the critique of Gadamerian hermeneutics associated with Jürgen Habermas, a philosopher in the tradition of the Frankfurt school of Marxist criticism. Although Habermas's critique is directed at Gadamer, it clearly has application also to traditional hermeneutics and the New Criticism. Habermas is sympathetic to Gadamer's anti-positivism; for example, his view of understanding as being always historically situated. But Habermas is worried that Gadamer's hermeneutic project involves reaching a consensus on meaning through a 'fusion of horizons' in which the language and perspective of the interpreter is extended in order to understand the text that is being interpreted. For Habermas this leaves out of account the question of ideology, that the consensus achieved may be systematically distorted. Gadamer, in focusing on truth does not consider the possibility, Habermas suggests, that 'truth' may have the ideological function of supporting repressive power structures. Gadamer, despite his criticism of the Romantic hermeneutics of Schleiermacher, is even more critical of the Enlightenment belief that one can attain a prejudice-free form of understanding. But for Habermas the Enlightenment tradition of thinking makes it possible to recognise the presence of ideology whereas the concept of understanding intrinsic to hermeneutics does not. One can make the separation between truth and ideology only by standing outside the hermeneutic perspective and focusing on what Habermas calls a 'reference system':

> *Social actions can only be comprehended in an objective framework that is constituted conjointly by language, labor, and domination.* The happening of tradition appears as an absolute power only to a self-sufficient hermeneutics; in fact it is relative to systems of labor and domination. Sociology cannot, therefore, be reduced to interpretive sociology. It requires a reference system that, on the one hand, does not suppress the symbolic mediation of social action in favor of a naturalistic view of behavior that is merely controlled by signals and excited by stimuli but that, on the other hand, also does not succumb to an idealism of linguisticality [*Sprachlichkeit*] and sublimate social processes entirely to cultural tradition.[16]

Gadamer has defended himself against this critique by claiming that the fact that 'truth' in hermeneutic terms cannot be dissociated from prejudice does not mean that hermeneutics is unaware of ideological considerations. He has also questioned how a critique such as Habermas's can exist beyond hermeneutics in such a way as to achieve a non-hermeneutic form of understanding.[17]

The Gadamer–Habermas debate, although not directly related to the question of literary interpretation, is nevertheless relevant to it. Whereas traditional hermeneutics, the New Criticism, and Gadamerian hermeneutics according to Habermas, are concerned with achieving a coherent reading of a text in its own terms without seeking to undermine that coherence, much contemporary critical theory believes that literary interpretation should abandon the concept of coherence and expose the incoherences that texts try to conceal. Perhaps the root of this division lies in aesthetics. Traditional historical critics, the New Criticism, and Gadamer, despite their differences, are united in regarding the literary text as an object of value in itself. Interpretation is therefore the means of enhancing the reader's appreciation of that intrinsic value. Contemporary critical theory tends on the other hand to regard aesthetics as a constraint on an uninhibited analysis of the literary text that must include aesthetics within its orbit. Before going on to discuss the various forms this new approach to interpretation takes in contemporary interpretative practice it is necessary to discuss another important element in contemporary criticism bearing on interpretation: namely the attack on interpretation itself as a legitimate form of literary criticism.

CHAPTER 4

Against interpretation

Although interpretation has played a dominant role in twentieth-century criticism, it has also met with strong opposition. As I suggested previously, Russian Formalism and Leavis's criticism were anti-interpretative but they did not attack interpretation directly. More recently, however, there have been explicit objections to interpretation as a critical approach. The best known attack is Susan Sontag's essay, 'Against interpretation', first published in 1964. Although this was an attack on interpretation in the arts in general, literary criticism was singled out as being particularly dominated by interpretation:

> To interpret is to impoverish, to deplete the world – in order to set up a shadow world of 'meanings'. . . .
>
> In most modern instances, interpretation amounts to the philistine refusal to leave the work of art alone. By reducing the work of art to its content and then interpreting *that*, one tames the work of art. Interpretation makes art manageable, comfortable.
>
> This philistinism of interpretation is more rife in literature than in any other art. For decades now literary critics have understood it to be their task to translate the elements of the poem or play or novel or story into something else.[1]

Susan Sontag's affiliations as a critic when this essay was published were with aestheticism and a formalism closer to Russian Formalism than to the kind of formalism associated with the early New Criticism, alternatives to interpretative criticism that had little support among literary critics of the time. She had also devoted comparatively little of her attention to literary criticism, yet this essay has been reprinted in collections of criticism and has had a considerable impact on literary critics. One of the main reasons for the power of the essay is that it appeared at a time when the sterility of the later New Criticism was becoming increasingly evident. What the New Critical tradition had apparently led to was the production of an endless stream of interpretations of the major works in the literary canon, but whether such unremitting interpretative activity was necessary or useful was seldom discussed. Interpretations of these works were also accumulating to such an extent that it was difficult even for specialists to find the time to read all the interpretative material being published.

Two factors were particularly responsible for creating this situation. By concentrating on interpreting the text itself with little emphasis being given to 'extrinsic' considerations such as authorial intention and historical context, the New Criticism inevitably produced self-contained interpretations of the works it discussed, interpretations which attempted to be as coherent, consistent and comprehensive as possible. But although the interpretations which were most comprehensive should theoretically be preferred, in practice, as I have suggested in Chapter 2, it was difficult to decide on degrees of comprehensiveness, as a totally comprehensive interpretation could never be achieved. What the New Criticism has revealed is that there are virtually no limits to the connotations of literary texts. This can be demonstrated by consulting bibliographies of criticism and looking at the articles published over the past twenty or thirty years on works by such writers as Shakespeare, Spenser, Milton, Dickens, Melville, Henry James, T. S. Eliot, Joyce. What such an exercise would show, I suggest, is that critics will always be able to discover in what are seen as major texts new or previously unnoticed connotations. And, given sufficient technical competence, the critic can then go on to create a new interpretation on the basis of these connotations that will possess some degree of coherence and comprehensiveness. Although the New Critics were opposed to relativism and appeared to believe that if one assembled together all the individual interpretations of a particular work, one would achieve something approaching a totally comprehensive interpretation, the evidence suggests that what the New Criticism led to in practice was an accumulation of interpretations which existed largely in their own terms. Critics might allude to other interpretations, usually in passing or in footnotes, but there was little sense of dialogue or debate, for what was important was to go on to create a new reading which accounted for data that previous readings ignored or dealt with inadequately.

But the fact that the New Criticism encouraged self-contained, internally coherent interpretations which tended to avoid dialogue or debate with other readings is not enough in itself to account for disillusionment with its critical approach. The problem was the sheer quantity of interpretations, especially of the major texts in the literary canon, that found their way into print. This made it inevitable that eventually questions would be raised as to the point of the interpretative enterprise. To understand why the New Criticism was used to generate so many interpretations, one must look at institutional factors affecting literary criticism, in particular the role of literary criticism in higher education.

By the 1950s the New Criticism had become the leading critical approach in American universities. Its pedagogical advantage over traditional scholarly and historical criticism led to English or literary studies becoming a major force in the humanities, which in turn created an expansion in staffing levels in literature departments to meet increasing student demand. The main criterion in appointments to full-time tenured posts in American universities is publication since this is seen as the only truly objective test. Thus prospective academics have to 'publish or perish'. Whereas in the era of scholarly criticism, a critic might have to spend years reading before venturing on publication, with the New Criticism one could embark on publication after having read closely only a comparatively few texts. The need to publish in order to secure employment or promotion encouraged academics to make use of New Critical techniques to produce as many interpretations as possible. (Of course, in publishing a book on the subject of interpretation I have to accept that I can be accused of being part of the phenomenon I am describing.) Whereas during the era of the early New Criticism, interpretation seemed to have an inner dynamic created by a combination of cultural, theoretical and aesthetic considerations, after the New Criticism had become established as the predominant academic approach, professionalism was the underlying force governing interpretation. This aroused the worry that if critics engaged in literary interpretation primarily for professional purposes, were their hearts really in it? Had the New Criticism not become mechanistic, the basis of a production-line which created interpretations primarily to serve the career purposes of academics?[2]

One critic who has made this connection between the New Criticism and professionalism and attacked both is Richard Levin, a supporter of traditional scholarly criticism. In his book *New Readings vs Old Plays* he expresses concern at the 'proliferation' of new interpretations in the field of Renaissance drama and blames this situation on 'the ascendancy of the New Criticism in our universities'[3] because it has the facility to generate an apparently never-ending series of new readings. This characteristic of the New Criticism interacts with the necessity to 'publish or perish' to create an uncontrolled profusion of interpretations:

> it is undeniable that many university teachers, particularly the younger ones, are powerfully driven to seek the rewards of publication – raises, promotions, tenure, fellowships, released time, invitations to speak, recognition by professional associations, and the like. And they know that their interpretations are not likely to be published unless they say something about the work that has never been said before, which all too often means . . . that they must say something very strange. (*New Reading vs Old Plays (NR)*, 196)

Since numerous academics are engaged in this activity, the result is a 'babel of conflicting new readings . . . at the expense of real dialogue between the critics' (*NR*, 197). Other interpretations are tolerated with 'indifference' if not 'downright cynicism' because publication is what counts. And Levin sees the situation as even worse than it appears: 'For every new reading accepted for publication, there must be at least ten still more dubious readings which make the rounds of the journals without finding a home' (*NR*, 197), not to mention those produced for teaching purposes which are not offered for publication.

Another critic who has attacked professionalism, Gerald Graff, has seen the root of the problem as the tendency of academic institutions to create isolated groups of specialists who do not interact or engage with each other, with the result that they produce 'routinized criticism' strictly for the consumption of fellow specialists:

> Relieved of having to engage in intellectual confrontation with their colleagues, professors naturally cultivate the techniques of running literature through the various available interpretive grids, holding themselves accountable only to others who use the same procedures. Routinization is the child of disconnection and isolation.[4]

Professionalism has been defended, however, by Stanley Fish, a critic perhaps more sympathetic to the ideology of *laissez-faire* than most. He argues that the activity of literary criticism can function only in professional terms:

> any reason one could come up with for doing literary criticism would be a professional reason, in the sense that it could only have occurred to someone already thinking within assumed goals. To say something new or different or corrective is not to perform at the suspect fringes of literary criticism: it is precisely to *do* literary criticism as that activity is understood at the present time.

Fish is not worried by the fact critics may produce new interpretations of texts purely for career purposes since he believes that there is no real distinction between 'what one understands as the attempt to come to terms with the text, and what one understands as a professional opportunity'.[5] A critic's motives, he implies, are irrelevant: an interpretation must be judged in its own terms. But this does not deal with the problem that critics' motives in promoting their careers have created such a proliferation of interpretations that this in itself has undermined confidence in interpretation as a critical activity.

In Britain the position has been somewhat different, for although the post-war period has seen, as in America, English expanding to become the leading subject within the humanities in terms of staff and student numbers, the policy of 'publish or perish' has not operated. (Recent trends in higher education suggest that this situation may be changing, not because of academic support for such a policy but because it can be used as a pretext to justify staff cuts at a time when government funding for higher education is being drastically cut.) As a result British academics have not tended to feel that it was necessary to publish if they were to survive, and even promotion often did not seem to require publication. This may have to a considerable extent prevented the professionalisation of literary criticism and the over-production of interpretations characteristic of the American situation, but there were also negative consequences. Although in America the policy of 'publish or perish' may have had adverse or distorting effects on criticism it had a crude utilitarian value in that it could lead to the survival of the fittest – even if one has doubts about the concept of the 'fittest' in this context – while the more relaxed British approach could allow the unfit or 'deadwood' to survive. Certainly the American critical scene since the war has seemed much more energetic and vital than the British, even allowing for differences in scale between American and British higher education.

The problem created by the uncontrolled and directionless accumulation of interpretations may not have been enough to undermine confidence in the New Criticism and interpretation if an alternative critical approach which called interpretation into question had not emerged. This alternative was structuralism, which had had a major impact in the field of social anthropology through the work of Claude Lévi-Strauss. In the 1960s in France, structuralism was being applied to the study of literature by such critics as Tzvetan Todorov, Gérard Genette and most famously by Roland Barthes. Although structuralism initially gained only a few adherents among Anglo-American critics, eventually it led to developments that have seriously challenged the ascendancy of the New Criticism in America, at least in the most prestigious universities.

Structuralists were not interested in the interpretation of particular works but in larger questions concerned with literature as a system or as a form of discourse. In an introductory essay on structuralism in relation to literary criticism Todorov argues that there are two dominant attitudes in literary studies: 'one sees the literary text itself as a sufficient object of knowledge; the other considers each individual text as the manifestation of an abstract structure'.[6] The first of these, which he calls interpretation, 'is defined . . . by its aim, which is *to name the meaning of the text examined*' (*Introduction to Poetics* (*IP*), 4). In order to achieve this, ideally the text itself should speak and the interpreter of the text and the drama of the text should be effaced. But this ideal must fail to be realised since 'it is impossible to interpret a work, literary or otherwise, for and in itself, without leaving it for a moment, without projecting it elsewhere than upon itself'. The ideal could be achieved only by interpretation espousing 'the forms of the work so closely that the two are identical': that is, by a word for word repetition of the work itself. But as soon as the critic forsakes the work to write independently he 'says something that the work studied does not say, even if he claims to say the same thing. By the fact that he writes a new book, the critic suppresses the one he is talking about' (*IP*, 4). The second attitude to literary criticism, Todorov goes on to argue, is concerned with 'the establishment of general laws of which this particular text is the product' (*IP*, 6). There are several variations of this attitude but 'All deny the autonomous character of the literary work and regard it as the manifestation of laws that are external to it and that concern the psyche, or society, or even the "human mind"' (*IP*, 6).

Todorov identifies a structuralist approach with 'poetics' and sees it as distinct from both interpretation and the search for general laws:

> In contradistinction to the interpretation of particular works, [poetics] does not seek to name meaning, but aims at a knowledge of the general laws that preside over the birth of each work. But in contradistinction to such sciences as psychology, sociology, etc., it seeks these laws within literature itself. Poetics is therefore an approach to literature at once 'abstract' and 'internal'. (*IP*, 6)

Todorov suggests that structuralism's closest links are with Russian Formalism by stating that the individual work is to be seen 'only as the manifestation of an abstract and general structure, of which it is but one of the possible realizations', while literary criticism is a scientific enterprise whose concern is 'with that abstract property that constitutes the singularity of the literary phenomenon: *literariness*' (*IP*, 7). He differentiates sharply the structuralist aim from interpretation: 'The goal of this study is no longer to articulate a paraphrase, a descriptive résumé of the concrete work, but to propose a theory of the structure and functioning of literary discourse . . . so that existing literary works appear as achieved particular cases' (*IP*, 7). Poetics is thus concerned with the more general aspects of literary works, such as 'those abstract structures which it names "description" or "action" or "narration"' (*IP*, 9). Todorov claims, however, that he is not opposed to interpretation as such: 'A massive imbalance in favor of interpretation characterizes the history of literary studies: it is this disequilibrium that we must oppose, and not the principle of interpretation' (*IP*, 12).

Gérard Genette's views are similar to Todorov's. He argues that 'there is no literary object strictly speaking, but only a *literary function*, which can invest or abandon any object of writing in turn'.[7] He is sympathetic to Russian Formalism although he recognises its 'excesses' in, at least temporarily, ignoring content: 'Literature had long enough been regarded as a message without a code for it to become necessary to regard it for a time as a code without a message' (*Figures of Literary Discourse (FL)*, 7). Genette reveals the connection between structuralism and semiotics or semiology:

> Structuralist method as such is constituted at the very moment when

one rediscovers the message in the code, uncovered by an analysis of the immanent structures and not imposed from the outside by ideological prejudices. This moment was not to be long in coming, for the existence of the sign, at every level, rests on the connection of form and meaning. (*FL*, 7)

He goes on to assert that 'structural analysis must make it possible to uncover the connection that exists between a system of forms and a system of meanings, by replacing the search for term-by-term analogies with one for overall homologies' (*FL*, 8). He illustrates this difficult concept by discussing a debate in literary criticism about whether or not vowels can be associated with colours. Some argued that this was a reality, a universal feature of all languages, while others claimed it was a myth because an investigation of particular languages revealed no agreement from one language to another about which vowels suggested which colours. Genette argues that structuralism can resolve this conflict by looking at the question in non-positivist terms:

> it is true that no vowel evokes, naturally and in isolation, a particular color; but it is also true that the distribution of colors in the spectrum . . . can find its correspondence in the distribution of vowels in a given language. Hence the idea of a table of concordance, variable in its details but constant in its function: there is a spectrum of vowels as there is a spectrum of colors; the two systems evoke and attract one another, and the overall homology creates the illusion of a term-by-term analogy, which each realizes in its own way by an act of symbolic motivation comparable to the one analyzed by Lévi-Strauss in the case of totemism. (*FL*, 8-9)

Whereas Russian Formalism had tended to ignore the question of meaning, Genette admits that 'semantic phenomena . . . constitute the essence of poetic language', but these are to be studied semiologically in relation to the ' "larger unities" of discourse, beyond the framework . . . of the sentence. . . . One would thus study systems from a much higher level of generality, such as narrative, description, and the other major forms of linguistic expression' (*FL*, 10). But like Todorov, Genette does not deny any role for hermeneutics in literary criticism: 'the relation that binds structuralism and hermeneutics together might not be one of mechanical separation and exclusion, but of complementarity' (*FL*, 15).

The leading advocate of structuralist criticism in the Anglo-American world, however, has been a harsher critic of interpretation than his French precursors. Jonathan Culler, in an essay entitled

'Beyond interpretation', first published in 1976, unleashed a strong attack on both interpretation and the New Criticism, and virtually suggested that interpretation should be banished from criticism:

> the most important and insidious legacy of the New Criticism is the widespread and unquestioning acceptance of the notion that the critic's job is to interpret literary works. Indeed, fulfillment of the interpretive task has come to be the touchstone by which other kinds of critical writing are judged, and reviewers inevitably ask of any work of literary theory, linguistic analysis, or historical scholarship, whether it actually assists us in our understanding of particular works. In this critical climate it is therefore important, if only as a means of loosening the grip which interpretation has on critical consciousness, to take up a tendentious position and to maintain that, while the experience of literature may be an experience of interpreting works, in fact the interpretation of individual works is only tangentially related to the understanding of literature. . . .
>
> Indeed, there are many tasks that confront criticism, many things that we need if we are to advance our understanding of literature, but if there is one thing we do not need it is more interpretations of literary works.[8]

In his book *Structuralist Poetics*, first published in 1975, Culler had defended and elaborated the critical position associated with such French critics as Todorov, Genette and Barthes during his structuralist period. At the end of that book, however, he attacked post-structuralism. This had emerged in France in the latter half of the 1960s, particularly in the writings of Jacques Derrida, who had subjected fundamental structuralist assumptions to a 'deconstructive' critique, as I shall discuss later. In Culler's more recent books, *In Pursuit of Signs* and *On Deconstruction*, his position has shifted significantly and he has reached an accommodation with Derridean deconstruction, although this has involved recognising that interpretation cannot be completely banished even if one adopts a structuralist approach to criticism. But structuralist interpretation is still, he contends, not interpretation in the New Critical sense: 'Even when structuralists engage in interpretation, their attempt to analyse the structure of the work and the forces on which it depends leads to concentration on the relation between the work and its enabling conditions and undermines, as the opponents of structuralism seem to sense, the traditional interpretive project.' He has to recognise, however, that deconstruction would appear to reinstate that project: 'One can certainly argue that American criticism has found in deconstruction reasons to deem interpretation the supreme

task of critical inquiry and thus to preserve some measure of
continuity between the goals of the New Criticism and those of the
newer criticism.' But he argues that such connections are only
superficial and claims that 'the goal [of deconstructive readings] is
not to reveal the meaning of a particular work but to explore the
forces that recur in reading and writing'.[9]

In an earlier discussion in *The Pursuit of Signs* he admits that
semiotics – understood in Saussurean terms and thus almost inter-
changeable with structuralism – has been destabilised by post-
structuralist thinking: 'The very conventions to which we appeal in
explaining literary meanings are products: products which, it would
seem, must have acts as their sources', so that meaning must be
accounted for 'not by prior conventions but by acts of imposition'.[10]
But he claims that semiotics is not thereby radically undermined,
since it exists in a 'tense interplay' with deconstruction: 'the first
perspective also deconstructs the second in its turn, for acts of
imposition are themselves made possible by the situations in which
they occur, and meanings cannot be imposed unless they are
understood, unless the conventions which make possible understanding are already in place' (*PS*, 39).

Culler attempts in *The Pursuit of Signs* to preserve structuralist
criticism in a post-structuralist climate by reformulating structuralist poetics as literary semiotics. Literary criticism should direct its
attention to semiotics – which, he claims, 'seeks to identify the
conventions and operations by which any signifying practice (such as
literature) produces its observable effects of meaning' (*PS*, 48) – as a
theory of reading. He is still hostile to interpretative criticism but,
rather than dismissing it as he had tended to do during his earlier
structuralist phase, he tries to incorporate it within his anti-
interpretative version of semiotics. He identifies 'the proliferation of
interpretations' of texts as a problem for criticism but rejects
attempts to solve it by trying to pin texts down to a single meaning.
What a semiotics of literature should focus on is this very openness
of literature to plurality of meaning: 'Instead of taking the proliferation of interpretations as an obstacle to knowledge, can one
attempt to make it an object of knowledge, asking how it is that
literary works have the meaning they do for readers?' (*PS*, 48).
Semiotics would not try to choose among the various conflicting
interpretations put forward but rather 'analyze the interpretive
operations that produce these disagreements' (*PS*, 48).

The object of semiotics as a theory of reading, therefore, 'would not be literary works themselves but their intelligibility: the ways in which they make sense, the ways in which readers have made sense of them' (*PS*, 50). In *Structuralist Poetics* Culler had formulated the concept of 'literary competence', using competence in a sense derived from its use in Chomskian linguistics, and it had been criticised for having excessively normative implications. He retains but modifies the concept in discussing a semiotics of reading:

> Not only does interpretation employ repeatable operations, but in one's attempt to interpret a text one is always implicitly appealing to norms. . . . These norms may remain vague and may vary from one situation to another and from one interpretive community to another, but the process of interpretation is incomprehensible without them, and one is usefully reminded of this by the allusion to norms implicit in the concept of 'literary competence'. (*PS*, 51)

A serious weakness of Culler's theory is that the relation between semiotics and interpretation is unstable. He claims that literary works 'provide conclusive evidence for the existence of a semiotic system which makes literature possible', but a 'semiotics of literature . . . does not interpret works but tries to discover the conventions which make meaning possible' (*PS*, 37). But the conventions do not have an existence independent of interpretations of literary texts: they are derived from interpretations which the semiotician brings together in order to abstract common elements which are then described as conventions or codes, since 'the semiotician attempts to discover the codes which make literary communication possible' (*PS*, 37).

It is clear that these conventions and codes are derived not from all the possible meanings and interpretations that can be elicited from literary texts, but only from what Culler calls 'a range of interpretations' (*PS*, 50). In other words, certain interpretations, or more exactly, interpretative approaches, have to be regarded as privileged in order for the semiotics of literature to have any stability, and by the same token others have to be excluded. Culler, for example, condemns the interpretative method of Norman Holland, based on ego-psychology, which involves an empirical investigation of the relation between how a reader responds to a text and the structure of that reader's identity. This version of reader-response criticism generates such a degree of variation in interpretation that Culler finds it unacceptable because it clearly destabilises his conception of semiotics.

A related problem for Culler's theory is that the focus is on the semiotic system that underlies interpretation and not on the interpretations and the interpretative approaches that have generated the system. Interpretations function rather like sentences in a linguistic system: they are the material that the semiotician uses in order to reveal the codes and conventions that constitute the grammar intrinsic to literary communication. Culler emphasises the parallel between semiotics in relation to the study of literature, and linguistics in relation to the study of language: 'the goal is to develop a poetics which would stand to literature as linguistics stands to language' (*PS*, 37). But whereas a linguist can view sentences as neutral data which are a universal feature of all languages, interpretations cannot be viewed in the same way. They are related to a whole series of factors and processes – cultural, historical, ideological – that cannot be left out of account. But Culler's concept of a semiotics of reading, by directing its attention to the system rather than to the processes which have created the building bricks of the system, would seem to have to ignore such questions, for the system cannot exist as a stable structure if one is taking its building bricks to pieces.

Culler might argue that even if one rejects his version of semiotics and concentrates on the cultural and ideological forces that lead critics to interpret literature in a particular way, one will only encounter semiotics at one remove, as it were. Hence the 'tense interplay' between semiotics and deconstruction which he refers to. But this suggests that there can be more than one approach to semiotics. Culler is concerned with signifying practices which remain stable in time and achieve sufficient fixity so that they can be understood in systematic terms. Thus the emphasis is on words like 'norms', 'conventions', 'codes'. This form of semiotics remains within the orbit of structuralism. But a different conception of semiotics is possible.

Julia Kristeva has argued that what is needed is a semiotics that directs its attention to the continual undermining of any system of signification – in other words a post-structuralist semiotics. She writes:

> Semiotics must not be allowed to be a mere application to signifying practices of the linguistic model – or any other model, for that matter. Its *raison d'être*, if it is to have one, must consist in identifying the systematic constraint within each signifying practice . . . but above all in going beyond that to specifying just what, within the practice, falls

outside the system and characterizes the specificity of the practice as such.

She claims that the semiotic approach that 'has made possible the systematic description of the social and/or symbolic constraint within each signifying practice' – that is, the approach associated with Saussure, Peirce, the Prague school and structuralism – is over. That approach aimed at creating a 'semiology of systems'. Kristeva advocates a semiotics that will be 'a theory of the speaking subject', a subject that is divided between the conscious and the unconscious. This new semiotics she calls 'semanalysis' and it 'conceives of meaning not as a sign-system but as a *signifying process*'. It will focus not so much on the norms, conventions and codes of any sign-system but on deviations and transgressions. For example, she sees poetic language as a signifying practice in which 'the *semiotic disposition* will be the various deviations from the grammatical rules of the language'. Thus 'The moment of transgression is the key moment in practice: we can speak of practice whenever there is a transgression of systematicity.'

Kristeva's semiotics thus shifts the emphasis to 'operations heterogeneous to meaning and its system'. She associates this heterogeneity with the fact that people are subject to the biological as well as to the social but claims that she is not merely replacing 'the semiotics of signifying systems by considerations on the biological code' as the latter also functions semiotically. The aim, rather, is 'to postulate the *heterogeneity* of biological operations in respect of signifying operations'. But since semiotics must function as a metalanguage, it can only 'postulate that heterogeneity; as soon as it speaks about it, it homogenizes the phenomenon, links it with a system, loses hold of it'. Kristeva's 'semanalysis', being based on 'a theory of the speaking subject as subject of a heterogeneous process', attempts to show what lies outside the operation of this metalanguage by studying 'each signifying system as a practice'.[11]

It is obvious that there are strong links between Kristeva's semanalysis and Derridean deconstruction, which sees meaning and the signifying system which is its basis as subject to 'différance' (a pun derived from the French verb, 'différer', which can mean both to differ and to defer). Meaning for Derrida can never be fixed by any system of signification since all such systems are subject to the temporal, to perpetually changing contexts. Saussurean linguistics and semiology emphasised the synchronic – the play of differences

that define any system within the one temporal plane – and relegated
in importance the diachronic: the changes that take place in any
signifying system such as language over time. Derrida questions this
marginalisation of the diachronic. He suggests that writing is the
best model for understanding how language, and by implication any
signifying system, works, since writing can continue to generate
meaning in an unlimited number of contexts and it cannot be limited
to a single, univocal meaning in any particular context. In other
words, the system with its differential, synchronic structure cannot
totally control or fix meaning since words possess meanings ('traces')
from their uses in earlier contexts which cannot be banished entirely.
Derrida, like Kristeva, recognises that one can never escape from
system: any undermining or destabilisation of a system or of a
structure of signs must function in semiotic terms and thus itself be
systematic. Derridean deconstruction plays off against each other the
systematic and those elements within any system that undermine it
in order to destabilise what he sees as the governing force in Western
metaphysics – the desire for 'presence' or 'logocentrism': that is, an
order and coherence that exists outside the play of signification.

Although Derrida is a philosopher, a great deal of his work is
devoted not to abstract analysis but to the discussion of texts,
particular texts by such literary authors as Rousseau, Mallarmé and
Genet, as well as by recognised philosophers such as Plato and
Husserl. One of the consequences of this has been that in much
deconstructionist criticism the interpretation of individual texts has
again become acceptable and those who oppose interpretation, such
as Culler, have been put on the defensive. However, whether
American deconstructionist literary interpretation in particular
breaks radically from the New Critical form of interpretation or is
essentially a continuation of it is a question about which there has
been much debate in contemporary critical theory. If deconstructionist criticism merely allows interpretation to become again the
central concern of literary criticism, then what one might call the
'interpretation mountain' will only be added to, thus exacerbating
the situation that obtained during the period of the later New
Criticism. But if Derridean deconstruction is the ultimate form of
interpretation beyond which one cannot go, might it not lead to the
end of the New Critical tradition, something that structuralists like
Culler as well as traditional historical critics like Hirsch and Levin
seem to desire? These questions cannot be confronted, however,

until one has considered the relationship between post-structuralism and interpretation.

CHAPTER 5

Post-structuralism and the question of interpretation

Before the emergence of post-structuralism, Anglo-American criticism had been dominated by the New Critical tradition and criticism that was historical or scholarly in approach, both of which coexisted amicably enough since they had evolved strategies by which to resolve their differences through compromise or tolerance. Alternatives to their power, such as archetypal criticism and structuralism, had not had sufficient impact to mount any serious challenge. But since the mid-1970s this situation has changed radically. Virtually all areas of criticism have had to recognise the threat posed to their most fundamental assumptions by post-structuralism. Even many of those who reject it have felt the need to enter into confrontation with it in order to justify their alternative approaches. It has created more dissension and conflict within criticism than has been seen since the early New Criticism emerged to challenge traditional scholarly and historical criticism.

The power of post-structuralism, particularly in America in the form of Derridean deconstruction, is surprising considering that structuralist criticism had had relatively little influence. Why then should post-structuralism have had such a powerful impact? Part of the reason for the fact that structuralism failed to have a strong influence on American critics may have been that Northrop Frye's attempt to establish a scientific form of criticism independent of both New Critical close analysis and traditional historical criticism had to some extent anticipated structuralism. Like such theorists as Todorov, Frye was interested less in individual works than in underlying structures. His aim in his major work, *Anatomy of Criticism*, is to establish a 'grammar of literary archetypes' which will show that literature is not a diverse collection of individual texts but a coherent and unified structure that can be analysed in 'scientific' terms. Like the structuralists, he shifts the emphasis away from those aspects of literature that can evoke an affective response towards what for him is more fundamental, namely the archetypal. He is, for example, critical of the concept of 'realism' and sees no basic difference between fantasy or romance and the realistic novel, although certain critical adjustments must be made: 'The presence of a mythical structure in realistic fiction, however, poses certain technical problems for making it plausible, and the devices used in solving these problems may be given the general name of *displacement*.' The potential conflict with the interpretation and close analysis of particular texts that had dominated Anglo-American criticism since Richards, Empson and the New Critics is revealed in his advocacy of the need to 'stand back' from the text:

> The further back we go, the more conscious we are of the organizing design. . . . If we 'stand back' from Spenser's *Mutabilitie Cantoes*, we see a background of ordered circular light and a sinister black mass thrusting up into the lower foreground – much the same archetypal shape that we see in the opening of the Book of Job. If we 'stand back' from a realistic novel such as Tolstoy's *Resurrection* or Zola's *Germinal*, we can see the mythopoeic designs indicated by those titles.[1]

But in practice Frye's archetypal criticism adapted itself to New Criticism and to the interpretation of individual texts more easily than the position he takes in *Anatomy of Criticism* might lead one to expect. In the critical works that followed the *Anatomy*, he tends to discuss the works of such writers as Shakespeare and Milton in ways which can be reconciled with interpretation. For American critics, paradoxically, French structuralism may have appeared both familiar, and therefore nothing new, and alien at the same time: it was not a radically new departure because of its affinities with Frye's *Anatomy*, but, unlike Frye, structuralism in operation was not easily reconcilable with interpretation and close reading of particular texts and as a result it could be regarded as outside the tradition of modern Anglo-American criticism. Post-structuralism, in contrast, at least in its Derridean form, did not seem to reject interpretation and close analysis of texts even if its approach to these was very different from that of the New Criticism. Thus perhaps a major reason that the most influential American form of post-structuralism – the Yale school of deconstructive criticism – has significant differences from

French and British forms of post-structuralism is because structuralist criticism had relatively little impact in America.

But where post-structuralism stands on the question of interpretation is not on the surface clear. Anyone attempting to find the answer to this question might conclude that confusion and contradiction reign. If one reads Fredric Jameson's book, *The Political Unconscious,* one is informed that 'hermeneutic or interpretive activity has become one of the basic polemic targets of contemporary post-structuralism in France',[2] and Jonathan Culler, generally regarded as a post-structuralist since the publication of his book *On Deconstruction,* remains as opposed to interpretation as he was during his structuralist period.[3] On the other hand, it is still widely believed that post-structuralism advocates 'freeplay' or complete liberty of interpretation. David Lodge writes, for example, that deconstruction 'opens up the text to multiple interpretations'.[4] Current critical debate on post-structuralism can hardly be conducted on an informed or rational basis if such apparent contradictions are not resolved. In the following discussion I shall concentrate on American deconstructive criticism because it is the form of post-structuralist criticism which is of greatest interest from the point of view of literary interpretation.

It is generally agreed that post-structuralism first appeared on the American critical scene at a conference held at Johns Hopkins University in 1966, when Derrida delivered a lecture entitled 'Structure, sign, and play in the discourse of the human sciences'. This essay has remained the best known post-structuralist text and one of its major concerns is the question of interpretation. Derrida drew a comparison between two types of interpretation:

> There are thus two interpretations of interpretation, of structure, of sign, of freeplay. The one seeks to decipher, dreams of deciphering, a truth or an origin which is free from freeplay and from the order of the sign, and lives like an exile the necessity of interpretation. The other, which is no longer turned toward the origin, affirms freeplay and tries to pass beyond man and humanism, the name man being the name of that being who, throughout the history of metaphysics or of onto-theology – in other words, through the history of all of his history – has dreamed of full presence, the reassuring foundation, the origin and end of the game. The second interpretation of interpretation, to which Nietzsche showed us the way, does not seek in ethnography, as Lévi-Strauss wished, the 'inspiration of a new humanism' (again from the 'Introduction to the work of Marcel Mauss').
>
> There are more than enough indications today to suggest we might

perceive that these two interpretations of interpretation – which are absolutely irreconcilable even if we live them simultaneously and reconcile them in an obscure economy – together share the field we call, in such a problematic fashion, the human sciences.[5]

This essay was widely interpreted to mean that the first form of interpretation was no longer valid, intent as it was on achieving 'full presence' and a 'reassuring foundation'. Only interpretation as Nietzschean freeplay had any authenticity. Critics devoted to traditional principles saw this as cutting the ground from virtually all forms of interpretation based on rational and historical principles. As M. H. Abrams put it:

> Derrida puts out of play, before the game even begins, every source of norms, controls, or indicators which, in the ordinary use and experience of language, set a limit to what we can mean and what we can be understood to mean. Since the only givens are already-existing marks, 'déjà écrit', we are denied recourse to a speaking or writing subject, or ego, or cogito, or consciousness, and so to any possible agency for the intention of meaning something ('vouloir dire'); all such agencies are relegated to the status of fictions generated by language, readily dissolved by deconstructive analysis.[6]

Hostility to conventional forms of interpretation has been widespread among post-structuralists, but this hostility needs to be looked at closely. One of the most interesting post-structuralist attacks on interpretation is to be found in an essay by Shoshana Felman on Henry James's *The Turn of the Screw*. Felman is particularly concerned with one of the best known interpretations of this novella, Edmund Wilson's Freudian reading, which argues that it must be read not as a ghost story but as a psychological study of its narrator, the governess. Felman argues that the efforts of critics to interpret or to explicate the meaning of the story are misconceived. She describes the work as being 'constructed as a *trap* designed to close upon the reader'.[7] Wilson, however, regards himself as superior to both James and the governess, both of whom he sees as 'self-deceived'. Only the critic, therefore, Felman suggests, is not a 'dupe'. She points out that this makes the critic similar to the governess, who is also determined not to be a dupe in relation to the children who are under her charge: 'Like Wilson, the governess is *suspicious* of the ambiguity of signs and of their rhetorical reversability; like Wilson, she thus proceeds to *read* the world around her, to *interpret* it, not by looking *at* it but by seeing *through* it, by demystifying and *reversing* the values of its

outward signs' ('Turning the screw of interpretation' ('TS'), 188).
But, equally, those who reject Wilson's reading, and who believe the
governess is right, are caught in the trap, since they behave like Mrs
Grose – who believes the governess – in the story. Both of these
opposed readings 'are themselves inscribed and comprehended in
the text' ('TS', 190), which 'thus constitutes a reading of its two
possible readings, both of which, in the course of that reading, it
deconstructs . . . the critic, like the governess, seeks to *stop* the
meaning, to *arrest* signification' ('TS', 190–1). In seeking to identify
the 'Master-Signifier' in the text, Wilson 'excludes, *represses*, the
very thing which led to his analysis, the very subject of his study: the
role of language in the text' ('TS', 192).

It is apparent, however, that Felman's attack on interpretation in
relation to *The Turn of the Screw* is not a rejection of interpretation as
such, in the manner of Jonathan Culler, for it is the text itself that
enacts this attack on interpretation since it is 'constructed as a *trap*
designed to close upon the reader', and she enlarges upon this later:

> '*Les non-dupes errent*' [non-dupes err], says Lacan. If James's text does
> not explicitly make such a statement, it enacts it, and acts it out, while
> also dramatizing at the same time the suggestion that this very sentence
> – which entraps us in the same way as does the 'turn of the screw' – this
> very statement, which cannot be affirmed without thereby being
> negated, whose very diction is in fact its own contradiction, constitutes,
> precisely, the position *par excellence* of *meaning* in the *literary utterance*:
> a rhetorical position, implying a relation of mutual subversion and of
> radical, dynamic contradiction between utterance and statement. ('TS',
> 200)

Meaning or interpretation, from a deconstructionist point of view,
cannot find a secure meta-position beyond the text by which to
stabilise itself. The text anticipates the critic's reading of it by
incorporating that reading within the play of its textuality. The
interpreter of a literary text – and for most American deconstructionists what makes a text 'literary' is this self-reflexivity – is in the
position of an interpreter of Epimenides the Cretan's paradox that
'all Cretans are liars'. That statement cannot be interpreted by
showing what it means: whatever meaning one puts forward has
been anticipated and undercut. All that the critic can do is to show
how the text enacts this play of undecidable meaning.

The Yale critics

This version of deconstruction has had a major impact on American criticism. It emerged first in an essay by Paul de Man in his book *Blindness and Insight*, first published in 1971, on Derrida's reading of Rousseau in *Of Grammatology*. On the face of it, Derrida in *Of Grammatology* is engaged in interpreting Rousseau in a manner fairly close to the first of the two senses which he describes in the 'Structure, sign, and play' essay. However, as Jonathan Culler has argued, even when Derrida engages in this form of interpretation he 'does not identify the thematic unity and distinctive meaning of any text but rather describes a general process through which texts undermine or reveal the rhetorical nature of the philosophical system to which they adhere'.[8] Even accepting that Culler is right, Derrida appears to be standing outside of the Rousseau text in order to reveal how the logic of the text works, and he then goes on to deconstruct that logic by revealing that what Rousseau wishes to exclude or marginalise in the interests of 'presence' cannot be done coherently. That which is excluded or marginalised in favour of what Rousseau regards as central can be shown, through deconstructive analysis, to have an equally legitimate claim to occupy the centre. 'Presence' or fullness of meaning is therefore destabilised. De Man's discussion of Derrida's deconstruction of Rousseau in his essay, 'The rhetoric of blindness: Jacques Derrida's reading of Rousseau', has been so influential that it must be looked at in some detail.

De Man makes it clear initially that he rejects structuralist attacks on interpretation. He refers to Todorov's view, which I discussed in the previous chapter, that the only adequate interpretation of a literary text would be a word for word repetition since 'every work constitutes its own best description' (*IP*, 4). De Man asserts that no interpretation can claim to be a description of a work: 'Because the work cannot be said to understand or to explain itself without the intervention of another language, interpretation is never mere duplication.'[9] For de Man there can be no escape from intrinsic criticism – treating the text itself as a self-enclosed form of discourse – which Todorov wishes to dismiss in favour of a structuralist poetics. He therefore approves of Derrida's interrogation of Rousseau's text and of his refusal to ignore ambivalences which conventional critics leave out of account or explain away. He summarises Derrida's reading of Rousseau as follows:

> Whenever Rousseau designates the moment of unity that exists at the
> beginning of things, when desire coincides with enjoyment, the self and
> the other are united in the maternal warmth of their common origin,
> and consciousness speaks with the voice of truth, Derrida's interpre-
> tation shows, without leaving the text, that what is thus designated as a
> moment of presence always has to posit another, prior moment and so
> implicitly loses its privileged status as a point of origin. (*Blindness and
> Insight* (*BI*), 115)

De Man claims, however, that Derrida's major contribution is to
show 'that Rousseau's own texts provide the strongest evidence
against his alleged doctrine . . . he "knew", in a sense, that his
doctrine disguised his insight into something closely resembling its
opposite' (*BI*, 116). Although de Man refers to Rousseau as 'he' –
which might imply that Rousseau is aware of what he is doing – de
Man argues that one is not concerned with Rousseau's consciousness
but with 'the knowledge that this language, as language, conveys
about itself, thereby asserting the priority of the category of language
over that of presence' (*BI*, 119). The author is 'blind' to what the
language of his text is doing. Certain figural elements in the text
undermine its 'literal' meaning so that the text cannot help but be
'misread' by those who are seeking a 'meaning' within the text itself.
Texts such as Rousseau's, therefore, become allegories of their own
misunderstanding, but the language of the text is not blind to this: 'it
follows from the rhetorical nature of literary language that the
cognitive function resides in the language and not in the subject. The
question as to whether the author himself is or is not blinded is to some
extent irrelevant' (*BI*, 137). Derrida, de Man claims, has remained
blind to the fact that his deconstruction of Rousseau has been
performed by the text itself.[10] Rousseau does not need deconstruction,
only his logocentric interpreters do: 'There is no need to deconstruct
Rousseau; the established tradition of Rousseau interpretation,
however, stands in dire need of deconstruction (*BI*, 139).

In order to reveal this deconstructive process at work in particular
texts, the critic must enter the text and participate in its textual play,
which means that the critic, even a de Manian deconstructive critic,
can never totally avoid blindness. De Man concludes his essay by
asserting that text and interpretation are dependent on each other:
'And since interpretation is nothing but the possibility of error, by
claiming that a certain degree of blindness is part of the specificity of

all literature we also reaffirm the absolute dependence of the interpretation on the text and of the text on the interpretation' (*BI*, 141). Literature and interpretation are therefore inseparable.

De Man's revision of Derridean deconstruction became the most powerful form of post-structuralism in America in the 1970s, with de Man being recognised as the leading theorist among the Yale deconstructionists. His influence is seen clearly in the work of Barbara Johnson, one of his former pupils, who treats the post-structuralist phase of Roland Barthes similarly to the way de Man had treated Derrida. During the first half of the 1960s Barthes had adopted a structuralist position somewhat similar to that of Todorov and Genette, most obviously in his book *Criticism and Truth* and such articles as 'Towards a structuralist analysis of narrative'. In the former he had stated: '[Literary science] cannot be a science of the content of works . . . but a science of the *conditions* of content, that is to say of forms'.[11] But in the later 1960s he gradually moved away from a structuralist position and with *S/Z*, first published in 1970, produced what is clearly a major work of post-structuralist literary criticism. Barbara Johnson's reading of *S/Z*, a study of Balzac's novella, *Sarrasine*, is similar to de Man's reading of Derrida on Rousseau.

S/Z has several parallels with Derrida. Barthes begins by repudiating his earlier structuralism. The attempt 'to see all the world's stories . . . within a single structure' and then to apply that to particular narratives is 'a task as exhausting . . . as it is ultimately undesirable, for the text thereby loses its difference'.[12] Criticism must focus on the single text and on interpretation: 'the single text is valid for all the texts of literature, not in the sense that it represents them . . . but in that literature itself is never anything but a single text: the one text is not an (inductive) access to a Model, but entrance into a network with a thousand entrances' (*S/Z* (*S/Z*), 12). There must thus be a return to interpretation but not in the sense of an attempt to discover a single meaning: 'To interpret a text is not to give it a (more or less justified, more or less free) meaning, but on the contrary to appreciate what *plural* constitutes it' (*SZ*, 5). Barthes's distinction between the 'writerly' (*scriptible*) and the 'readerly' (*lisible*) has affinities with Derrida's two forms of interpretation. The 'writerly' text, the goal of which 'is to make the reader no longer a consumer, but a producer of the text' (*SZ*, 4) has obvious parallels with the form of interpretation which 'affirms freeplay and tries to pass beyond man and humanism', whereas the 'readerly' text, or the 'classic text', has only a limited plurality and is therefore not beyond interpretation in a more traditional sense.

As with Derrida in relation to Rousseau, Barthes directs his attention to a 'readerly' text in order to reveal the 'difference' at work within the text. He relates this difference to the space between denotation and connotation in a text, connotation being 'a correlation immanent in the text . . . one may say that it is an association made by the text-as-subject within its own system . . . connotations are meanings which are neither in the dictionary nor in the grammar of the language in which a text is written' (*SZ*, 8). Barthes claims that 'denotation is not the first meaning, but pretends to be so; under this illusion, it is ultimately no more than the *last* of the connotations (the one which seems both to establish and to close the reading)' (*SZ*, 9). Adopting Derridean terminology, one might say that connotations are marginalised in the 'classic text'. In revealing that the text is a plurality of levels of connotation, with 'denotation' having no separate existence, the critic dismantles the text's 'presence' and in the process dismantles the 'I' who reads the text: 'This "I" which approaches the text is already a plurality of other texts, of codes which are infinite or, more precisely, lost (whose origin is lost)' (*SZ*, 10). Subjectivity is only a 'deceptive plenitude . . . merely the wake of all the codes which constitute me' (*SZ*, 10). Barthes calls his 'step-by-step' method of working his way through the text, which he divides into units of meaning or 'lexias', disclosing the various levels of connotation and the codes which constitute them, 'the *decomposition* (in the cinematographic sense) of the work of reading' (*SZ*, 12), As with Derrida on Rousseau, Barthes appears to stand outside the text in order to unravel a textual logic that the text itself is apparently blind to.

In her essay on *S/Z* in her book *The Critical Difference*, Barbara Johnson develops the concept of 'difference' which Barthes had mentioned without elaborating on its significance. She emphasises that it is not a difference 'between' entities of the text but a difference 'within' them which subverts a text's claim to identity or integrated wholeness. Deconstructive criticism she defines as proceeding by 'the careful teasing out of warring forces of signification within the text itself'.[13] The text is not undermined by this, only 'the claim to unequivocal domination of one mode of signifying over another' (*The Critical Difference* (*CD*), 5). She suggests, however, that Barthes's approach in *S/Z* is not so much deconstructionist as 'anti-constructionist' and raises the question 'whether in the final analysis a certain systematic level of textual difference is not also lost and flattened by Barthes's refusal to reorder or reconstruct the text' (*CD*, 7).

Johnson suggests that what *Sarrasine* shows is that the distinction Barthes makes between the 'writerly' and the 'readerly' text – a difference between – collapses to a difference within when one realises that the characteristics Barthes associates with the 'writerly' are evident in this 'readerly' text: 'Like the readerly text, Sarrasine's deluded image of La Zambinella is a glorification of perfect unity and wholeness. . . . But like the writerly text, Zambinella is actually fragmented, unnatural and sexually undecidable' (*CD*, 8). Barthes, she claims, has chosen this text because it thematises oppositions between the readerly and the writerly, but in the process of demonstrating this, 'The traditional value system that Barthes is attempting to reverse is thus already mapped out within the text he analyzes' (*CD*, 8). The main character of the novella, Sarrasine,

> In thinking that he knows where difference is located – between the sexes – is blind to a difference that cannot be situated between, but only within. In Balzac's story, castration thus stands as the literalization of the 'difference within' which prevents any subject from coinciding with itself. (*CD*, 10)

The text itself, therefore, 'demystifies the logocentric blindness' of Sarrasine's interpretation of La Zambinella, a castrated man who appears to be a woman, and Johnson concludes that Balzac's text has already deconstructed the readerly ideal of 'perfect wholeness and unequivocal femininity': 'Balzac has already in a sense done Barthes's work for him. The readerly text is itself nothing other than a deconstruction of the readerly text' (*CD*, 11). Whereas Barthes 'fills in the textual gaps with a name' and 'erects castration into *the* meaning of the text, its ultimate signified', the text itself 'does not simply reverse the hierarchy between readerly and writerly by substituting the truth of castration for the delusion of wholeness; it deconstructs the very possibility of naming the difference' (*CD*, 11–12).

Johnson and J. Hillis Miller are probably the leading exponents of the practice of deconstructive criticism: that is, of applying Derridean theory as revised by Paul de Man to the interpretation of particular texts. Both reject Barthes's attempt to create a fundamental distinction between modernist or postmodernist and 'classic' texts. Johnson's deconstructive approach is applied to both Mallarmé and Melville, and Hillis Miller discusses Hardy's fiction in the same terms as that of Conrad and Virginia Woolf. Whereas Johnson focuses on two concepts of 'difference', Miller directs his attention in his study of seven English novels to two forms of 'repetition'. The interpretation of fiction is founded on 'the identification of recurrences and of meanings generated through recurrences'.[14] Whereas in traditional criticism, attention is directed at what these recurrences or repetitions have in common in order to justify an interpretation that attempts to encompass the whole text, Miller argues that recurrences are as important for their differences as for their similarities. As well as repetition based on correspondence or copying, there is a 'Nietzschean mode of repetition' which 'posits a world based on difference' (*Fiction and Repetition (FR)*, 6) and which is 'ungrounded'. He compares it to the operation of involuntary memory or dreams in which 'one thing is experienced as repeating something which is quite different from it and which it strangely resembles' (*FR*, 8). It is clear that Miller's two forms of repetition have much in common with Johnson's 'difference between' and 'difference within'.

This is not surprising since in his essay 'Steven's rock and criticism as cure, II', Miller had defined deconstruction in very similar terms to Johnson:

> Deconstruction as a mode of interpretation works by a careful and circumspect entering of each textual labyrinth. . . . The deconstructive critic seeks to find, by this process of retracing, the element in the system studied which is alogical, the thread in the text in question which will unravel it all, or the loose stone which will pull down the whole building.[15]

Although many have argued that American deconstructive criticism is only a variation of the New Criticism, Miller argues that it is fundamentally different. Whereas the New Criticism endeavoured to demonstrate that literary texts possess organic unity, deconstructive criticism is concerned with 'heterogeneity of form in literary works' (*FR*, 5), the 'oddnesses' of a work that resist comprehensive interpretations. Applying this to the study of seven English novels Miller asserts: 'The heterogeneity of these texts lies in the fact that both forms of repetition are present, though the two forms can be shown to be incompatible' (*FR*, 17). Deconstructive interpretation is also fundamentally different from the New Criticism since it is 'more concerned with the relation of rhetorical form to meaning than with thematic paraphrase' (*FR*, 3). Miller's focus is 'not "what is the meaning?" but "how does meaning arise from the reader's encounter with just these words on the page?"' (*FR*, 3). With the novel this involves showing how the dimension of the words on the page undermines the coherence of the other two dimensions of fiction: 'representation' – the conventions of story-telling, modes of consciousness in the novel – and 'human reality' (*FR*, 20).

In discussing such novels as Conrad's *Lord Jim* and Hardy's *Tess of the d'Urbervilles* Miller shows that the presence of repetitions does not serve to support coherent and comprehensive interpretations of the novels: differences among the various elements of the works reveal heterogeneity and not organic unity. *Lord Jim* resembles 'a dictionary in which the entry under one word refers the reader to another word which refers him to another and then back to the first word again, in an endless circling' (*FR*, 39). In *Tess* the reader is confronted by 'multiple incompatible explanations of what happens to Tess. They cannot all be true, and yet they are all there in the words of the novel' (*FR*, 128). The novel thus deconstructs the assumptions of traditional critical approaches to interpretation based as they are on

> the presupposition that a novel is a centered structure which may be interpreted if that center can be identified. This center will be outside the play of elements in the work and will explain and organize them into a fixed pattern of meaning deriving from this center. (*FR*, 140)

Here one sees the influence of Derrida's 'Structure, sign, and play' essay which had criticised 'classical form concerning structure' for believing that the centre, which 'constitutes the very thing within a structure which governs the structure',[16] itself escapes structurality. Critical interpretation can therefore never arrive at any fixed meaning of a text. Meaning for Miller 'is suspended within the interaction among the elements. It is immanent rather than transcendent' (*FR*, 127).

This deconstructive approach has been criticised from several different viewpoints. Marxists, for example, have attacked it for cutting the text off from social and political questions, and a purist Derridean such as Rodolphe Gasché has claimed that it is merely an offshoot of the New Criticism. Gasché attacks de Man's identification of deconstruction with the self-reflexivity of the text. The de Man version of deconstruction entails that 'literariness, writing, and the text are understood according to the model of a conscious subjectivity, that is, a self-reflexive presence', whereas, argues Gasché, *'writing,* a notion which has, as a result of a deconstruction, an irreducible non-phenomenal meaning, deconstructs and disrupts all reflexivity'. Ideas of self-reflection and self-referentiality, claims Gasché, 'are essentially metaphysical and belong to logocentrism'.[17] Christopher Norris, however, has replied that one cannot separate deconstruction from the thematics of the text, as Gasché wishes to do: 'Derrida's chosen texts are those which more or less explicitly *thematize* the deconstructive logic at work within them.'[18] Gasché himself offends against the spirit of deconstruction, Norris believes, in trying to limit it to the philosophical sphere, whereas Derrida is concerned to break down the barriers between disciplines like philosophy and literature.

It seems certain, however, that Derridean deconstruction, as interpreted by de Man, has achieved the power it has in America because there is continuity with the New Criticism. In both forms of criticism close analysis of the literary text has priority over contextualist considerations even though the deconstructive critic's concern is to demonstrate heterogeneity rather than organic unity. As with the New Critics, the critical discourse employed by deconstructionist critics such as Johnson and Miller is relatively traditional in style, constructing a coherent argument, avoiding word-play and the use of 'literary' devices. This raises the issue of the status of the deconstructive critic's own discourse: does it not have an organising centre which escapes structurality? can it not therefore be deconstructed in turn? For example, the readings of Felman, Johnson and Miller, which demonstrate that the works they discuss undermine any systematic interpretation, are themselves interpretations which cannot help but claim to be coherent and systematic, as in this comment by Miller on *Tess*: 'My following through of some threads in the intricate web of Hardy's text has converged toward the conclusion that it is wrong in principle to assume that there must be some single accounting cause' (*FR*, 141). Likewise, Felman in her discussion of *The Turn of the Screw*, attacks the efforts of critics to impose fixed interpretations on literary texts but her own reading of the novel as a text which resists interpretation has a similar fixity, somehow outside the play of meaning which undermines other readings.

A particularly striking instance of this contradiction within deconstructive criticism itself can be seen in Miller's critique of M. H. Abrams's book *Natural Supernaturalism*. Miller argues that Abrams's view of Romanticism is seriously flawed, particularly because it fails to take account of a figure like Nietzsche and his radical ideas on language and interpretation. As evidence that Abrams's book implies the acceptance of a 'metaphysical scheme' Miller refers to the book's use of citations. These are employed

> to illustrate some straightforward point with a quotation which is not 'interpreted', in the sense of being teased for multiple meanings or implications. . . . The assumption is that a text has a single meaning which is more or less independent of the play of relations, repetitions, and differentiations within the work itself.

Nietzsche is held by Miller to be the philosopher who does most to refute this view: 'For Nietzsche there is no "objective" interpretation. The reading of a work involves an active intervention on the part of the reader. Each reader takes possession of the work for one reason or another and imposes on it a certain pattern of meaning.' Miller proceeds to cite several passages from Nietzsche's writings to support these points, such as the following: 'Ultimately, man finds in things nothing but what he himself has imported into them'; 'In fact interpretation is itself a means of becoming master of something'.[19] But these quotations merely illustrate the point Miller is making. There is no sense of their 'being teased for multiple meanings or implications'. Miller's use of citation is therefore no different from Abrams's and thus undermines the logical basis of his critique.

The root of the problem here is that Miller and other deconstructive critics like Johnson and Felman employ a discourse with a fixed centre. Although they are concerned with the play of signification that undermines stable meaning in the texts they discuss, the centre of their own discourse is immune from that play of meaning. This makes them vulnerable to their own critique since it is comparatively easy, as I have tried to show, to expose this situation. One response to the problem is to accept such contradiction as unavoidable. It is admitted that one can never entirely close the circle, even if one must try to make the gap as small as possible, but it is denied that any deconstructive form of criticism is thereby invalidated.[20] Another response is to adopt a different style of critical discourse in which there is scope for textual 'freeplay' so that there is no stable centre vulnerable to deconstructive critique.

Two critics who have been associated with the Yale school of deconstruction – Geoffrey Hartman and Harold Bloom – can be aligned with this second response. Hartman and Bloom, however, have refused to go all the way with deconstruction. Indeed, Bloom has vehemently denied that he is a deconstructionist. Hartman has described their position in the following terms (referring to himself in the third person, a device perhaps to expose his own status as 'text'):

> Bloom and Hartman are barely deconstructionists. . . . For them the ethos of literature is not dissociable from its pathos, whereas for deconstructionist criticism literature is precisely that use of language which can purge pathos, which can show that it too is figurative, ironic or aesthetic.[21]

For Hartman the merit of Derrida's work is that it undermines any fundamental difference between literary and critical texts: 'Since we ourselves are the text, there is no point to the antinomy between *Dichter* (creative writer) and *Denker* (critical thinker).' He believes that critical writing should become as demanding as literature, should not limit itself to commentary, and should employ the same rhetorical and figurative devices which are associated with literary texts. He urges that literary criticism reject any 'subordinate, service function' and aspire to literary status. Hartman's criticism, most notably in his book, *Saving the Text*, a study of Derrida's *Glas*, has displayed an attention to style and word-play that makes any deconstruction of it by exposing the stable centre extremely difficult. For him a critical essay should combine being an 'intellectual poem' with the close analysis and attention to detail characteristic of modern criticism.[22] Whether this overcomes the problem of the stable centre or merely exhibits the instability of a form of critical discourse that falls between two stools is open to debate.

Harold Bloom's criticism does not normally aspire to the play of meaning at the level of texture that is a feature of much of Hartman's writing. It is in the ambition of its organisation and structure and in the terminology he employs that one discerns an imaginative play uncharacteristic of conventional critical discourse. Although Bloom directs his attention to the poet and psychology rather than to the question of textuality, like the deconstructionists he is concerned to undermine the concept of 'presence' and the organicist aesthetics which New Criticism advocated. He also believes that approaches based on structuralist poetics have little of value to contribute to literary criticism: 'the anti-humanistic plain dreariness of all those developments in European criticism . . . have yet to demonstrate that they can aid in reading any one poem by any poet whatsoever.'[23] He accepts, like deconstructionists, that 'poems are not things but only words that refer to other words, and *those* words refer to still other words, and so on, into the densely overpopulated world of literary language',[24] but for him this makes the poetic text a 'psychic battlefield' in which the poet struggles to achieve 'the divinating triumph over oblivion' (*Poetry and Repression (PR)*, 2). The poet cannot avoid the influence of his predecessors but equally the 'strong poet' cannot accept it either. Poetry for Bloom is constituted by this struggle of the strong poet for an imaginative liberation even if it is impossible to achieve.

In summarising his position Bloom indicates that the critic is not outside this struggle. The critic, or 'strong reader', resembles the strong poet:

> Influence, as I conceive it, means that there are *no* texts, but only relationships *between* texts. These relationships depend upon a critical act, a misreading or misprision, that one poet performs upon another, and that does not differ in kind from the necessary critical acts performed by every strong reader upon every text he encounters. The influence-relation governs reading as it governs writing, and reading is therefore a miswriting just as writing is a misreading. As literary history lengthens, all poetry necessarily becomes verse-criticism, just as all criticism becomes prose-poetry.[25]

Bloom, therefore, sees criticism as 'misprision' or 'creative misreading' (*PR*, 4), and he constructs a series of what he calls 'revisionary ratios', by which the use of tropes and rhetoric in poetry is seen as a psychic defence against accepting the necessity of influence. Rhetoric is 'a mode of interpretation that is the will's revulsion against time, the will's revenge, its vindication against the necessity of passing away' (*PR*, 10). The strong poet 'will not tolerate words that intervene between him and the Word, or precursors standing between him and the Muse' (*PR*, 10).

Bloom's 'strong' interpretations of the poets he discusses stand apart from orthodox criticism. Discussing the first verse of Tennyson's 'Mariana' Bloom argues that 'sexual anguish' is 'a mask for influence-anxiety': 'Mariana is herself a poetess, her true affliction is the Romantic self-consciousness of Keats and

Shelley . . . what Mariana is longing for is not her belated swain but a priority in poetic invention' (*PR*, 151). Mariana's predicament parallels that of Tennyson:

> What then is Mariana repressing? Why, that she doesn't want or need the other who cometh not. . . . And what is Tennyson the poet repressing? Only that the most dangerous and powerful and authentic part of his own poetic mind would like to be as perfectly embowered as Mariana's consciousness, but of course it can't. (*PR*, 153)

Bloom continually creates relationships between Tennyson's poem and other poems, written both before and after: 'Mariana'

> can be regarded as a catachresis of the Romantic crisis-ode, as a hyperbolic version of Coleridge's *Dejection* or Keats's *Nightingale*. . . . Let us think of Mariana as Tennyson's Stevensian Interior Paramour or Shelleyan epipsyche, and be prepared to find her hovering elsewhere in his poetry. (*PR*, 155)

This is obviously not orthodox literary criticism that attempts to create a persuasive interpretation in the ordinary sense. Bloom as a 'strong reader' is engaged in an imaginative struggle with the poets he discusses, refusing to read them in their own terms. This is a risky enterprise. Like Hartman, Bloom does not accept literary criticism as a kind of service industry. It is production as much as literature is. It may be that Bloom's readings will be seen in the future as so imaginatively powerful in themselves that his work takes its place in the tradition of Romantic writing and will be studied on an equal basis with Shelley, Keats and Tennyson. Or it may be dismissed, as one unsympathetic commentator on Bloom puts it, as 'unilluminating criticism'.[26] Conventional literary critics – that is, those who see themselves as playing a role secondary to the works they write about – know that there is some possibility of their readings surviving if they are seen as particularly enlightening or innovative, even it critical fashion moves on. Even those critical texts which fail to find any place in the canon of literary criticism may be read in the future by assiduous Ph.D students. Perhaps the best the orthodox interpreter of literature can hope for is that, like Bradley's *Shakespearean Tragedy*, his or her work will continue to be read as exemplifying a particular critical approach which retains a good deal of its power to serve the text even if most later critics no longer accept its assumptions. But Bloom refuses to accept such critical parasitism; he appears to demand equality with the literary text or nothing. Thus his work may fall between two stools: failing to achieve equal status with canonic literary texts yet not being 'illuminating' enough in conventional terms to be read for its critical usefulness.

The later work of Derrida and de Man

The critic who has gone further than any other to practise in the mode of Derrida's second form of interpretation as 'freeplay' is Derrida himself. Since the major writings of the late 1960s, such as *Of Grammatology* and *Writing and Difference*, he has published a series of works which depart radically from ordinary forms of critical discourse in form and style, *Glas* being the most notable example. Vincent B. Leitch gives the following account of this phase of Derrida's work:

> Focusing on the structuration of systems or on the crossing points of networks, Derrida seeks to intervene and open destabilizing and permanent doubleness, continuous and irresolvable bifurcations. Strategically, his writing itself manifests such doubleness – sometimes in double columns, sometimes in paleonymic italics, and sometimes in other split formats. . . .
>
> Not only does Derrida examine numerous versions of betweenness, but he tries to occupy that space. He attempts to lodge his own discourse in the between. In this effort, he seeks not resolution but undecidability, not clarity but unreadability. To avoid being thematized or categorized, the vigilant deconstructor constructs his own doubled text. In *Glas*, Derrida observes 'if I write two texts at once, you cannot castrate me'.

Whereas reading in the traditional sense 'seeks to clarify the meaning and ethical value of texts; in the new deconstructive sense, reading searches out and celebrates contradictions and undecidables, turning up and aside simultaneously an arbitrary and one sided, a masterful and inclusive system of valuation.'[27]

Derrida, by going further than any other deconstructionist in attempting to create a discourse that is not itself exposed to deconstructive critique, is in consequence the least vulnerable to the charge of self-contradiction that can be directed at critics like Miller who use relatively conventional critical discourse. But although this may counter logical objections to deconstruction, it leads to problems at a more pragmatic level. It is significant that only a few deconstructive critics have attempted to emulate Derrida in this phase of his writing and that his most influential work remains the texts he produced in the late 1960s. A common response to Derrida's later, more 'writerly' texts, as it were, is that they are impenetrable.[28] Just as Joyce's *Finnegans Wake* has been seen as a kind of *reductio ad absurdum* of the modernist novel which gave many later novelists, as they saw it, little alternative but to return to pre-modernist conventions, there is a possibility that *Glas* and other later texts will be generally regarded as so inaccessible that their influence on critical practice will be minor. Further, if such a form of writing is what deconstruction logically leads to, even deconstructive criticism that is less radical in form and style may suffer some discredit by association.

Certainly in the late 1980s deconstruction of the Yale type seems to be a less powerful force than it was ten years ago; the death of Paul de Man in 1983 was a severe blow and recent revelations that in the early 1940s he wrote articles which express some sympathy with Nazi ideas are likely to harm deconstruction, at least in the short term. Various 'new' forms of critical approach, more straightforwardly committed to interpretation, have emerged in the 1980s and have perhaps seized the initiative – neo-Marxism, the new historicism, new pragmatism – although all of these have felt the influence of deconstruction. It may be that this situation is only temporary, however, and that deconstruction will regain its former power, for it has changed significantly in the 1980s primarily as a result of Paul de Man's later writing: *Allegories of Reading*, published in 1979, and essays published in the early 1980s. The phenomenological language of his earlier writing gave way in his later essays to a more rhetorical terminology. Instead of talking of the relation between 'blindness' and 'insight', for example, he now refers to that between rhetoric as trope and rhetoric as persuasion or to the gap between the constative and performative functions of language. This shift reminds one of the early New Critics' translation of Richards's psychological terminology in his discussion of poetry into linguistic terms.

Deconstruction is redefined in de Man's later work as rhetorical criticism. To read a text rhetorically is to read it non-thematically. Interpretation of the text is still involved but it is a mode of interpretation that does not concern itself with meaning or unity and rejects organicist forms of aesthetics which identify literary value with the work of art's capacity to overcome difference or contradiction.

Rhetorical interpretation, rather, demystifies such concepts by revealing how they are effects of the working of language. It also combines theory and practice, for

> the object of discussion is no longer the meaning or the value [of literary texts] but the modalities of production and of reception of meaning and of value prior to their establishment – the implication being that this establishment is problematic enough to require an autonomous discipline of critical investigation to consider its possibility and status.[29]

This redefinition of deconstruction in rhetorical terms may seem on the surface to reinforce objections to it as a negative, formalistic kind of criticism, at best apolitical, at worst nihilistic. Such a perception of deconstruction was one of the main reasons why it lost ground in the last decade to interpretative modes that attempted to make literary criticism directly pertinent to political or ethical issues. But, paradoxically, deconstruction in this rhetorical form may undermine such objections, for de Man claims that such textual scrutiny has a powerful political application:

> What we call ideology is precisely the confusion of linguistic with natural reality, of reference with phenomenalism. It follows that, more than any other mode of inquiry, including economics, the linguistics of literariness is a powerful and indispensable tool in the unmasking of ideological aberrations, as well as a determining factor in accounting for their occurrence.[30]

Deconstruction as rhetorical interpretation may develop into a form of intrinsic criticism that can also explore the extrinsic relations of literature, thus overcoming one of the most serious divisions in criticism.

Of course, the thorny problem of de Man's own 'ideological aberration' in his early career must be faced. On the surface, the discovery of his wartime writings might seem to confirm the claims of those who see deconstruction as rooted in extreme right-wing ideology. Yet to see such a simple relation between de Man's early and later writings is surely to regress to a crude, positivistic form of interpretation that modern literary critics, especially, should be suspicious of. A different interpretation seems to me more persuasive.

De Man's relentless determination to expose the operations of rhetoric and to undermine aesthetic concepts can be seen as a reaction, perhaps an over-extreme one, to his own seduction by the language of Nazi ideology, sometimes described as an aestheticising of politics. Both his theory of language and the interpretative practice that is related to it are difficult to separate from his own situation as the author of writings in his earlier life that would seem to associate him incontrovertibly with Nazism. De Man had formulated his theory that language is a collection of pure signifiers and thus, as Knapp and Michaels put it, 'a meaningless structure to which meanings are secondarily (and in de Man's view illegitimately) added' in the context of discussing an episode in Rousseau's *Confessions* in which an apparently incriminating speech act is perpetrated when the word 'Marion' is uttered. He writes: 'Rousseau was making whatever noise happened to come into his head; he was saying nothing at all. . . . In the spirit of the text one should resist all temptation to give any significance whatever to the sound "Marion".' It is difficult to believe that personal factors did not have an influence on this vision of 'the absolute randomness of language, prior to any figuration or meaning'. The theory is also open to objection on intellectual grounds. Knapp and Michaels write:

De Man's separation of language and speech acts rests on a mistake. It is of course true that sounds in themselves are meaningless. It is also true that sounds become signifiers when they function in language. But it is not true that sounds in themselves are signifiers; they become signifiers only when they acquire meanings, and when they lose their meanings they stop being signifiers.[31]

De Man's readings of certain texts, particularly the view he takes of how the language of Romantic poetry functions, can perhaps also be related to his earlier 'ideological aberration'. He took the view that the early Romantics were 'the first modern writers to have put into question, in the language of poetry, the ontological priority of the sensory object'.[32] In one of his major essays on Romanticism, 'The rhetoric of temporality', which anticipates his later emphasis on rhetoric, he identifies irony in Romantic poetry with pure negation. But Anne K. Mellor has argued that this view of the Romantics is unbalanced, for Friedrich Schlegel's Romantic irony is a

movement back and forth between enthusiastic creation and sceptical de-creation [that] mimics the abundant chaos and never-ending process of life. . . . De Man privileges negation at the expense of creation – and thus arbitrarily confines post-Enlightenment allegoric figuration to a temporal process of de-mystification, even though the greatest literary allegories have prefigured a union of self with an other, whether nature or God.[33]

The existence of de Man's wartime writings, makes it virtually impossible to read his criticism as a disinterested form of discourse. Of course, no form of critical discourse is purely disinterested, and one should be aware of that, but one can usually ignore this fact for practical purposes. In de Man's case this is no longer an option. But however one interprets the relation between the early and the later writings, de Man seems certain to remain a central figure in contemporary criticism whose work has had and is likely to continue to have a major influence on literary interpretation.

Postmodern hermeneutics

It has been argued by deconstructive critics that deconstruction is interpretation allied to semiotics – how texts mean – rather than to hermeneutics – what they mean, although deconstruction has been described as 'negative hermeneutics'. Recently Hillis Miller, revealing the influence of the later de Man, has defined the practice of deconstructive or rhetorical interpretation as 'critique': that is, 'a testing of the medium from which the bridge between theory and practice is made'. Such 'critique' should be identified neither with hermeneutics nor poetics, although closer to the latter; it 'is a testing of the grounding of language in this or that particular text'.[34]

Not all post-structuralist criticism, however, has sought to distance itself from hermeneutics. Several critics associated with the journal *boundary 2* have asserted their commitment to what they have called 'postmodern hermeneutics'. William V. Spanos, the editor of the journal, sees strong connections between the Heidegger of *Being and Time* and Derridean deconstruction. However, he attacks de Man's revision of Derrida which he sees as still in the grip of the spatial concepts that, he asserts, have dominated the New Criticism, structuralism, the Geneva school, Frye's archetypal criticism, and which lead these critical schools to deny the text's temporality by seeing the end and the beginning of the text as coexisting at the same point in time. He rejects de Man's view in *Blindness and Insight* that deconstruction takes place within literary texts of virtually any period by arguing that literature from the Greeks to Modernism has been governed by logocentrism. Only postmodernist literature has succeeded in escaping it – that is, a literature which

> exists primarily to deconstruct and demystify the logocentric or, as I prefer to put it, spatialized literary texts of the tradition . . . and thus to deconstruct, to phenomenologically reduce by violence, the traditional privileged or spatial frame of reference of the modern reader.[35]

Whereas deconstructionists like de Man and Miller emphasise the heterogeneity or play of meaning within the text, Spanos's main concern is with the Heideggerian concept *Dasein* or being-in-the-world. This shifts the focus from text to reader: 'Hermeneutics . . . does not discover anything radically new as such. It dis-covers what the interpreter (the inquirer) by his very nature as *Dasein* already has as a whole . . . in advance, but is unaware of until the traditional interpretive instrument breaks down.'[36] The interpreter, in accepting the hermeneutic circle, discovers 'repetition', but this is a somewhat different concept of repetition from that of Miller since it is 'a process of dis-covering and re-membering the primordial temporality of being and thus of the truth as *a-letheia* (un-hiddenness), which metaphysical understanding and interpretation . . . in *closing time off . . .* and hardening this closure into "tradition", covers over and forgets' ('Heidegger, Kierkegaard, and the hermeneutic circle' ('HK'), 122). The hermeneutic circle as repetition '*lets* the being of a text be . . . lets it *say* how it stands with being. It is, in short, dialogic' ('HK', 122). The use of the word 'dialogic' suggests that there is a connection between Spanos's Heideggerian criticism and the work of Mikhail Bakhtin, with whom the term 'dialogic' is associated.

Spanos's interpretation of particular works has two main tendencies. He exposes those texts which are governed by the spatialising metaphysics he rejects and celebrates postmodernist texts which undermine spatial concepts in favour of Heideggerian temporality. Thus in an essay on the detective story he argues that this literary form

> has its ground in more than merely a belief in the susceptibility of nature to rational explanation. It is based, rather on a monolithic certainty that immediate psychic or historical experience is part of a comforting, even exciting and suspenseful well-made cosmic drama or novel.

As a reaction against this

> the paradigmatic archetype of the postmodern literary imagination is

the anti-detective story (and its anti-psychoanalytical analogue), the formal purpose of which is to evoke the impulse to 'detect' and/or to psychoanalyze in order to violently frustrate it by refusing to solve the crime (or find the cause of the neurosis).

Similarly postmodernist texts systematically subvert plot, which, since Aristotle, has been seen 'to be the most important of the constitutive elements of literature'.[37] When he writes on Sartre's *La Nausée*, which he interprets as postmodernist, he shows how the text is written from a postmodern perspective, but his interpretation tends to be conventionally thematic in approach even though he is attempting 'a *dis-covering* or *dis-closing* of the be-ing of the novel covered over or closed off from view and thus forgotten by the spatial-izing hermeneutics . . . of the Western literary tradition'.[38] The real value of postmodernist texts in terms of Spanos's approach is that they actively undermine the reader's logocentrism, and it is difficult to see how this could happen other than as a unique experience on the part of the reader which cannot be communicated in conventional critical terms. All that criticism would seem able to do is to destabilise the reader's logocentrism and encourage him or her through the reading process to enter into a dialogic relation with the text in order to experience the temporality of being-in-the-world.

Deconstructionists of the Yale school could argue that postmodern hermeneutics, although it might be radical from a philosophical standpoint, is essentially committed to thematic inter-pretation and thus is unable to do justice to the rhetorical complex-ities of literary texts. Defenders of Spanos might reply that his approach allows him to connect criticism with wider cultural and political issues which deconstructionism, up until recently, at least, has failed to address. Spanos can create connections between the issues he discusses in his criticism and events like the Vietnam war. He sees, for example, the CIA as 'the international detective agency whose job it is to coerce the reality under investigation to conform to a preconceived order'.[39] His emphasis on the being of the reader, however, the text existing not so much as a play of signifiers but as an event in the reader's life, indicates that Heidegger is very much the dominant figure in his criticism and that there are fundamental disagreements with Derridean and de Manian deconstruction.

Another critic associated with the *boundary 2* group has attempted to hold Heidegger and Derrida in balance. Joseph N. Riddel is probably the leading American deconstructionist outside of the Yale critics. In a long review of a book by Riddel on William Carlos Williams, Hillis Miller severely criticised Riddel's version of deconstruction, and implied that there is little difference between him and Spanos. Miller is doubtful whether any reconciliation between Heidegger and Derrida is possible. He claims that Riddel is fundamentally committed to a mimetic concept of language that refuses to face the heterogeneity of the text. Since Riddel agrees with Spanos that postmodernism constitutes a fundamental break from previous literary approaches, Miller argues that he fails to realise that the major literary texts of the past are ahead of their critics: 'They have anticipated explicitly any deconstruction the critic can achieve.'[40] In a reply to Miller Riddel argues that de Man's revision of Derrida, which underlies Miller's critique, is a domestication of Derrida designed to elevate literature and the 'exemplary text':

> Like de Man's reading of Rousseau who writes the allegory of all future misreadings of his text, Miller offers his own version of the retrieved ontology of a text which, though defined by its heterogeneity, is as hermetic as the New Critic's 'precious object', a monad of self-sufficiency.

For Riddel, 'This puts a hedge around Derrida's "Nietzschean joy" of open, endless interpretation, and even around his "Heideggerian hope". It ironizes Derrida, and in spite of what Miller says, it "thematizes" his questioning.'[41] Riddel suggests that criticism should attempt to combine Derridean 'freeplay' with a Heideggerian concern with being.

This is an important debate, with implications beyond the question of whether de Man or Riddel is right about the relevance of Derrida's work for literary critics. De Man's interpretation of Derrida has had such a powerful impact because, in suggesting that literary texts had anticipated Derridean deconstruction, it was possible for deconstruction to operate within literary texts from virtually any period. Thus the power of literature and the importance of literary criticism were enhanced without any fundamental undermining of the literary canon taking place. In Riddel's version of Derrida, since only postmodernist texts exemplify deconstructionist principles, deconstruction would apply only at the level of philosophical critique to non-postmodernist texts, which might appear to offer too narrow a basis for literary criticism. Yet it depends where one locates narrowness, for while the Yale form of deconstruction seldom extends beyond the literary–critical sphere to confront wider cultural and political issues, it is clear from Riddel's association with the *boundary 2* group that for him deconstruction as a mode of literary criticism is inseparable from a more general cultural critique.

The critic who has probably been most active in seeking to create a post-structuralist literary criticism that both has affinities with Yale textualism and displays a fundamental concern for cultural and political issues is Edward W. Said. It is significant that Said's book *Beginnings* was very favourably reviewed by Miller[42] yet he has also been published in *boundary 2*. For Said textuality must not become dissociated from history: 'As it is practiced in the American academy today, literary theory has for the most part isolated textuality from the circumstances, the events, the physical senses that made it possible and render it intelligible as the result of human work.'[43] Like the *boundary 2* critics he is not afraid to connect criticism and politics. Thus, discussing deconstruction, he sees 'the emergence of so narrowly defined a philosophy of textuality and critical noninterference' (*The World, the Text, the Critic* (*WT*), 4) as related to the rise of Reaganism and the dominance of right-wing attitudes in the late 1970s and 1980s. Said, in contrast, 'affirms the connection between texts and the existential actualities of human life, politics, societies, and events' (*WT*, 5). He recognises the importance of 'method and system' in criticism, yet they become a danger if 'their practitioners lose touch with the resistance and the heterogeneity of civil society' and convert 'everything into evidence for the efficacy of the method, carelessly ignoring the circumstances out of which all theory, system, and method ultimately derive' (*WT*, 26). Thus Derrida's textualism must be combined with Foucault's preoccupation with the relation between discourse and power, and Foucault in turn connected with the concrete political concerns of a thinker like Gramsci. Said's aim, then, is to make criticism 'oppositional' (*WT*, 29) and thus 'to reinvest critical discourse with something more than contemplative effort or an appreciative technical reading method for texts as undecidable objects. . . . Criticism cannot assume that its province is merely the text, not even the great literary text' (*WT*, 224–5).

When one looks at Said's criticism as applied to the practice of interpretation, however, one becomes conscious of a division. When he writes of literary texts 'method and system' appear to dominate and it is difficult to see how they relate in any direct way with political and social questions. The analyses of particular texts in his book *Beginnings* are concerned with the temporality of the text, with the interpreter of the text not being a seeker after truth but a constructor of a meaning that cannot be dissociated from the interpreter's own temporal situation. But in his discussion of such works as Dickens's *Great Expectations* or Hopkins's poetry this does not lead on to a political or social dimension that is intrinsically connected with his literary analysis. Similarly his essay on Conrad in *The World, the Text, the Critic* reads like a straightforward piece of literary criticism, and the writer he seems happiest with in that book is Swift, an author whose work does not easily fit into orthodox literary categories.

Where Said has been able successfully to combine post-structuralist literary critical method with political and cultural concerns has been in that area of his work which breaks away from literature in the narrow sense, notably in his book *Orientalism*, which concentrates on historical texts or literary texts that have been generally regarded as not of the first rank, although some major figures, such as Flaubert, are discussed. But as yet Said has failed to demonstrate in his analyses of 'canonic' literary texts that a textualist analysis can be combined with the political and cultural critique which he thinks essential if literary criticism is to have any serious social and political impact. Of course, some critics, Terry Eagleton being an obvious example, would argue that criticism should reject the whole concept of 'canonic' texts and devote itself to the analysis of textuality in a much wider sense. Said, however, shows no sign of rejecting high art as a legitimate category. The problem for criticism, he suggests, is rather to do justice to the complexity of the major works of the literary and high cultural canon, in the manner of textualist modes of criticism, while also showing that 'even when they appear to deny it, they are nevertheless a part of the social world, human life, and of course of the historical moments in which they are located and interpreted' (*WT*, 4).

The critical approach which has been most committed to combining literary criticism and politics is, of course, Marxism. Marxists would no doubt argue that Said's difficulty has been created by his refusal to adopt a Marxian perspective. Said is not anti-Marxist but he believes 'Marxism is in need of systematic decoding, demystifying, rigorous clarification' (*WT*, 29). He finds it difficult to reconcile an acceptance of Marxism with the preservation of 'criticism'. Yet though he believes criticism must be 'oppositional', it is difficult to see how criticism can mount a serious attack on entrenched political and social ideologies if it defines itself only negatively as 'reducible neither to a doctrine nor to a political position on a particular question' (*WT*, 29). Whether Marxist or Marxist-influenced interpretation can reconcile criticism in Said's sense – the most rigorous form of which at the present time is deconstruction with its relentless scrutiny of the semiotic and rhetorical operations of texts – with a political, social, and even existential critique is a question that must be pursued in the next chapter.

CHAPTER 6

Marxist criticism, cultural materialism, the new historicism

A significant development of contemporary criticism has been the acceptance of Marxism as central to critical debate. Marxist criticism has, of course, a long history but until fairly recently it tended to be taken seriously, at least in Britain and America, only by those adhering to a Marxist political perspective. This is no longer the case. Many contemporary critics and theorists who would not profess to being Marxists at the level of political commitment recognise that Marxism has a crucial role to play in many of the major issues in current theory and interpretation. Why has this change taken place?

One important reason is that Marxist criticism has to a large extent turned away from the kind of criticism that interpreted literary works in reflective terms as being directly determined by socio-economic forces. Many Marxist critics refer to this critical approach as 'vulgar Marxism'. One finds examples of this form of Marxist interpretation in Christopher Caudwell's book, *Illusion and Reality*, when, for instance, he writes of Tennyson's *In Memoriam*: 'The unconscious ruthlessness of Tennyson's "Nature" in fact only reflects the ruthlessness of a society in which capitalist is continually hurling down fellow capitalist into the proletarian abyss.'[1] Although reflective Marxist interpretation of the Caudwell type may oversimplify, its directness still has considerable appeal, especially in a contemporary critical context in which interpretations are becoming more and more intricate.

A critic such as Georg Lukács can certainly not be dismissed as a 'vulgar Marxist' – indeed the range of his works constitutes a major contribution to twentieth-century criticism – but Lukács's support for socialist realism during his 'Stalinist' phase and his lack of sympathy for the Modernist tradition of writing have tended to reduce his influence on contemporary criticism. Even Lukács adhered to the position that literature reflected socio-economic reality although he saw the relation between the one and the other as less straightforward than, for example, Caudwell did. He viewed the major nineteenth-century novelists as not merely reproducing reality in terms of bourgeois ideology but also using the form of the novel to reveal the contradictions within that ideology. Bourgeois literary forms were not merely reflective but could incorporate an implicitly Marxist critique.

A major change that has taken place in contemporary Marxist theory has been a move away from the position that literary works reflect socio-economic reality towards a fundamentally different view of the relation between the literary work and historical reality. The key figure in effecting this change has been the French Marxist philosopher Louis Althusser who attacked Hegelian or humanistic readings of Marx and directed his attention to the later Marx's attempt to found a 'scientific' system. Two formulations introduced by Althusser into Marxist theory were particularly important in providing the basis for a radical revision of the reflection model. Althusser claimed that works of art possess 'relative autonomy' and that rather than being causally determined by socio-economic forces they are 'overdetermined': that is, they are the product of a complex network of factors that cannot be interpreted in simple terms. Althusser refers to society as a 'social formation', the various levels of which are not a reflection of any controlling centre such as the economy but exist in conflict with each other and embody inner contradictions. Only 'in the last instance' can the economy be seen as a determining force. This suggests that before the relation of the work of art to the social and cultural forces that produced it can be understood, it is necessary to focus on formal and technical consider-ations in a way that previous Marxist criticism – with the exception of the Bakhtin school – had tended to ignore. Althusser is often said to have created an alignment between Marxism and structuralism, and this has been another important factor in promoting greater interest in Marxist criticism among non-Marxists. That Marxist and structuralist literary criticism could be effectively combined has been most clearly demonstrated by another French philosopher who had collaborated with Althusser, Pierre Macherey, in his book *A*

Theory of Literary Production.

Although this book was published as early as 1966, Macherey's position has also several affinities with post-structuralism, which increases its interest. Discussing the relation between critic and text he writes that 'the critic, employing a new language, brings out a *difference* within the work by demonstrating that it is *other than it is*'.[2] In his concern with what a work does not say, he quotes Nietzsche, the major philosophical influence on post-structuralism, in support of his position: 'When we are confronted with any manifestation which someone has permitted us to see, we may ask: what is it meant to conceal?' (*A Theory of Literary Production (TL)*, 87). He also attacks the idea of plenitude of meaning and asserts: 'Conjecturally, the work has its *margins*, an area of incompleteness from which we can observe its birth and its production' (*TL*, 90). Thus he rejects univocal meaning in favour of dissemination:

> Constrained by its essential diversity, the work, in order to say one thing, has at the same time to say another thing which is not necessarily of the same nature; it unites in a single text several different lines which cannot be apportioned. (*TL*, 99).

He also stresses the importance of intertextuality, a text's relation to other texts: 'the work never "arrives unaccompanied"; it is always determined by the existence of other works, which can belong to different areas of production' (*TL*, 100).

A particularly important connection between Macherey and structuralism is that he is opposed to interpretation in the conventional sense as a comprehensive reading of a text. Like Todorov he sees this form of interpretation as repetition or copying, or as a reduction of the work to a hidden meaning which leaves it 'threadbare' (*TL*, 76). For Macherey authentic criticism seeks knowledge of the text, and such knowledge is achieved not through interpretation but by 'explanation [which] recognises the necessity that determines the work but which does not culminate in a *meaning*' (*TL*, 77-8). The work has a multiplicity of meanings and criticism 'measures the *distance* which separates the *various* meanings' (*TL*, 79). Since the work is therefore 'decentred', 'The structure of the work, which makes it available to knowledge, is this internal displacement, this caesura, by which it corresponds to a reality that is also incomplete, which it shows without reflecting' (*TL*, 79). Whereas 'interpretation' attempts to demonstrate totality of meaning, 'explanation' shows that the work is not independent but is the product of several incompatible meanings and thus

> bears in its material substance the imprint of a determinate absence which is also the principle of its identity. . . . In seeing how the book is made we see also what it is made *from*: this defect which gives it a history and a relation to the historical. (*TL*, 80)

Macherey's approach is a kind of Marxist semiotics in which one is concerned with 'how' rather than 'what' the text signifies.

Like earlier Marxist critics Macherey focuses on the relation between literature and ideology but he has a very different conception of that relation. He sees a historical period as not producing 'a single, monolithic ideology, but a series of ideologies determined by the total relation of forces' (*TL*, 115). Ideology in a literary text should not be seen in terms of the consciousness which produced the work but as independently constituted, as '*encountered*' (*TL*, 115) in the author's work. Ideology cannot be considered separately from the question of form since a literary work 'is not directly rooted in historical reality, but only through a complex series of mediations' (*TL*, 118). He modifies Lenin's theory of reflection by arguing that if the work is a mirror that reflects historical reality, the mirror is partial, selective, and the selection 'is symptomatic; it can tell us about the nature of the mirror' (*TL*, 120). Criticism has to decipher the images in the mirror in the same way as Freud deciphers dream imagery. History is thus like the Freudian unconscious: it can be revealed only indirectly through the interpretation of such phenomena as dreams, and this is done by grasping '*relationships* in contradiction' (*TL*, 126). The divisions within the work constitute its unconscious, 'the unconscious which is history, the play of history beyond its edges, encroaching on those edges' (*TL*, 94). Since the work is an 'ensemble' of contradictions, it is wrong to say 'that the contradictions of the work are the *reflection* of historical contradictions; rather they are the consequences of the absence of this reflection' (*TL*, 128). Thus the work has 'a self-sufficient meaning' which 'results from the disposition of partial reflections within the work and a certain impossibility of reflecting. The function of criticism is to bring this to light' (*TL*, 128).

One can perhaps illuminate this by drawing a comparison with the position that Erich Auerbach takes in his book *Mimesis*. Auerbach is concerned with how reality is represented in texts ranging from the Bible and Homer up to Virginia Woolf. What his investigation reveals is that virtually all literary representation is under the control of some system or other, but he takes the view that reality cannot be contained by any single system and that systematic attempts to represent reality can never achieve completeness. Reality emerges, then, to use Macherey's terms, in the fissures or gaps that one discerns in the systems that govern literary representation. Reality is thus an absence in the text. For Macherey the relation is not between system and reality but between ideology and history; nevertheless his position is fundamentally similar to Auerbach's: 'To know what an ideology means, to express this meaning, we must therefore go beyond and outside ideology; we must attack it from the outside in an effort to give form to that which is formless' (*TL*, 132). By giving ideology a determinate image and form, the text enables ideology 'to speak of its *own absences*' and makes it possible 'to escape from the false consciousness of self, of history, and of time' (*TL*, 132).

Macherey sees criticism as a scientific enterprise in which the aim 'is not an interpretation of its objects; it is a transformation, an attribution of significations which the objects themselves did not initially possess' (*TL*, 149). But the object is left intact in the process, since analysis does not paraphrase what a work says but explores its silences, denials, resistances – the conditions that made it possible – in an effort to produce new knowledge. Again he compares the critic's concern with the relation between the text and history with Freud's investigation of the unconscious, which Macherey views not as a reality but as 'a concept . . . a peculiar speechless language from which nothing will ever emerge but structures, the images of the discourse and the words of the dream' (*TL*, 150-1). The question criticism should ask of a work is: '*In what relation to that which is other than itself is the work produced?*' (*TL*, 154). The apparent order of a work is only an 'imagined order', based as it is on 'the fictive resolution of ideological conflicts' (*TL*, 155), and the critic's role is to reveal the incoherences, fissures, absences, which are inevitably part of that resolution since ideology can never be totally systematic. These are not defects in the sense of being faults, since they are 'indispensable informers' (*TL*, 155). Macherey concludes: 'In the defect of the work is articulated a new truth: for those who seek to know this truth it establishes an original relation to the real, it establishes the revealing form of a knowledge' (*TL*, 155-6).

One of the authors Macherey discusses to illustrate his theory is Balzac. Although the focus is on one work, *Les Paysans*, Macherey shows his affinities with structuralist criticism by being especially interested in understanding the 'langue' or underlying system of Balzac's fiction, with the single text being treated as 'parole' or product of the system. Like Barthes in *S/Z* he refuses to accept Balzac as a realist in a mimetic sense. Macherey sees 'literary discourse as parody, as a contestation of language rather than a representation of reality' (*TL*, 61). The critic's role is to display but not to try to resolve the conflict between meanings which 'produces the radical otherness which shapes the work' (*TL*, 84). Ideology must be the critic's central concern since it exists to efface contradictions but is by definition made up of contradictions. A novelist like Balzac 'confronts *an* ideological utterance with *a* fictional utterance' (*TL*, 261).

Macherey argues that the major dislocation in Balzac's fiction lies in his use of two types of utterance corresponding to his desire both to know and to judge, although they are fused together in the text. As an example of this incompatibility Macherey cites a comparison Balzac draws between the man of the people and the savage, a comparison Macherey finds incoherent since it brings together 'a knowledge which is distinct and an ideology which is confused' (*TL*, 287). Balzac's fictional project, Macherey claims, is divided between the creation of diversity in order to show the complex reality of bourgeois society – that is, knowing – and the creation of literary types, such as the savage, which indicate that this society is being judged in accordance with a theory or ideology. Meaning is in constant movement from one sphere to the other. This creates a 'gap' in the work, 'a complexity which makes it *meaningful*' (*TL*, 296). Criticism which concentrates just on the artistic aspect of the work or on the political creates 'false readings' since it is the play of meaning in and between each sphere and the gap between one sphere and another that constitute the work's literary identity. Politics and art are thus inseparable in literature, Balzac's fiction being a production or working of both, and it is this which should be the focus of the attention of the critic through concentrating on what the text cannot know for itself since it is concealed within the gaps and silences of the work. Marxist theory can then be employed to explain their significance.

Although I have argued that Macherey has several connections with post-structuralist criticism and clearly makes a radical break from reflection theory, the fact that he dismisses 'interpretation' in favour of 'explanation' and sees criticism as a 'science' suggests that he continues to operate within what Derridean critics would call 'logocentrism' – the assumption that there is a fixed centre outside the play of meaning – Marxism, for him, being a science which is beyond ideology and which can yield true knowledge. It is in relation to Marxism as a fixed centre that the 'gaps' and 'silences' in texts can be discerned and explained. But does Marxism itself not exist as a set of texts open to interpretation? Again one can draw a comparison with Auerbach's *Mimesis* where it is clear that his categorisation of certain modes of thought of the past as 'systems' is itself based on certain 'systematic' assumptions, in his case broadly empiricist and liberal–humanist in basis, but which are not seen as systematic. What distinguishes post-structuralism and the work of such critics as Stanley Fish from Macherey is a self-consciousness about the critical process. Thus deconstructionists are concerned with the 'blindness' – as Paul de Man puts it – of the critical text as well as of the literary text. There has been much discussion of whether literary and critical discourse can be clearly separated and Fish has contended that there can be no critical standpoint that is outside interpretation, that 'interpretation is the only game in town'.[3] Although I suggested in the previous chapter that post-structuralist critical practice is vulnerable to its own critique, Macherey's position perhaps creates greater difficulties since he seems to ignore this whole question.

Althusser and Macherey have also been criticised from within Marxism itself. Although Terry Eagleton has clearly been strongly influenced by them in one of his most important theoretical works, *Criticism and Ideology*, he does not wish to see Marxist criticism becoming completely dissociated from its traditional basis in reflection. He criticises Althusser's view that authentic art achieves 'an *internal distantiation*' from ideology and thus exposes it and reveals its contradictions.[4] Eagleton believes that for Althusser and Macherey 'the aesthetic must still be granted mysteriously privileged status, but now in embarrassedly oblique style' (*Criticism and Ideology* (*CI*), 84). He agrees with Macherey's view that ideology being put to work within a text exposes the gaps and silences within the ideology which can then be made to speak, and sees the task of criticism then being 'to install itself in the very incompleteness of the work in order to *theorise* it – to explain the ideological necessity of those "*not-saids*" which constitute the very principle of its identity' (*CI*, 89). The critic's object is thus the work's 'unconsciousness', the space which is articulated by the coming together of the work's meanings, creating the gaps and silences that are produced by the relationship between ideology and history. Ideology is 'hollowed' – as Macherey puts it – in the text and transformed into literary discourse.

But although Eagleton goes part of the way with Macherey he is unhappy with his concept of 'absence', which he criticises as 'an essentially *negative* conception of the text's relation to history' (*CI*, 93). Even if the relation between the contradictions in the text and historical contradictions may not be one of direct reflection, Eagleton wishes to preserve some connection: 'In yielding up to criticism the ideologically determined conventionality of its modes of constructing sense, the text at the same time obliquely illuminates the relation of that ideology to real history' (*CI*, 101). Instead of focusing on gaps and absences, Eagleton is concerned with the complex mediations that govern the relation between history and literary text. History can be present in the text only as ideology since its material is not drawn directly from reality but from how reality is signified. Reality in the text is therefore 'pseudo-reality'. Drawing on Althusser, he sees the relation between text and history as 'overdetermined' since the text is an imaginary construction produced from representations which are themselves productions. Criticism is therefore concerned with examining 'in conjuncture two mutually constitutive formations: the nature of the ideology worked by the text and the aesthetic modes of that working' (*CI*, 85) and it can aspire to the status of a science only on the basis of 'the science of ideological formations' (*CI*, 96): that is, studying 'the laws of the production of ideological discourses as literature' (*CI*, 97). This creates 'a ceaseless reciprocal *operation* of text on ideology and ideology on text, a mutual structuring and destructuring in which the text constantly overdetermines its own determinations', so that instead of the structure of the text reflecting historical reality, it is 'the *product* of this process, not the reflection of its ideological environs' (*CI*, 99). Both language and argument seem strained here, suggesting that Eagleton is finding it a struggle to preserve traditional Marxism's concern with the relation between text and history, given that the theory of reflection in its straightforward form must be sacrificed.

He goes on to consider the work of a number of writers, including George Eliot. Her work and that of other writers such as Arnold, Dickens and Conrad is seen in relation to a problem that faced bourgeois ideology in the nineteenth century: because the culture could not sustain 'a set of potently affective mythologies which might permeate the texture of lived experience of English society' it was necessary to construct an ideology from the Romantic tradition, a 'nebulous compound of Burkean conservatism and German idealism . . . a tradition which offered an idealist critique of bourgeois social relations, coupled with a consecration of the rights of capital' (*CI*, 102). George Eliot's work is an attempt 'to resolve a structural conflict between two forms of mid-Victorian ideology' (*CI*, 111): the belief in individualism and the need for the existence of a set of social laws which prevent individualism taking anarchic or socially irresponsible forms, with any collision between the two ideologies being 'consistently defused and repressed by the forms of Eliot's fiction' (*CI*, 112). This results in the recasting of 'the historical contradictions at the heart of Eliot's fiction into ideologically resolvable terms' (*CI*, 112).

As against criticism of the Caudwell type, Eagleton tries to avoid reducing George Eliot's consciousness to ideological terms. George Eliot signifies for him 'the insertion of certain specific ideological determinations – Evangelical Christianity, rural organicism, incipient feminism, petty-bourgeois moralism – into a hegemonic ideological formation which is partly supported, partly embarrassed by their presence' (*CI*, 113). He also seeks to avoid suggesting that these ideological contradictions are directly incorporated in her fiction. One must take account of 'the relatively autonomous level of the mutation of literary forms' since 'it is the mutual articulation of these discourses within the text which *produces* these ideological forms as literary signification' (*CI*, 113). Thus he attempts to accommodate Althusser and Macherey.

However, in his discussion of individual works of George Eliot, Eagleton produces readings which are more like straightforward interpretations than Macherey's criticism, although his aim is to reveal unresolved contradiction and conflict rather than the artistic and thematic unity of conventional forms of interpretation. Thus *Adam Bede* is 'allowed to advance into more richly individualised consciousness . . . without damage to his mythological status as organic type, an admirable amalgam of naturalised culture and cultivated nature' (*CI*, 114). Macherey's criticism endeavoured to bring together the political and the aesthetic, it being impossible in his view to separate them. This aesthetic dimension is given little emphasis by Eagleton and whereas Macherey exposes the contradictions in Balzac's work without implying a negative judgement of them or that it would have been better if they had been avoided, Eagleton's criticism is riddled with explicit and implicit negative judgements and has affinities with what Macherey calls 'normative' criticism, even though Eagleton appears to agree with Macherey and dismisses 'the typical gesture of "normative" criticism [which] is to inscribe a "Could do better" in the work's margin' (*CI*, 91). Thus there are references to 'the nostalgic organicism of Eliot's historically backdated rural fiction' (*CI*, 116), 'the aggressive modes of working-class consciousness caricatured in *Felix Holt*' (*CI*, 119), the 'ideologically insufficient' solution of the 'abnegation of the ego' (*CI*, 121) in *Middlemarch*, 'the desperate recourse of adopting a mystical epistemology to resolve [*Daniel Deronda's*] problems' (*CI*, 123) and the 'effusive celebration of the *status quo*' and 'jingoist reaction' (*CI*, 125) of *Impressions of Theophrastus Such*. This suggests that not only is Eagleton's Marxism, like Macherey's, beyond ideology, but that the 'vulgar Marxist' tendency to criticise works and writers for failing to adopt a Marxist position has not been completely transcended.

Jameson's Marxist synthesis

If Eagleton in *Criticism and Ideology* is seeking to reconcile traditional Marxist ideological criticism with Althusser and Macherey, the leading American Marxist critic, Fredric Jameson seeks a similar reconciliation between Althusserian Marxism and the Hegelian Marxist critical tradition that would include Georg Lukács and the later work of Jean-Paul Sartre. Jameson's ambition is, however, greater since his aim in *The Political Unconscious* is to create a totalising Marxist criticism that can subsume not only Althusser and Macherey but also structuralism and post-structuralism, formalistic and archetypal criticism and virtually all other significant critical schools.

In contrast to Macherey Jameson is committed to interpretation. He recognises that structuralist and some post-structuralist critics have attacked interpretative criticism, in particular Freudian and traditional Marxist criticism, as reductive since it in effect rewrites complex texts in terms of a 'master code' or 'master narrative'. In their book *Anti-Oedipus*, Gilles Deleuze and Felix Guattari writing from a broadly post-structuralist position had distinguished between 'transcendent' interpretation, such as Freudian and Marxist readings which they equate with allegorising, and 'immanent' interpretation – the kind of criticism that refuses to look for meanings beyond the text – and they argue that only 'immanent' criticism is defensible. Jameson's response is to deny the validity of this distinction. All 'immanent' criticism can be shown to be governed by a 'master code': 'even the most formalizing kinds of literary or textual analysis carry a theoretical charge whose denial unmasks it as ideological'.[5] He claims, for example, that the New Criticism, the major Anglo-American form of 'immanent' criticism, was governed by a philosophy of history even if most of the New Critics themselves and their readers had little awareness of the fact because the underlying ideology had such power over them.

Criticism cannot, therefore, avoid allegorising. Jameson accepts, however, that allegory in the conventional sense is reductive and impoverishing. But he argues that Marxist criticism is a non-reductive form of allegorisation because it can be equated with the four levels of allegory that governed much medieval literature, with the fourth or anagogical level in his Marxist version being history as understood in terms of a kind of Marxist apocalypse in which both history and individuality in the Western sense cease. At this ultimate allegorical level there is no further need for interpretation.

In order to reinstate interpretation as central to Marxist criticism, Jameson has to come to terms with Althusser's attack on 'expressive causality': that is, the doctrine that the products of the superstructure, such as works of literature, can be rewritten in terms of some more fundamental or 'hidden master narrative' (*The Political Unconscious (PU)*, 28) which has its basis in the economic base or infrastructure. Expressive causality is particularly associated with the practice of one of the critics Jameson most admires, Lukács. Althusser's attack on it was related to his criticism of another central traditional Marxian concept, mediation: that is, the idea that since all levels of the superstructure are reflections of the infrastructure or economic base, they must all be essentially similar in structure despite their apparent differences. Althusser reformulates the relation between infrastructure and superstructure in structuralist terms, rejecting causality in any traditional sense; he substitutes a relational for a causal model. The economic base is no longer the hidden 'cause' of the superstructure but exists within the superstructure itself. Its relation to the superstructure is then seen in terms of 'overdetermination' and not in terms of traditional determinism. Thus he replaces 'expressive causality' with 'structural causality' which allows the various levels of the superstructure, such as art, law, religion, 'relative autonomy' rather than being mere reflections of the economic base.

Jameson goes part of the way with Althusser but he wants to retain mediation in a modified form. He claims that Althusser's concern with the 'interrelatedness of all elements in a social formation' but relating them

> by way of their structural *difference* and distance from one another, rather than by their ultimate identity . . . is *also* a form of mediation. Althusserian structural causality is therefore just as fundamentally a practice of mediation as is the 'expressive causality' to which it is opposed. (*PU*, 41)

But the real value of Althusser's analysis as far as Jameson is concerned is that since infrastructure and superstructure are no longer two separate realms, history does not exist separately from its products but only within the relations between them. History is therefore an 'absent cause' and this leads Jameson to the concept of a 'political unconscious' which can be penetrated only by interpreting such cultural products as literary texts. As I have suggested above this idea was anticipated by Macherey and Eagleton but Jameson greatly develops it and makes it part of his much more ambitious system. In his interpretation of it, it entails 'that all literature must be read as a symbolic meditation on the destiny of community' (*PU*, 70).

The implicit psychoanalytical model which underlies Jameson's concept of history also shapes his concept of ideology. Ideologies are not conceived of, as in traditional Marxism, as consciously held and inauthentic sets of ideas or beliefs but as '*strategies of containment*' (*PU*, 53) which repress or refuse to acknowledge contradictions that have their basis in history, history being understood by Jameson as 'a single great collective story . . . the collective struggle to wrest a realm of Freedom from a realm of Necessity' (*PU*, 19), a struggle which has led to perpetual class conflict. The most complex products of these 'strategies of containment' are works of art and for Jameson the importance of the political unconscious in literary criticism is that it enables the critic to restore 'to the surface of the text the repressed and buried reality of this fundamental history' and to 'explore the multiple paths that lead to the unmasking of cultural artifacts as socially symbolic acts' (*PU*, 20). Literary works for Jameson develop complex strategies either to deny the exploitation and oppression that are the reality of history or to find some way to shut out the pain and suffering they have caused. Jameson lays particular stress on Walter Benjamin's assertion that 'There has never been a document of culture which was not at one and the same time a document of barbarism.' (One wonders whether Benjamin's position may owe more to Nietzsche and his claim, in *Beyond Good and Evil*, that 'Almost everything that we call "higher culture" is based upon the spiritualizing and intensifying of *cruelty*' than to Marx.) Continuing to follow this psychoanalytical model, literary analysis proceeds by looking for clues or symptoms which indicate the ways in which literary texts evade the realities of history or refuse to recognise or acknowledge its contradictions. Yet it is only this method of procedure that can give one an insight into history itself since history 'as an absent cause . . . is inaccessible to us except in textual form, and . . . our approach to it and to the Real itself necessarily passes through its prior textualization, its narrativization in the political unconscious' (*PU*, 35).

Literary criticism, instead of being a relatively unimportant activity that has little connection with the realities of history and politics, is thus elevated in significance as the means by which one discovers the truths about history which are hidden within texts that are ideological through and through. It seems clear that the doctrine of reflection has not been completely banished from Jameson's criticism since literary works function in terms of ideologies as strategies of containment, but reflection can no longer be seen as simple mirroring:

> The type of interpretation here proposed is more satisfactorily grasped as the rewriting of the literary text in such a way that the latter may itself be seen as the rewriting or restructuration of a prior historical or ideological *subtext*, it being always understood that that 'subtext' is not immediately present as such . . . but rather must itself always be (re)constructed after the fact. (*PU*, 81)

There is thus always 'some active relationship' between literary work and the 'Real'. However, the 'Real' does not remain inert but is drawn into the work's texture in such a way that 'language manages to carry the Real within itself as its own intrinsic or immanent subtext' (*PU*, 81). Jameson claims that this view of the relation between literary text and reality avoids both the 'ideology' of structuralism and vulgar materialism, the one denying that any referent exists which has any relation to the text as a symbolic act and the other claiming that the text is the product of passive reflection of the economic base.

Criticism for Jameson therefore involves revealing that literary works attempt to resolve in symbolic terms contradictions which have their basis in history and only Marxism makes possible insights which are the 'ultimate *semantic* precondition for the intelligibility of literary and cultural texts' (*PU*, 75). Interpretation functions in terms of three 'distinct semantic horizons'. These

> mark a widening out of the sense of the social ground of a text through the notions, first, of political history . . . then of society . . . and, ultimately, of history now conceived in its vastest sense of the sequence of modes of production and the succession and destiny of the various human social formations. (*PU*, 75)

Within the first horizon the text is treated as an individual work in conventional analytic terms except that it is 'grasped essentially as a *symbolic* act' (*PU*, 76). The second semantic horizon brings the text into dialectical relationship with the social order so that the individual work is 'reconstituted in the form of the great collective and class discourses of which a text is little more than an individual *parole* or utterance'. Here the focus is on 'the *ideologeme*, that is, the smallest intelligible unit of the essentially antagonistic collective discourses of social classes'. Obviously Jameson is drawing an analogy with linguistics in which ideology is 'langue', the literary text 'parole' and the smallest unit of ideology functions like a phoneme to create the system of differences that makes meaning possible. At the third semantic horizon of history in a totalising sense

> both the individual text and its ideologemes know a final transformation, and must be read in terms of what I call the *ideology of form*, that is, the symbolic messages transmitted to us by the coexistence of various sign systems which are themselves traces or anticipations of modes of production. (*PU*, 76)

Jameson's use of the term 'trace' with its Derridean connotations suggests that he hopes to accommodate deconstruction within his system. He acknowledges that a major influence on his theory of interpretation is Lévi-Strauss's readings of myths in which 'the individual narrative, or the individual formal structure, is to be grasped as the imaginary resolution of a real contradiction' (*PU*, 77).

In *The Political Unconscious* Jameson applies this system to Balzac, Gissing and Conrad, with the Conrad essay clearly being the most substantial. His particular aim is to account for the stylistic and formal aspects of literary texts in Marxian terms – something that earlier Marxist criticism had failed to do convincingly – and the works of Conrad, a writer who has strong connections with Modernism, offer a greater challenge from this point of view than fiction in the realist tradition. He sees two strategies of containment at work in Conrad: Nietzsche's concept of *ressentiment* and existentialist metaphysics. These 'allow Conrad to recontain his narrative and to rework it in melodramatic terms, in a subsystem of good and evil which now once again has villains and heroes' (*PU*, 216). He argues that Conrad's and Henry James's concern with the technical question of point of view should also be seen in ideological terms, as 'part of the more general containment strategy of a late nineteenth-century bourgeoisie suffering from the aftereffects of reification' (*PU*, 221). Point of view is both 'a protest and a defense against reification', but it 'ends up furnishing a powerful ideological instrument in the perpetuation of an increasingly subjectivized and psychologized world' (*PU*, 221).

Jameson relates Conrad's style to impressionism, normally thought of as anti-positivist. But Jameson argues that both positivism as 'ideological production' and impressionism as 'aesthetic production' are responses to 'rationalization and reification in late nineteenth-century capitalism' (*PU*, 225). Style is thus dissociated from idealist forms of aesthetics and redefined as 'stylistic production' which should be read 'as a projected solution, on the aesthetic or imaginary level, to a genuinely contradictory situation in the concrete world of everyday life' (*PU*, 225). Jameson believes a reinstatement of 'mediation' through the adoption of mediatory codes central to Marxism, such as reification or mode of production or alienation, helps to connect phenomena which are normally regarded as belonging to quite different aspects of reality and thus to restore social unity. Conrad's style should not be regarded as aesthetically autonomous but as an '*aestheticizing strategy*' (*PU*, 230) and Modernism is viewed 'as a late stage in the bourgeois cultural revolution . . . whereby the inhabitants of older social formations are culturally and psychologically retrained for life in the market system' (*PU*, 236). Jameson, however, wants to go beyond a merely negative critique, since Modernism can also be read 'as a Utopian compensation for everything reification brings with it'. Thus Conrad's stylistic practice is 'ideology and Utopia all at once' (*PU*, 236) in that Conrad is engaged in a symbolic act which seeks to transform a reified reality. Marxist criticism must go beyond a 'negative hermeneutic function' towards a 'positive hermeneutic' (*PU*, 292) and show that a cultural artifact also possesses a 'Utopian power as the symbolic affirmation of a specific historical and class form of collective unity' (*PU*, 291).

The ambition and totalising impulse informing Jameson's criticism obviously make it vulnerable to attack from several perspectives. At the most general level Jameson's system can be seen as another search for a 'key to all mythologies' and thus open to the criticism that it merely selects elements from a great variety of sources which happen to fit in with Jameson's project and constructs out of these a system that is no more solid than a house of cards. Certainly some of Jameson's arguments seem to resemble the ontological argument for the existence of God, namely, that since no being more perfect than God can be conceived, and since it is better to exist in fact than in imagination, then God must exist. Jameson argues along similar lines that dialectical thought is 'the anticipation of the logic of a collectivity which has not yet come into being', so that 'to project an imperative to thought in which the ideological would be grasped as somehow at one with the Utopian, and the Utopian at one with the ideological, is to formulate a question to which a collective dialectic is the only conceivable answer' (*PU*, 286–7). Nor is it clear why, if Nietzsche's *ressentiment* is an ideological product, certain comparable Marxian concepts, such as alienation, are not equally ideological. His view of the relation between text and history can also be accused of exhibiting hermeneutic circularity. History is an absence which is only accessible in textual form, but Jameson appears to know already what history is: it is class struggle, oppression, what hurts. Thus it is no surprise that this is the history which he finds repressed in literary texts.

Yet unlike Macherey and Eagleton, Jameson does not talk of Marxist criticism as a 'science' or suggest that his interpretative approach is superior because it has a scientific basis. Nor does he draw back from connecting Marxism with religious forms of thinking. He even risks mockery by confronting the problem of death for Marxists: if or when Marxism triumphs politically 'people will still grow old and die', but death in a 'future communal social life . . . will have lost its sharpness and pain and be of less consequence' (*PU*, 261). But in his view alternatives to Marxism, even science itself, have no better claim to total objectivity. Influenced by Jean-François Lyotard's discussion in *The Postmodern Condition* of the relation between scientific and narrative knowledge, Jameson believes that the 'great master-narratives' persist in the unconscious and subsume scientific knowledge.[6] Thus, since he is unable to claim scientific superiority for his interpretative approach it can be judged only in relation to the alternatives which are in conflict with it, and he is content that it be assessed on the basis of the readings it produces. He denies that the question of interpretative validity can be usefully discussed and justifies his interpretations on the grounds that they are 'strong misreadings' (*PU*, 13). His ambitious system is in some ways, then, more modest than those of Macherey and Eagleton, for it does not seek to compel submission by claiming scientific objectivity but to convince through its explanatory power: its attempt to fuse intrinsic, ethical and political criticism.

It should be pointed out that both Macherey and Eagleton have moved on from the positions that I have discussed above, largely through the influence of a later essay by Althusser, 'Ideology and ideological state apparatuses',[7] which breaks radically with the view that ideology is something mental and adopts the uncompromising materialist position that ideology exists within a system of social practices, produced by the functioning of those 'apparatuses' which are dominant in the state. For Althusser and Macherey the most powerful state apparatus is the educational system, and this has led Macherey to focus his attention on the ideological use to which literature is put in the school.[8] Although such apparatuses as the school and the family may appear to be benign and do not employ outward force, their function, in Althusser's view, is to construct malleable subjects whose relation to the real, oppressive relations of production is imaginary and who thus serve the interests of the capitalist system.

Eagleton in his more recent work takes a similar view of the study of literature: 'Departments of literature in higher education . . . are part of the ideological apparatus of the modern capitalist state', even if they are unreliable in serving the interests of that apparatus. He believes the category 'literature' should be discarded since virtually any text can be analysed using literary–critical methods, and that a mode of study should be created which would be concerned with 'the kinds of *effects* which discourses produce, and how they produce them', in order to grasp discursive practices 'as forms of power and performance'.[9] Above all one should be concerned with why one wants to engage in discourse analysis and this will determine the texts studied and how that study will proceed. For a Marxist it can be a worthwhile activity only if it is directed by the aim of emancipating humanity by means of a socialist transformation, and this aim should also determine how traditional literary texts should be interpreted.

Although Eagleton is hostile to what he sees as the underlying ideology of post-structuralism, his critical practice since the publication of *Walter Benjamin or Towards a Revolutionary Criticism* in 1981 has clearly been influenced by Derrida and might be described as post-Derridean Marxist interpretation, and his rejection of the concept of literature has not prevented him from recently writing a book on the most 'canonic' of writers, Shakespeare. He describes this study as 'an exercise in political semiotics, which tries to locate the relevant history in the very letter of the text'. Deconstruction pervades both the ideas and language of the book:

> When language is cut loose from reality, signifiers split from signifieds, the result is a radical fissure between consciousness and material life. Macbeth will end up as a bundle of broken signifiers, his body reduced to a blind automaton of battle.
>
> The complexity of Shakespeare's ideological dilemmas . . . arises from the fact that they do not take the form of 'simple' contradictions, in which each term is the polar opposite of the other; on the contrary, in 'deconstructive' fashion, each term seems confusingly to inhere in its antagonist.[10]

It is this willingness to make use of contemporary theory rather than merely to condemn or dismiss it that has been to a large extent responsible for revitalising Marxist criticism.

Cultural materialism and the new historicism

Macherey, Eagleton and Jameson are convinced Marxists but one of the most significant developments in recent literary criticism has been the emergence of forms of historical interpretation that are strongly influenced by Marxism yet which keep a certain distance from it as a system. The most notable of these are what has become known as 'cultural materialism' in Britain and 'the new historicism' in America, though 'the new historicism' is being increasingly used to cover both. They have been seen as more or less the same but, as one might expect, cultural materialism is more openly Marxian in approach, whereas the influence of Marxism on the new historicism is more understated. The work of Althusser is particularly important for cultural materialism, while the new historicism draws considerably on Foucault's cultural theory.

A major influence on cultural materialism is Raymond Williams, a critic who adopted an explicitly Marxist position only towards the end of his career, although he seems to prefer Bakhtinian dialogical thinking to the Marxian dialectic. Williams coined the term 'cultural materialism' in his book *Marxism and Literature*, published in 1977. His support for a materialist approach to literature is apparent in an earlier book like *Keywords*, first published in 1976, where it is clear he is opposed to the identification of literature with a 'canon' of exemplary texts that are of particular artistic merit. Williams argues that this concept of literature is of very recent origin, that previously the term 'literature' referred to books and writing in a more general sense. Williams's hostility to a narrow concept of literature that equates it with high culture is particularly evident in his discussion of 'aesthetic' in *Keywords*. He sees the separation of art from its social and cultural dimensions as 'damaging, for there is something irresistibly displaced and marginal about the now common and limiting phrase "aesthetic considerations" '.[11] Williams had always been concerned with literature in its social context, but in his later writings, which I am concerned with here, he becomes convinced that criticism should reject any tendency to allow the literary text to transcend the culture that produced it and argues that it should be thoroughly situated in its cultural matrix. He defines cultural materialism as 'the analysis of all forms of signification, including quite centrally writing, within the actual means and conditions of their production'.[12]

Williams is aware, however, of the problems with early Marxist criticism and reflection theory, and probably his major theoretical contribution to materialist criticism is to produce a different way of looking at the relation between base and superstructure. For him the idea that social being determines consciousness is central but he believes this exists in an unsatisfactory relation with the traditional Marxist proposition that the economic base determines the super-structure, although he does not wish wholly to reject this proposi-tion. Thus he argues that base and superstructure need to be reinterpreted, superstructure being seen in terms of 'a related range of cultural practices' and base as 'the specific activities of men in real social and economic relationships, containing fundamental con-tradictions and variations and therefore always in a state of dynamic process'.[13] He believes the concepts of base and superstructure need to be combined with the concepts of totality and hegemony, the latter understood in Gramsci's sense as a dominant ideology that permeates a society to such an extent that it is not perceived as ideology in the traditional sense.

Yet Williams argues that even the concept of hegemony needs to be developed further by being related to a real social process; it must not be seen as static. There will be oppositional elements in any social formation that resist the dominant ideology, but these opposit-ional elements are also not static. Williams defines them in terms of 'residual' and 'emergent' cultural forces, the 'residual' representing 'experiences, meanings and values' (*Problems in Materialism and Culture (PM)*, 40) which are the product of a previous social formation but which continue to have power, and the 'emergent' representing 'new meanings and values, new practices, new signifi-cances and experiences [which] are continually being created' (*PM*, 41). Williams suggests that this revision of traditional Marxist formulations makes possible a reconciliation with the idea that social being determines consciousness, and he draws the further conclusion that

> we cannot separate literature and art from other kinds of social practice, in such a way as to make them subject to quite special and distinct laws. They may have quite specific features as practices, but they cannot be separated from the general social process. (*PM*, 44)

Thus in looking at any specific literary work one should be aware of its connections with dominant, residual and emergent cultural forces and the complex and changing interplay between them. This means that literature cannot be seen in isolation but must be related to other social practices. He also believes this makes possible a break from theories of art which assume that the work of art is an object to be consumed in favour of an understanding of art as a social practice.

Most of Williams's specific literary interpretation predates his advocacy of cultural materialism. The book which has closest affinities with it is *The Country and the City*, in which, for example, Jane Austen's works are discussed along with the writings of William Cobbett and Gilbert White, provoking the question 'what was the social substance of her precise and inquiring personal and moral emphases?'.[14] Williams rejects the view that the social context of the novels can be seen as mere background so that one can then interpret her fiction as concerned with 'purely personal relationships'. He contends that her major concern is 'personal *conduct*: a testing and discovery of the standards which govern human behaviour in certain real situations' (*The Country and the City* (*CC*), 113). He sees her novels as having a direct connection with the contradiction at this historical period between two types of improvement: 'improvement of soil, stock, yields, in a working agriculture', and 'improvement of houses, parks, artificial landscapes' (*CC*, 115) in the spirit of consumption and indulgence. The theme of improvement in Jane Austen's fiction has a similarly double nature: 'The working improvement, which is not seen at all, is the means to social improvement, which is then so isolated that it is seen very clearly indeed' (*CC*, 116), and not in flattering terms. He concludes by claiming that although the perspectives of Cobbett, Jane Austen and Gilbert White are very different, each of their ways of observing is social and each illuminates the other.

Despite the connections between *The Country and the City* and Williams's later, more theoretical writings, it is obvious that it is not a fundamental departure from conventional literary interpretation which has always had a place for connecting the literary work with its social context, even though Williams is attempting both to make that connection more integral and to interpret it in political terms. British critics who have wholly identified with cultural materialism, such as Jonathan Dollimore and Alan Sinfield, have presented a more direct challenge to conventional criticism by advocating a much more openly political form of interpretation. Central to this is the attack on what they call 'essentialism'.

The fullest account of this is to be found in Dollimore's reading of Renaissance drama in his book *Radical Tragedy*. This is to a large degree a polemical book and therefore more vulnerable to objections than Williams's criticism, which almost always is prepared to recognise and not over-simplify difficulties. Dollimore argues that conventional Christian and humanist readings of Renaissance drama posit an essentialist ideology by assuming that 'man' possesses an unalterable essence and thus transcends history and society. Dollimore advocates a 'materialist' conception of the subject which sees it as the product of specific historical conditions and social relations. He argues that conventional criticism has projected essentialist ideas on to the interpretation of Renaissance drama and has ignored the degree to which anti-essentialist ideas can be found in some of the major writers and thinkers of the period, such as Montaigne, Machiavelli, Raleigh, Burton. Indeed, he goes so far as to suggest that Montaigne's view of 'custom' has much in common with Althusser's conception of ideology. In his interpretation of *King Lear*, for example, Dollimore rejects both Christian and humanist readings, which emphasise such ideas as pity and redemption, as based on mystification, and argues that the play is fundamentally concerned with power and property. The influence of Williams is apparent in Dollimore's view that Edmund's scepticism represents the 'emergent' although his engagement in the struggle for power and property shows how 'a revolutionary (emergent) insight is folded back into a dominant ideology'. Dollimore concludes that the play 'offers . . . a decentring of the tragic subject which in turn becomes the focus of a more general exploration of human consciousness in relation to social being – one which discloses human values to be not antecedent to, but rather in-formed by, material conditions'.[15]

Anti-essentialism has been associated with a variety of modern thinkers, such as Heidegger, Derrida, Thomas S. Kuhn, Richard Rorty. For example, Rorty writes of pragmatism and William James:

> My first characterization of pragmatism is that it is simply anti-essentialism applied to notions like 'truth', 'knowledge', 'language', 'morality', and similar objects of philosophical theorizing. . . . Those who want truth to have an essence want knowledge, or rationality, or inquiry, or the relation between thought and its object, to have an essence. Further, they want to be able to use their knowledge of such essences to criticize views they take to be false, and to point the direction of progress toward the discovery of more truths. James thinks these hopes are vain. There are no essences anywhere in the area.[16]

Anti-essentialism is often associated with 'anti-foundationalism' and there is an important debate between the latter and 'foundationalism', the belief that one can or should try to base 'reason' or 'truth' on a firm foundation, a position whose most powerful current defender is Jürgen Habermas.

Dollimore's anti-essentialism has little in common with that of Rorty or with anti-foundationalist thought generally and his use of the term 'essentialism' to categorise what he wants to attack creates therefore a somewhat misleading picture of cultural materialism. The cultural materialist position seems much closer to that of Habermas and his view that, as Christopher Norris puts it, 'there *must* be certain positive norms – structures of rational understanding – which allow thought to criticize the current self-images of the age'.[17] In the foreword to their book, *Political Shakespeare*, Dollimore and Sinfield write that cultural materialist criticism 'registers its commitment to the transformation of a social order which exploits people on grounds of race, gender and class',[18] and their interpretations of texts are informed by this commitment. Rather than being anti-essentialist in a Derridean or Rortian sense, cultural materialism is better seen as opposing liberal–humanist essentialism with a neo-Marxian alternative, which in Rorty's terms would be equally essentialist. Thus liberal–humanist interpretations of *King Lear* in terms of 'man' or 'nature' are rejected as false by Dollimore in favour of what he appears to regard as the 'true' reading, namely that it is 'above all, a play about power, property and inheritance'.[19]

By focusing on 'resistances' within a text which destabilise the prevailing ideology that the text would appear to support, cultural materialist critics use literary interpretation to promote social and political change. As with Jameson, they exploit elements from a variety of intellectual sources – such as Althusser, Foucault, Williams, Derrida – but unlike Jameson these are not incorporated in an ambitious alternative system. Rather, cultural materialists adopt those concepts and ideas which are most useful from their point of view and discard the rest. In contrast to the complexity of Jamesonian readings, interpretations by Dollimore and Sinfield are much more direct and straightforward in approach. Thus they have created an interpretative mode that has something of the force of a critic like Caudwell's reflective Marxist criticism but with a more sophisticated theoretical base.

American new historicism appears to be less politically committed. Its leading practitioner, Stephen Greenblatt, has argued in an influential essay[20] that in Renaissance texts the resistances or subversive elements, which on the surface undermine the ideological discourse of such texts, function rather to immunise that discourse against being seriously threatened since subversion is both generated and contained by the dominant ideology. This view, clearly, does not lead to his form of historical criticism positively furthering social change, as cultural materialism seeks to do, but Greenblatt could still argue that it promotes change indirectly by revealing how this process operates. The reader of such criticism is then in a better position to understand his or her contemporary cultural situation and can act to alter it.

Greenblatt's book, *Renaissance Self-Fashioning*, is widely regarded as the major work to date of the new historicism. Like Jameson, he is committed to interpretation and sets forth the principles of interpretation on which his criticism is based in the introduction. His position in relation to essentialism and anti-essentialism is more complex than Dollimore's. He begins with the anti-essentialist statement that human nature is determined by culture: 'the cultural system of meanings . . . creates specific individuals by governing the passage from abstract potential to create historical embodiment'.[21] He goes on to argue that literature has three 'interlocking functions' within this cultural system that creates individuals: 'as a manifestation of the concrete behavior of its particular author, as itself the expression of the codes by which behavior is shaped, and as a reflection upon those codes' (*Renaissance Self-Fashioning* (*RS*), 4). In attempting a kind of criticism that tries to take account of all three Greenblatt aims to create 'a more cultural or anthropological criticism', a criticism 'conscious of its own status as interpretation and intent upon understanding literature as a part of the system of signs that constitutes a given culture', the goal of which 'is a *poetics of culture*' (*RS*, 4–5). Since both social actions and the language of literary texts are

> always embedded in systems of public signification . . . our interpretive task must be to grasp more sensitively the consequences of this fact by investigating both the social presence to the world of the literary text and the social presence of the world in the literary text. (*RS*, 5)

More recently Greenblatt has used the term 'negotiation' to describe the process by which the work of art is produced: 'the work of art is the product of a negotiation between a creator or class of creators, equipped with a complex, communally shared repertoire of conventions, and the institutions and practices of society.' Thus criticism should reject the notion of textual autonomy and the mimetic theory of art and

> construct in its stead an interpretative model that will more adequately
> account for the unsettling circulation of materials and discourses that
> is . . . the heart of modern aesthetic practice. It is in response to this
> practice that contemporary theory must situate itself: not outside
> interpretation, but in the hidden places of negotiation and exchange'.[22]

Unlike Dollimore, however, Greenblatt openly acknowledges that
he cannot escape from the hermeneutic circle:

> I should add that if cultural poetics is conscious of its status as
> interpretation, this consciousness must extend to an acceptance of the
> impossibility of fully reconstructing and reentering the culture of the
> sixteenth century, of leaving behind one's own situation: it is every-
> where evident in this book that the questions I ask of my material and
> indeed the very nature of this material are shaped by the questions I ask
> of myself. (*RS*, 5)

The first part of that sentence strikes an obvious Gadamerian note
but the end of the sentence suggests that Greenblatt may be
conscious of Habermas's criticism of Gadamerian hermeneutics on
the grounds that it makes it impossible to achieve a position outside
of historical meaning from which one can adopt a critical stance and
thus create change. Greenblatt's criticism can be seen as, in effect,
attempting to reconcile Gadamer and Habermas. This makes his
criticism particularly interesting, although it also creates difficulties.

He admits that certain concepts that derive from his own culture
determine how he views the sixteenth century as a cultural system:
'the resonance and centrality we find in our small group of texts and
their authors is our invention and the similar, cumulative inventions
of others' (*RS*, 6). Influenced by the work of twentieth-century
cultural theorists, especially Clifford Geertz and Foucault, he sees
culture in terms of power, 'power at once localized in particular
institutions . . . and diffused in ideological structures of meaning,
characteristic modes of expression, recurrent narrative patterns' (*RS*,
6). However, although he concedes that he has only selected from the
period 'a handful of arresting figures who seem to contain within
themselves much of what we need', he believes that the fact that they
do so is not 'entirely our own critical invention' (*RS*, 6) since one can
take certain things for granted. For example, art in the sixteenth
century did not claim to be autonomous, 'the written word is self-
consciously embedded in specific communities, life situations,
structures of power' (*RS*, 7). But the fact that particular writers are

chosen for discussion in relation to 'what we need' indicates that the purposes of the present are uppermost in his literary interpretations.

In practice, Greenblatt's approach to interpretation operates in terms of a sophisticated intertextuality. The literary text which is the focus of his critical concern is discussed in the context both of other texts of its time, usually with one particular non-literary text highlighted, and of modern texts which may only be implicitly present but which govern how Greenblatt interprets his historical texts, literary and non-literary. In a chapter on *Othello*, for example, he discusses passages from Marlowe's *Tamburlaine*, Spenser's *The Faerie Queene*, and Machiavelli's *The Prince* as conventional historical critics might do, but he shows how far he departs from such critics by placing much more emphasis on a text that seems quite unrelated to *Othello*, an account by Peter Martyr of how Spanish colonisers responded to a labour shortage in the gold mines of Hispaniola. He also refers to the work of a modern sociologist and implicitly exploits the theory he has derived from such writers as Geertz and Foucault.

The interpretation of *Othello* is governed by the way in which Greenblatt interprets the Martyr text, particularly with regard to how the Spanish persuaded natives on a neighbouring island to Hispaniola to go there and work in the gold mines. Iago, he argues, is able to gain power over Othello in the same way that the Spanish imposed their will on the natives: by a combination of empathy and improvisation. This interpretation of both the Martyr text and the play is clearly dependent on modern ideas. Greenblatt claims that Martyr's account suggests that the Spanish were able to enter into the natives' religion in a theatrical sense through empathy and improvisation after having grasped this religion as 'an ideology' that bore 'a certain structural resemblance' (*RS*, 228) to their own religion of Catholicism. Thus the natives' religion 'is conceived as analogous to Catholicism, close enough to permit improvisation, yet sufficiently distanced to protect European beliefs from the violence of fictionalization' (*RS*, 229). He implicitly criticises the Spanish since he suggests that they failed to draw the conclusion that their own religion could also be seen as 'a manipulable human construct', and they thus exhibited an 'absence of reciprocity' (*RS*, 229).

As I discussed in Chapter 3, fundamental to Gadamerian hermeneutics is the concept of a 'fusion of horizons' in which the historical text and the perspective and interests of its modern interpreter come together in the interpretative act, making it impossible to separate one element from the other. With Greenblatt's interpretations there is little sense of such a fusion: rather the emphasis is on the perspective of the modern interpreter. Thus Greenblatt takes a critical stance to the Spanish colonisers' 'absence of reciprocity' because as a twentieth-century person he accepts cultural relativism. To adopt a 'fusion of horizons' approach would deny Greenblatt a position from which he can criticise the Spanish colonisers and by extension Western imperialism. But from a Gadamerian position it could be argued that in adopting a critical perspective towards imperialism Greenblatt in effect bypasses the hermeneutic circle and in doing so becomes vulnerable to the kind of critique he makes of the Spanish: as they privilege their belief in Catholicism to serve the purposes of their own time, so he privileges cultural relativism to serve the purposes of his time.

Another indication of Greenblatt's implicit rejection of the concept of a 'fusion of horizons' and his privileging of his own modern perspective is his use of a mode of critical discourse that could only be understood in a twentieth-century intellectual context. Discussing the consequences of Othello's storytelling, he writes: 'Othello is pressing up against the condition of all discursive representations of identity. He comes dangerously close to recognising his status as a text, and it is precisely this recognition that the play as a whole will reveal to be insupportable' (*RS*, 238). Although from a Gadamerian point of view the modern interpreter cannot transcend his or her own time and its language and discourses, it seems clear that Greenblatt goes beyond this and is quite deliberately interpreting the past from a modern, implicitly political point of view and refuses even to attempt to achieve a fusion of horizons. This makes Greenblatt's new historicism vulnerable to attack from both Gadamerian hermeneutics and orthodox historical critics like E. D. Hirsch, who could argue that new historicist interpretations have more in common with the radical unhistorical criticism of a critic such as Jan Kott in his book *Shakespeare Our Contemporary*, which quite explicitly interprets the plays in relation to twentieth-century issues, than with a criticism that attempts to understand texts written in the past in historical terms.

However, that kind of objection ignores the difficulty of Greenblatt's interpretative project: the attempt to combine a Gadamerian form of hermeneutics with a political and cultural critique. It may be that any such combination will always be vulnerable to incoherence or instability, but struggling to overcome that, even if not entirely successfully, can produce more exciting criticism than settling for one or the other. What perhaps makes the work of Raymond Williams more interesting than that of his cultural materialist disciples is that his writing embodies a similar conflict rather than settling for a too easy commitment to political critique. Another way of putting this is that Williams and Greenblatt write criticism in which both foundationalist and anti-foundationalist impulses are strong. Although this may create unresolved tensions in Greenblatt's interpretations along the lines I have suggested, by grappling with such tensions he has produced some of the most interesting interpretative criticism being written at the present time.

CHAPTER 7

Reception theory and reader-response criticism

The development in Britain and America of a theorised historical interpretation has been paralleled to some extent in Germany by the work of a group of critics based at the University of Konstanz, although their concern is more with literary history than with the relation between literature and social and political history. The approach of these critics has come to be known in the English-speaking world as reception theory, with Hans Robert Jauss being generally regarded as its most important representative. I suggested in the previous chapter that Gadamerian ideas, particularly his positive acceptance of the hermeneutic circle, underlay some of the theoretical assumptions of a new historicist such as Stephen Greenblatt. Gadamer is a powerful and more direct influence on Jauss, who is one of his former pupils. But whereas, as I have already argued, Gadamer's 'fusion of horizons' is implicitly rejected by new historicists and cultural materialists it is crucial to Jauss's work.

Another basic difference relates to aesthetics. Although the major concern of cultural materialism and the new historicism has been with canonic works of literature, with the plays of Shakespeare being given particular attention, there has been a strong tendency to deny literary texts special status and to see them as being on the same level as non-literary texts. But aesthetics remains fundamental for reception theory, as the German term *Rezeptionästhetik* – the aesthetics of reception – indicates. The main publication series of the Konstanz theoreticians is entitled 'Poetics and hermeneutics', a juxtaposition which suggests that for reception theory questions of meaning and interpretation cannot be separated from such literary considerations as the special nature of poetic language and literary form.

Jauss's most influential essay is entitled 'Literary history as a challenge [*Provokation*] to literary theory'. Adopting a communication model in which the receiver of a message is as important as the sender, Jauss argues that the literary work exists only when it has been re-created or 'concretised' in the mind of its reader. Both the role of the author of the work and the work as an object in itself are less important for Jauss than the work's reception or impact. The work also cannot be legitimately confined to the period which produced it since it continues to affect later generations of readers, nor can it simply be appropriated by modern readers as transcending its own time. Jauss sees the Marxist theory of reflection as inadequate because the literary work is consigned to 'a merely *copying* function',[1] whereas in his view it continues to live through its influence, and thus can have a formative effect on history. Formalist criticism – and for Jauss this means primarily and somewhat limitedly Shklovsky's concept of 'defamiliarisation', by which literary forms and styles need to renew themselves continually in an effort to resist 'automatization' (*Toward an Aesthetic of Reception* (*TA*), 17) – is also inadequate because it does not 'see the work of art in *history*, that is, in the historical horizon of its origination, social function, and historical influence' (*TA*, 18).

Jauss attempts to create a new kind of literary history which can accommodate both Marxist and Formalist criticism through focusing on the reception and influence of the literary work. He sees the relation between the work and its succession of audiences as 'dialogical' at both the aesthetic and the historical levels:

> The aesthetic implication lies in the fact that the first reception of a work by the reader includes a test of its aesthetic value in comparison with works already read. The obvious historical implication of this is that the understanding of the first reader will be sustained and enriched in a chain of receptions from generation to generation; in this way the historical significance of a work will be decided and its aesthetic value made evident. (*TA*, 20)

The concept of a 'horizon of expectations' is central to Jauss's thinking. All readers read literary works with certain expectations derived from reading other works, especially works in the same genre. Whereas works of little literary interest will tend to conform to the original reader's expectations and thus remain within his or her horizon, the literary work will disrupt or undermine these expectations and thus cannot be accommodated within that horizon.

This last point explains why Jauss places such great emphasis on reception. In the course of time literary works which were not reconcilable with their original audience's horizon of expectations become assimilated by the literary culture and conform with rather than disrupt their readers' expectations. If these works are to retain their power as literature – defined by Jauss as works 'whose reception can result in a "change of horizons" through negation of familiar experiences or through raising newly articulated experiences to the level of consciousness' (*TA*, 25) – modern readers have to make an effort to recover and experience the original reception of these works. Consequently 'it requires a special effort to read them "against the grain" of the accustomed experience to catch sight of their artistic character once again' (*TA*, 26). Thus an aesthetics of reception 'demands that one insert the individual work into its "literary series" to recognize its historical position and significance in the context of the experience of literature' (*TA*, 32). In order to know why a particular text was not within the horizon of its original audience's expectations, one needs to know what expectations that audience had and why it had them, which entails making connections between art and ideology, though this point is only implied by Jauss:

> The new is thus not only an *aesthetic* category . . . [it] also becomes a *historical* category when the diachronic analysis of literature is pushed further to ask which historical moments are really the ones that first make new that which is new in a literary phenomenon. (*TA*, 35)

At the end of the essay Jauss discusses wider questions concerning the social and existential functions of literature. He argues that

> The social function of literature manifests itself in its genuine possibility only where the literary experience of the reader enters into the horizon of expectations of his lived praxis, preforms his understanding of the world, and thereby also has an effect on his social behavior. (*TA*, 39)

He draws a comparison between the concept of the horizon of expectations and Karl Popper's philosophy of science in which scientific progress results from hypotheses having to withstand continual testing. Popper regards it as a particularly valuable and positive consequence of scientific practice when expectations (which are intrinsic to hypotheses) prove to be unfounded, since such an experience makes the scientist aware of the otherness of a 'reality' that resists subjective construction. For Jauss literature has a similarly liberating function: 'The experience of reading can liberate one from adaptations, prejudices, and predicaments of a lived praxis in that it compels one to a new perception of things' (*TA*, 41), with the result that 'a literary work with an unfamiliar aesthetic form can break through the expectations of its readers and at the same time confront them with a question, the solution to which remains lacking for them in the religiously or officially sanctioned morals' (*TA*, 44). Literary history can thus bridge the gap between 'aesthetic and historical knowledge' by discovering 'in the course of "literary evolution" that properly *socially formative* function that belongs to literature as it competes with other arts and social forces in the emancipation of mankind from its natural, religious, and social bonds' (*TA*, 45).

Both cultural materialism and the new historicism can also be related to a philosophy of liberation in their emphasis on the real as a construction by dominant discursive practices which can be challenged or contested by competing discursive practices. The role of the critic is to show this conflict taking place within specific texts so that both literature and criticism can become the means of furthering social change. But whereas this philosophy of liberation is social and political Jauss's is centred on the individual consciousness. In his later work he connects the pleasure of reading, which happens at the level of the individual, with human freedom since there is no necessity to read literary texts.[2] Reading literature is therefore a free act in which one confronts texts which by definition question or undermine dominant ideologies.

An obvious problem with Jauss's theory is whether it applies to all periods of literature. Certain major works of literature – Virgil's *Aeneid* would be an example – would appear to have the function of reinforcing the official ideology and there is little or no evidence to suggest that they were not read in that way. Cultural materialists and new historicists, with their theory of society as a struggle for power, can nevertheless discern conflict and division within such literature even though authors and readers may not have been aware of this. It would seem necessary to Jauss's theory, however, that actual contemporary readers experienced a literary work intended to reinforce the dominant ideology as subverting their expectations, an idea that does not seem particularly persuasive. A possible defence of Jauss is that in such cases the horizon of expectations should be understood as referring primarily to the formal aspect of literature, and that even literary works which ostensibly reinforce the official ideologies of their cultures at a semantic level create a style or a formal structure which conflicts with the audience's horizon of expectations. These stylistic and formal features, when interpreted by literary historians, can be shown to have a semantic significance, which original readers may not have been able to conceptualise, in conflict with the work's apparent meaning. It is doubtful, however, whether this defence would work for the literature of every period, especially in certain non-Western cultures, and a critic like Jameson would no doubt argue that stylistic and formal innovations can also have the function of providing only a more subtle or devious support for dominant ideologies.

Although Jauss sees some similarities between reception theory and structuralism and semiotics, all of which are concerned with poetics, an important difference is that interpretation of individual texts remains central in reception theory. But the aim of interpretation is not 'the tracing of a text back to its "statement", to a significance hidden behind it, or to its objective meaning'; rather 'the meaning of a text [is] a convergence of the structure of the work and the structure of the interpretation which is ever to be achieved anew'.[3] However, he does not view literary texts as different in kind from other texts in regard to how they should be interpreted. Interpretation is tri-partite, consisting of understanding (*intellegere*), interpretation or explanation (*interpretare*) and application (*applicare*), with the question one asks of a text being integrally connected with any meaning one derives from it. This is a traditional approach to interpretation which Jauss gives Gadamer the credit of reviving after it had been discarded in favour of positivist and historicist alternatives. One must understand the literary text at a semantic and aesthetic level, explain or interpret it, and then apply that reading in a particular context. These three activities are interconnected since the application will determine the form of the explanation and understanding cannot be entirely dissociated from explanation:

> *Application* includes both acts of understanding and interpretation insofar as it represents the interest in transporting the text out of its past or foreignness and into the interpreter's present, in finding the question to which the text has an answer ready for the interpreter, in forming an aesthetic judgment of the text which could also persuade other interpreters.[4]

Although applications are without limit, Jauss denies that there is any danger of subjectivism since the connection with the text's original reception is maintained and the appeal to aesthetic judgement encourages intersubjectivity. He argues that treating the text as an object separated from history is much more likely to encourage subjectivism.

Jauss applies his interpretative approach to a poem by Baudelaire, 'Spleen II'. There are three horizons of reading corresponding to the three aspects of interpretation described above, although Jauss believes some adaptation of Gadamer's model is necessary to deal with 'texts of an aesthetic character' (*TA*, 140). The first horizon consists of 'immediate understanding within aesthetic perception', the second 'reflective interpretation' (*TA*, 141) arising from that. With the poetic text 'aesthetic understanding is primarily directed at the process of perception' (*TA*, 141), a process that often requires repeated readings. The second interpretative phase 'always presupposes aesthetic perception as its pre-understanding' (*TA*, 142). Jauss believes that his interpretative method can combine structuralist and semiotic analysis – integral to the first horizon – with the phenomenological and hermeneutic forms of interpretation integral to the second. Jauss objects to traditional historical interpretation or, as he calls it, 'historical–philological hermeneutics', on the grounds that the interpreter has to dismiss his or her own historicity and seek a purely objective meaning in the text while also privileging the historical over the aesthetic. For Jauss the aesthetic is crucial because it acts as a 'hermeneutic bridge' to the past through works which continue to be accessible in a fully human way, something lacking, he argues, in conventional historical documents or relics. But the historical aspect of the literary text is equally important since it 'prevents the text from the past from being naively assimilated to the prejudices and expectations of meaning of the present, and thereby . . . allows the poetic text to be seen in its alterity' (*TA*, 146). Thus the interpreter must seek out 'the questions (most often unexplicit ones) to which the text was a response in its time' (*TA*, 146), and connect these with the original audience's horizon of expectations at the level of both form and meaning. But the interpreter must also ask questions of the text from his or her own historical perspective: ' "What did the text say?" ' becomes transformed into ' "What does the text say to me, and what do I say to it?" ' (*TA*, 146).

Jauss believes the kind of interpretation associated with a critic like Roland Barthes which emphasises 'the interminable play of a free-floating intertextuality' creates readings which are 'neither historical nor aesthetic' (*TA*, 147). Literary hermeneutics, in contrasts, 'poses the hypothesis that the concretization of the meaning of literary works progresses historically and follows a certain "logic" that precipitates in the formation and transformation of the aesthetic canon' (*TA*, 147). It also makes possible discriminations between 'arbitrary interpretations and those available to a consensus' (*TA*, 147-8).

Jauss's literary hermeneutics is open to attack from 'new pragmatists' like Knapp and Michaels on the grounds that since interpretation makes no sense unless it assumes texts are the product of human intention, it can only be historical in its basis. Jauss's assumption that one can choose to reject a text's historicity, even if only partially, in interpreting is therefore incoherent. It follows that differences among interpreters – such as traditionalists, Barthes, Jauss – derive not from their possessing different theories of interpretation but from their opposed views about whether or not the modern interpreter can escape his or her historical situation when interpreting texts written in the past. Traditional historicists believe one can, Barthes thinks one cannot, and Jauss that a 'fusion of horizons' takes place. But all of them must attempt to interpret texts as historical and intentional products otherwise, Knapp and Michaels would argue, their interpretative activities are meaningless.

When Jauss looks in detail at the Baudelaire poem, he discusses its formal coherence and stylistic patterning in the first stage of interpretation. At the second stage he connects the formal and thematic levels and emphasises how the poem's use of allegory brings together form and meaning. The function of such phrases as 'Je suis un cimetière' and 'Je suis un boudoir' is 'to make visible the overpowering of the self through the alien, or (as one may now put it) the ego through the id' (*TA*, 168). The last part of that comment, with its Freudian connotations, reveals Jauss's concern to make the poem relevant to the reality of its modern reader. In discussing the third horizon of interpretation, the history of the poem's reception, Jauss deals with the responses of a number of critics, particularly Gautier's contemporary response. Initially, he says, one wants to ask such questions as the following: 'Which expectations on the part of its contemporary readers can this "Spleen" poem have fulfilled or denied? What was the literary tradition, and what was the historical and social situation, with which the text might have come to have a relation?' (*TA*, 170).

Jauss recognises that a materialist reading might want to go further than looking at the response of a 'perceptive eyewitness', such as Gautier, and relate the poem to historical processes and conditions, but Jauss believes this would be possible only through resorting to allegory, or as Jauss puts it, 'the method of allegoresis' (*TA*, 172), which cannot be dissociated from the subjectivity and partiality of the interpreter. Jauss would rather stress the poem's break with Romanticism and its anticipations of psychoanalysis, which make Baudelaire 'the poet of modernity' (*TA*, 174).

He goes on to discuss the responses of various later commentators, which illuminate both the poem and the cultural interests of these commentators. In looking at the history of a work's reception, one should not, he argues, be primarily concerned with showing that certain interpretations are wrong. An interpretation can be judged to be wrong if it asks 'falsely posed or illegitimate questions' of the work: 'questions are legitimate when their role as initial comprehensions for the sake of interpretation is borne out in the text' (*TA*, 185). The different responses which create 'the historically progressive concretization of meaning in the struggle of interpretation' testify to 'the unifiability of legitimate questions' (*TA*, 185), and unposed questions give scope for future interpretation.

Jauss's hermeneutics is probably more systematic than any of the interpretative approaches discussed previously, with the possible exception of Jameson, although it does not have the disadvantage of Jameson's eclecticism. Deconstructionists and contemporary Marxists might argue that the emphasis on aesthetics commits Jauss to the concepts of coherence and unity – he refers, for example, to 'the achieved whole of the form' and 'the harmony of a coherence of meaning' (*TA*, 161) – and thus to an implicitly conservative position which imposes constraints on freeplay and ignores fissures or impasses in the text. Thus, although Paul de Man admires Jauss, he refers to 'linguistic factors that threaten to interfere with the synthesizing power of the historical model'. De Man believes textuality cannot be contained by aesthetics. For him poetics should be equated with rhetoric, in which the play of the signifier can undermine the grammatical and logical dimensions of language, rather than with aesthetics. He also sees Jauss's objections to allegory as 'a breaking of the link between poetics and history'.[5] Another objection one can make is that, although Jauss places such emphasis on reception, he does not seem interested in the empirical problem of discovering contemporary responses to a work. Further, if there are conflicting contemporary responses how does one decide between them? With 'Spleen' Jauss seems content to take one response and use that as the basis of his consideration of the work's contemporary reception. But the question as to whether Gautier's response was characteristic of his period or whether there were alternative contemporary responses is not raised. This suggests that there is an underlying idealism in Jauss's conception of history, that his interest is not in what is historically representative or typical but in past responses that happen to be interesting from a modern point of view.

Jauss's work has been less discussed in the English-speaking world than that of the other major reception theorist, Wolfgang Iser. While Gadamer is the main influence on Jauss, Iser's work has strong affinities with the phenomenological criticism of Roman Ingarden. The major difference between Jauss and Iser is that with Iser the emphasis is more on the reading process than on a work's historical reception. Like Jauss, Iser rejects interpretation as the discovery of an objective meaning or hidden significance in the text: 'If texts actually possessed only the meaning brought to light by interpretation, then there would remain very little else for the reader.' The meaning of the text, claims Iser, 'is in itself nothing more than an individual reading experience which has now simply been identified with the text itself'. The New Criticism had used interpretation to reveal meanings hidden in the text, but Iser objects: 'one cannot help wondering why texts should indulge in such a "hide-and-seek" with their interpreters; and even more puzzling, why the meaning, once it has been found, should then change again, even though the letters, words and sentences of the text remain the same.' The critic should renounce the search for meaning, recognise that any reading is only 'one of the possible realizations of a text', and admit that meanings 'are the product of a rather difficult interaction between text and reader and not qualities hidden in the text'.[6]

The critic's object, therefore, should be 'not to explain a work, but to reveal the conditions that bring about its various possible effects. If he clarifies the *potential* of a text, he will no longer fall into the fatal trap of trying to impose one meaning on his reader, as if that were the right, or at least the best interpretation'.[7] Literary texts, Iser believes, possess a plurality of meanings but that plurality is not produced by the text as such but by the text's interaction with its readers. Iser, like Jauss, emphasises the reader's expectations, the various norms and codes which the reader brings to the text but which the text negates or calls into question. This entails that the reader's imagination is brought into play in the process of reading rather than merely passively consuming the text. His main departure from Ingarden is that whereas for Ingarden concretisation – the reader's need to complete or fill out what Ingarden calls the 'schematised structure' of the text – functions in terms of an aesthetic of artistic unity and harmony, for Iser concretisation does not involve eliminating the indeterminacies in the text, the gaps and blanks that exist between the text's various schematic layers. Such textual indeterminacy is central to Iser's conception of aesthetics.

René Wellek had pointed to a relationship between Ingarden's phenomenological criticism and New Critical organicist aesthetics,[8] but Iser connects it with Russian Formalism since he argues that the reader's encounter with the text's indeterminacies is defamiliarising. Reading is conceived of as a dynamic process in which the norms and codes that govern the reader's thinking and perception may be called into question by having to confront textual gaps and blanks, thus making it possible for reading literature to be liberating. But as with Jauss, such liberation operates at the individual rather than the social level.

Iser's theory implies that indeterminacy must exist as a potential of the text as object although it is activated only during the process of reading. The ability of the text to communicate also depends on indeterminacy:

> There are . . . two basic structures of indeterminacy in the text – blanks, and negations. These are essential conditions for communication, for they set in motion the interaction that takes place between text and reader, and to a certain extent they also regulate it. (*The Act of Reading (AR)*, 182)

The reader's relation to the text assumes 'connectability' but blanks 'break up this connectability' (*AR*, 183). Connectability relates both to text and to reader since it is intrinsic to the text as a structure 'and can be equated with the concept of *good continuation* used in the psychology of perception' (*AR*. 185). Iser uses Fielding's *Tom Jones* to provide an example of a textual blank:

> When Captain Blifil deceives Allworthy, the interlinking segments of two different character perspectives give rise to the idea that the perfect man lacks discernment because he trusts in appearances. But this image

soon has to be abandoned, when Tom sells the horse Allworthy has given him. The two pedagogues are horrified by the obvious baseness of such a deed, but Allworthy forgives Tom because, despite appearances, he discerns the good motive underlying the action.

Thus the idea of the perfect man lacking in discernment is proved to be wrong, and the original image has to be abandoned; the new image is of the perfect man who lacks the ability, necessary for good judgment, to abstract himself from his own attitudes. (*AR*, 186)

Blanks in the text, 'by suspending the *good continuation*, condition the clash of images, and so help to hinder (and, at the same time, to stimulate) the process of image-building. It is this process that endows them with their aesthetic significance' (*AR*, 187). Negations create more fundamental dislocations, so that the reader 'is blocked off from familiar orientations, but cannot yet gain access to unaccustomed attitudes' (*AR*, 213).

As with Jauss a difficulty for Iser's theory arises in relation to those texts written before the modern period which appear to reinforce the prevailing ideologies of their time and to conform to generic norms. Iser must either find a way of introducing indeterminacy into such texts or else judge them as artistically inferior to texts written in the modern period. A related problem is that repeated readings of a work would seem to reduce its indeterminacy and thus diminish its aesthetic interest. Iser might counter such arguments by utilising Jauss's reception theory to situate texts historically by relating them to their original readers' expectations and thus revealing indeterminacies in the reader–text interaction which might not be apparent from a modern point of view. He might also argue that his theory can account for readers losing interest in certain works because they are no longer able to experience a sufficient degree of indeterminacy in their reading of them. But in general, certain texts from earlier eras, particularly the classical and medieval periods, would seem to place Iser's theory under some strain.

In focusing on gaps, blanks, negations in the text, Iser's theory has certain similarities to that of Macherey but, in contrast to Iser, Macherey sees gaps in the text not in relation to the reader's consciousness or to aesthetic experience but as symptoms of a repressed history which the text's ideology endeavours to conceal and which the critic should be concerned to expose. This reveals a fundamental difference of view about the function of literature. Terry Eagleton attacks Iser in the following terms: 'Iser's reception theory, in fact, is based on a liberal humanist ideology: a belief that in reading we should be flexible and open-minded, prepared to put our beliefs into question and allow them to be transformed.' He claims that Iser's good reader 'would *already* have to be a liberal: the act of reading produces a kind of human subject which it also presupposes'.[9] Indeterminacy in Eagleton's view also only leads to the desire to create a new kind of unity not to an interrogation of the whole concept of aesthetic coherence and harmony. But Iser would no doubt reject both Eagleton's assumption that to accept the provisionality of belief means 'we only hold our convictions rather lightly in the first place' and his accusation that reader-based theories 'betray a liberal distaste for systematic thought'.[10] For Iser such claims would be signs of a doctrinaire Marxism which is committed to a fixed notion of truth in relation to which literature should be judged, and that Eagleton's real objection to Iser's theory is its implication that truth and ideology cannot be separated. The function of literature in Iser's view is essentially negative and critical: continually to undermine ideology, whereas for critics in the Marxist tradition literature's negativity is a bourgeois phenomenon; when Marxism triumphs politically, the negative function of literature will eventually, one assumes, cease and criticism will become a positive form of hermeneutics.

Reader-response criticism

There are also significant differences between reception theory and reader-response criticism which I shall illustrate in discussing the work of Norman N. Holland and Stanley Fish. In a critique of Iser, Holland, a psychoanalytic critic in the 'ego-psychology' tradition, argues that although the role of the reader is given great emphasis in reception theory, Iser does not discuss the responses of actual readers to literary texts. Holland believes that Iser's concept of the 'implied reader', a term which 'incorporates both the prestructuring of the potential meaning by the text, and the reader's actualization of this potential through the reading process',[11] has little substance if it does not take account in empirical terms of real readers' responses. He defines Iser's model in which 'a sequence of schemata in the text stimulates us "to constitute the totality of which the schemata are aspects" ' as 'bi-active'.[12] Holland contrasts this model in which the text controls the reader's responses to it with his 'transactive' model in which the reader both initiates and creates the response. In Holland's version of reader-response criticism reading is a personal transaction of the reader with the text in which there is no fundamental division between the text's role and the reader's role.

Holland reveals the consequences of this theory for interpretation in an essay on Poe's 'The purloined letter'. Since his theory denies any fundamental separation between text and reader, interpretation functions in terms of personal association. Thus the text triggers a personal association which Holland then goes on to develop:

> Dupin reminds me . . . of Prometheus, whose name means 'forethought' and who stole a sacred object, black and red like this royal letter, a fragment of glowing charcoal hidden in a giant fennel stalk. . . . This Dupin-Prometheus thus restores the connection between the gods and men, between the miraculous and the natural, between man and woman.[13]

Holland also adopts a very personal tone, spelling out his relation to the story in the most subjective terms: 'I love this story, as I love the Holmes stories, because I can be both the Dupin one admires and the relater who loves and is loved of Dupin' ('Re-covering "The purloined letter" ' ('RP'), 359). He even goes so far as to associate the story's concern with having something to hide and the fact that when he was 13 his indulgence in masturbation also gave him something to hide. He interprets the readings by other critics as equally having a personal basis even if the critics appear to be responding to the text in objective terms. Thus 'Lacan seeks, as does Dupin himself, the hermeneutical decoding of the text, but for Lacan it is psychoanalysis – Lacanian psychoanalysis – that occupies the place of Dupin' ('RP', 361); 'Derrida, I think, writes out of a need not to believe, a need to *dis*trust' ('RP', 362).

Holland goes on to reflect theoretically on his interpretative practice. In transactive criticism 'the critic works explicitly from his transaction of the text', but he is different from other critics only in that he accepts that the critic has no other choice and 'explicitly builds on his relationship to the text' ('RP', 363). Fundamental to the model of reading that emerges from this is the fact that although the text is the same for everybody 'everyone responds to it differently' ('RP', 363). Whereas Iser's concept of the implied reader tries to eliminate the reader's personal associations, Holland accepts them. He claims that the 'text-active' theory of reading, common to both traditional criticism and the New Criticism, which

> assumes that there is a normal response to a text, which the text itself
> causes . . . simply does not fit what we know of human perception:
> namely, that perception is a constructive act in which we impose
> schemata from our minds on the data of our senses. ('RP', 364)

A 'bi-active' theory, such as Iser's reception theory or Stanley Fish's
affective stylistics, 'in which a text and its literent (reader, viewer, or
hearer) act together to cause the response' ('RP', 365), is a great
advance but still has two difficulties for Holland: 'First, it is really
two theories, a new theory of reader activity plus the old text-active
theory in which the text does something to the reader', and secondly,
it is not borne out by perception theory: 'I do not first see the lines
and then decide that I will interpret them as though they were
perspectives of rectangles. I do it all in one continuous transaction. I
never see the lines without a schema for seeing them' ('RP', 366).

Holland claims that if readers' free responses to texts are collected
they have virtually nothing in common and that where shared
responses exist they are created by such factors as the authority of
teachers. Readers should accept interpretation as a personal transaction between the reader's 'unique identity' and the text. Such a
transactive theory of reading fits in with contemporary psychological
theory, he argues, and accounts 'both for the originality and variety
of our responses and for our circumscribing them by conventions'.
One can then go on to use psychoanalytic concepts such as identity
to 'connect literary transactions to personality' ('RP', 367). Holland
also argues that this does not lead to relativism but to
intersubjectivity: 'I can give you my feelings and associations and let
you pass them through the story for yourself to see if they enrich
your experience' ('RP', 368). Whereas orthodox critics resist the
knowledge that we all read differently, the transactive critic
embraces this truth joyfully: 'Instead of subtracting readings so as to
narrow them down or cancel some . . . let us use human differences
to add response to response, to multiply possibilities, and to enrich
the whole experience' ('RP', 370).

The objection to his theory Holland claims he is most often
confronted with is that it has the consequence that every reading of a
text becomes totally subjective. The term 'subjective' does not
trouble him but he denies that for him interpretation is purely
random. But whereas for Iser the text exerts controls, for Holland
controls exist within the reader. Fundamental to his view of the

reader is the psychoanalytic concept of 'identity'. He accepts the conception of the subject which is central to ego-psychology, namely that the ego seeks to harmonise the demands of both the external and the internal world, but modifies it by claiming that identity functions in relation to a dialectic of sameness and difference. Identity is thus both theme – the persistent stamp of one's personal style in what one does – and variations on that theme. Literature enables us to re-create our identities by allowing us to transact with the text in four ways: defence, expectation, fantasy and transformation, which Holland reduces to the acronym 'DEFT':

> One can understand *expectation* as putting the literary work in the sequence of a person's wishes in time, while *transformation* endows the work with a meaning beyond-time. Similarly, I learn of *defenses* as they shape what the individual lets in from outside; while *fantasies* are what I see the individual putting out from herself into the outside world.

He tries to avoid the problem of the theorist's role in understanding and describing this process, since his theory must also apply to himself as interpreter of the reader, by arguing that 'my reading of your identity must be a function of my own. Identity, then, is not a conclusion but a relationship: the potential, transitional, in-between space in which I perceive someone as a theme and variations.'[14]

Although readers' responses to literature are variable, Holland argues that the concept of identity allows one to find a pattern in these variations. Thus, studying the responses of a group of academics to a poem, he finds that although their readings are the same in some respects and different in others, their common need to re-create their identities has generated their readings, both to 'factual' questions concerning the poem and questions that elicited varieties of response. Thus he concludes: '*Both objective and subjective responses emerge from a process in which subjectivity shapes objectivity.*' Identity functions in terms of a feedback loop:

> In short, a person – an identity – *uses* hypotheses with which to sense the poem. The poem responds to those hypotheses, and the individual *feels* whether it is a favorable or unfavorable response and so closes the loop, preparatory to sending another hypothesis out around it.[15]

Holland has continually modified his theory over the years to counter objections. This testifies to the fact that the theory has to struggle against the knowledge that most readers find it counter-intuitive, since there is a deep-seated resistance among readers, both sophisticated and unsophisticated, to giving up the idea that the literary text has objective qualities. Holland's theory also offers little scope for interpretative debate since the focus is switched from text as object to reader response. These difficulties do not necessarily invalidate the theory, and indeed the objections Holland is constantly being confronted with may point to a fear on the part of critics that he could be right. Critics have been used to exerting their mastery over texts through the power of interpretation, but in Holland's theory the text strikes back and interprets the interpreter, so that it is the critic who is exposed as much as the text. Critics' resistance to this seems likely to deny Holland's theory wide support within the literary institution.

On a more strictly theoretical level one might argue that although Holland is right in his view that the text is a construction by the reader he places too much emphasis on the reader as an individual and fails to take sufficient account of the fact that any text one reads is already a social production and any relation that the reader has with it will also be socially defined. The transaction with a literary text cannot therefore depend purely on individual identity. The text has otherness not as a pure object with a meaning in itself but in the sense that there is general social agreement as to the kind of discourse it is and the kind of constraints that determine meaning within that discourse. When one reads a text, therefore, it has already, as it were, been subject to a social reading which has a determining effect on semantic meaning and contextualisation and which provides the text with a sense of otherness that is at least partially independent of the reader. The reader has theoretical freedom to ignore this and to allow the words to trigger off whatever associations come into his or her mind and to dismiss generic or period considerations, but in practice very few will either desire or be able to do this, unless of course they are part of one of Holland's experiments in free association. Readers will continue, and I think justifiably, to see the text as other even though Holland is right to argue that in interpretation subject and object cannot be separated.

Another problem is that Holland's view of the reader-text relation depends on a particular psychoanalytic theory. An opposing psychoanalytic theory – one that posited, for example, that the ego is irretrievably divided against itself – will lead to a different view of how the reader transacts the text. Holland's concept of identity could, for example, be attacked as 'essentialist' by Lacanians. Debate is therefore likely to be centred so much on the validity or invalidity of different psychoanalytical theories that any secure application to literary texts will be perpetually deferred. In that context there is something to be said for Iser's attempt to define the reader phenomenologically since this at least avoids the problem of having to decide among various psychoanalytic theories of the subject. It should be remarked, however, that Holland is not merely concerned with the theory and practice of literary interpretation for their own sake but with using literature for therapeutic purposes through examining readers' responses by means of his DEFT method. Thus one merit of his theory is that responses to literature and the critic's interpretation of them could come to play a role in psychoanalysis similar to the interpretation of dreams.

As I mentioned above, Stanley Fish is the leading exponent of 'affective stylistics', which Holland characterises as a 'bi-active' theory. It is doubtful whether Fish, at least from his most recent theoretical position, would accept that affective stylistics as a form of interpretation is a bi-active theory. Virtually all of the contemporary critics I have discussed have seen themselves as combining theory and practice in their criticism, but Fish has argued that theory and practice should be seen as quite separate activities since he believes that theory has no consequences. Looking at Fish's career, what one sees is a series of developments at the theoretical level but a continuing commitment to affective stylistics as a form of inter-pretative practice. Change at the theoretical level, however, has led to a different view of and justification for that practice.

Fish gives a useful account of affective stylistics and the develop-ment of his theoretical position in the introduction to his book, *Is There a Text in This Class?*. Affective stylistics shifts the literary focus from text to reader, and Fish admits that in the beginning he saw the text as an entity separate from the reader, a position similar to that of Iser. Fish's interest is in reading as a temporal process and in his early work he had to confront the New Critics' dismissal of the subjectivity of the reader by means of the 'affective fallacy'[16] and their commitment to spatial form, the view that the language of the literary text should be seen as coexisting at a single temporal point rather than developing in time. He argues that meanings are actualised in the process of reading – that is, temporally – and thus emerge from the interaction between the text and 'the reader's expectations, projections, conclusions, judgments, and assumptions'.[17] Meaning in being 'redefined as an event rather than an entity' (*Is There a Text in This Class? (IT)*, 3), is thus to be identified with the reader's experience of the text. The major practical effect of this is that meanings that can be generated from within syntactic units should not as a matter of principle be held in abeyance until one has reached a point of syntactic closure when they should be modified or discarded in favour of the meaning of the whole. The fact that one might have to revise a meaning one had initially formulated when one arrives at a point of syntactic closure does not abolish the earlier meaning. This interplay of meaning is a feature of literary texts and consequently justifies a temporal approach to reading, such as affective stylistics, since New Critical formalism would miss such interplay entirely.

Fish admits, however, that he was placed on the defensive by objections to his method and was forced to resort to arguments which, from his later theoretical position, were unsatisfactory. For example, to counter the argument that to introduce the subjectivity of the reader opens the door to relativism he had to claim that all readers' responses to the text were essentially the same and that differences arose only when one reflected later on matters of interpretation, a position 'in essence . . . no different from the formalism to which it was rhetorically opposed' (*IT*, 7), since a text to which response was uniform had to be assumed: 'I retained the distinction between description and interpretation and by so doing affirmed the integrity and objectivity of the text' (*IT*, 8). This distinction was required because he believed the subjectivity of the reader had to be controlled.

The first stage in his abandonment of this position was his rejection of the view that the language of literature was fundamentally different from that of other discourses: 'while literature is still a category, it is an open category, not definable by its fictionality, or by a disregard of propositional truth, or by a predominance of tropes and figures, but simply by what we decide to put into it' (*IT*, 11). Thus 'it is the reader who *makes* literature' (*IT*, 11), but the reader has power to 'make' literature only when he or she is part of a community of readers. This led on to the view that the distinction between text and reader should be abandoned since neither had independent status: 'interpretive strategies are not put into execution after reading: they are the shape of reading, and because they are the shape of reading, they give texts their shape, making them rather than, as is usually assumed, arising from them' (*IT*, 13). These 'interpretive strategies' are not purely subjective but proceed from 'interpretive communities', groups of readers who share the same 'interpretive strategies'; thus Fish denies that his theory opens the door to subjectivism and relativism. He further claims that his theory is easily able to account for both agreement and disagreement about interpretation.

Much of Fish's theoretical work has been devoted to showing that both 'text-active' and 'bi-active' theories of interpretation, to use Holland's terms, are incoherent and can be reformulated in Fishian terms. Thus in a critique of Iser he argues that Iser's distinction between the literary text as incorporating aesthetic directions or potentialities and the reader as actualising or producing the aesthetic object in the process of encountering these is incoherent. He illustrates his argument by examining Iser's account of Allworthy in *Tom Jones*, which I quoted earlier. Iser's position, Fish claims, depends on human perfection being incompatible with being taken in by a hypocrite 'for only then will the "Allworthy perspective" and the "Blifil perspective" be perceived as discontinous'.[18] But Fish argues that it is quite easy to imagine a reader for whom there is no incompatibility between perfection and vulnerability. For such a reader, therefore, the blank in the text which Iser points out would not exist. Iser believes such blanks or gaps exist in the text itself even though they have to be actualised by the reader but Fish argues that it is Iser's 'interpretive strategies' which create the gaps he discovers in the text and concludes: 'if gaps are not built into the text, but appear (or do not appear) as a consequence of particular interpretive strategies, then there is no distinction between what the text gives and what the reader supplies; he supplies *everything*'.[19]

But Fish attacks Iser only at the level of theory not at the level of his interpretative practice. Iser's critical approach reformulated in Fish's terms would presumably be quite acceptable, and indeed it has many similarities to Fish's own, since both are within the 'interpretive community' of reader-response criticism. Thus Iser's interest in gaps in the text can be compared with Fish's concern with dislocations in the reading process caused by premature closures of meaning. Reading as a temporal process is integral to both methods. Fish argues, for example, that Herbert's poetry works 'by inviting the reader to a premature interpretive conclusion, which is at first challenged, and then reinstated, but in such a way as to make it the vehicle of a deeper understanding'.[20]

Another implication of Fish's view that practice and theory are separate is that one does not need to read in the way that he does. Indeed, he argues that his theory has no consequences for other forms of critical practice, although he would claim that it accounts for all forms of critical practice. Why one chooses to engage in one form of interpretation rather than another, therefore, depends not on a general theory of interpretation but largely on one's view of what the value of interpreting literature is. Fish has made it clear that it is reading as a human activity that he values and that he objects to the implied anti-humanism of formalist approaches. Related to that is the idea that the interaction between reader and text can cause the reader to question his or her most fundamental assumptions and expose deep-rooted self-interest. Thus discussing a passage from *Paradise Lost*, Book IV, lines 9–12, he writes:

> the passage would seem to be assigning the responsibility of the Fall to Satan. . . . This understanding, however, must be revised when the reader enters line 12 and discovers that the loss in question is Satan's loss of Heaven. . . . The understanding that the reader must give up is one that is particularly attractive to him because it asserts the innocence of his first parents, which is, by extension, his innocence too. (*IT*, 4)

Such experiences encourage the reader to reflect on his or her own responses, so that criticism and self-criticism become inseparable. Expectation must clearly be intrinsic to this process, but whereas for Iser the text is a virtual structure which can both arouse and undermine expectations, for Fish expectations are integral to the 'interpretive strategies' the reader brings to the text.

Fish has probably been attacked more than any other recent critic or theorist, particularly over his claims that the text has no separate existence from the reader and that theory has no consequences. Fish has, I think, successfully rebutted total rejections of his position, but his contention that the interpreter also 'writes' the text that he or she interprets is difficult to accept without qualification. To justify this view he recounts how a class he was teaching, which expected to deal with seventeenth-century English religious poetry, proceeded to read a list of names he happened to have written on the board for a previous class as a seventeenth-century religious poem. He concludes: 'Interpretation is not the art of construing but the art of constructing. Interpreters do not decode poems; they make them'

(*IT*, 327). On the surface Fish seems to be conferring total power on the reader, but on the next page, discussing whether or not it would have made any difference if the list of names had been different, he remarks:

> Given a firm belief that they were confronted by a religious poem, my students would have been able to turn any list of names into the kind of poem we have before us now, because they would have read the names within the assumption that they were informed with Christian significances. (*IT*, 328)

The significant phrase here is 'Given a firm belief', because this qualification does much to undermine the apparent extremism of Fish's position, for I would argue that 90 per cent of the time the text itself has a considerable degree of power over the reader's beliefs.

This can be easily illustrated by returning to Fish's list of names. It is surely indisputable that if one added to the list the names 'Hitler' or 'Beethoven' or 'Jimi Hendrix' even a reader who possessed only a minimal knowledge of seventeenth-century religious poetry would not believe that he or she was confronted by a poem of that period. Of course, these names would have to be constructed by the reader before they could be construed, bearing out Fish's general argument, but the reader's power of construction is limited by the fact that the names have already been socially and historically constructed which prevents the reader from constructing them in such a way as to see them as part of a seventeenth-century religious poem even if the reader has expectations of encountering such a poem. Fish's extreme position might have held if he had confined it to poetry in general but in using a particular period of poetry to illustrate his point the limitations on the reader are exposed, for any reader capable of understanding the concept of seventeenth-century religious poetry will *ipso facto* possess the means of recognising, at least at the most basic level, when a piece of language does not belong to that category.

The weakness of Fish's theoretical position is that it appears to suggest that the text cannot present any resistance to the reader, even if Fish denies that this is his intention. He never concedes that the language the reader encounters will already have been socially and historically constructed, and although there will be an interaction between the reader's interests and the socially and historically constructed words of the text which will modify the power of the latter, the reader's power – unless the reader is psychotic – to impose his or her interests or the interests of an 'interpretive community' totally on the text will also be limited. In other words, the text has a degree of otherness even if that otherness is the product of social and historical construction rather than 'pure' otherness.

Fish has denied that his theory entails relativism and scepticism on the grounds that

> one cannot, properly speaking, *be* a skeptic for the same reason that one cannot be a relativist, because one cannot achieve the distance from his own beliefs and assumptions that would result in their being no more authoritative *for him* than the beliefs and assumptions held by others or the beliefs and assumptions he himself used to hold. (*IT*, 361)

But although relativism as a belief is contradictory, in the sense that if one holds such a belief by the same token one ceases to be a relativist, this will not stop someone using relativism as a reason for refusing even to play the game of interpretation. Fish is right when he argues that as soon as one enters into the discourse of interpretation, one is inevitably involved in preferring one reading to another on the basis of certain principles, but an effect of his emphasis on a literary institution divided into separate 'interpretive communities' which write the text by means of their 'interpretive strategies', together with his refusal to allow the text any degree of otherness, seem to me to encourage relativist and sceptical arguments that literary interpretation is not a worthwhile activity because there is nothing 'other' to interpret.

Fish's claim that theory has no consequences, which has had a major influence on the 'new pragmatists', is powerfully argued although it depends on a very narrow definition of theory as being

> an attempt to *guide* practice from a position above or outside it . . . and . . . an attempt to *reform* practice by neutralizing interest, by substituting for the parochial perspective of some local or partisan point of view the perspective of a general rationality to which the individual subordinates his contextually conditioned opinions and beliefs.[21]

Fish claims that theory in this sense 'will never succeed: it cannot help but borrow its terms and its content from that which it claims to transcend, the mutable world of practice, belief, assumptions, point of view, and so forth' ('Consequences' ('C'), 438). And since theory can never succeed it cannot have the consequence 'of guiding and/or reforming practice' ('C', 438). Any practice will itself have certain rules built into it and these will be sufficient for it to function. If these rules of practice are defined as theory then theory will embrace virtually everything so that it will be impossible to make any useful distinction between theoretical and non-theoretical activity. He admits that no practice can be carried on without some set of beliefs but 'beliefs are not theories. A theory is a special achievement of consciousness; a belief is a prerequisite for being conscious at all' ('C' 443). He rejects the view that only theory can lead to the 'fore-grounding of beliefs and assumptions' ('C', 447) and by so doing guide or alter practice since this assumes either that one can somehow achieve a position that does not depend on beliefs or assumptions, which Fish believes impossible, or that such fore-grounding can promote the ends of theory by inducing critical self-consciousness which Fish denies on the ground that virtually anything can cause one to reconsider one's most fundamental beliefs and assumptions, not just theory. Finally he argues that although it is clear that the practice of certain critics has been altered by theory what this reveals 'is that thematizing remains the primary mode of literary criticism and that, as an action, thematizing can find its materials in theory as well as in anything else' ('C', 451). Although this is a consequence of theory, Fish asserts that it is not a theoretical consequence: theory has merely become a form of practice but it does not inform practice.

Fish's position on the separation of theory and practice is justified in the sense that as soon as theory is used as the foundation for a form of practice it is transformed into belief. It can always be reactivated by questions being posed about the presuppositions underlying practice. In exploring and attempting to justify these presuppositions belief will again become theory. One might compare theory with metaphor. All language use can be seen as having its basis in metaphor but this is not perceived because the great majority of metaphors are dead metaphors: they are treated as if they merely described reality. Similarly, all discourse can be seen as having its basis in theory but in being applied to practice theory has become 'dead' and functions as belief. Fish's view is that theory must always stop for practice to take place and thus always becomes belief. Even if one seeks continually to interrogate belief so that it remains theory, when it is applied to practice it will stop and change into belief. Belief, therefore, always gets behind theory. Contemporary theorists like Derrida are aware of this and have attempted to construct a theoretical discourse that continually doubles back on itself by coining new terms and concepts and employing playful or oblique language, as I discussed previously. Theoretical language has bequeathed to us the equivalent of dead metaphors – ideology, will to power, objective correlative – which are used as if their meaning was quite straightforward. Even Derrida has been unable to escape this process, for those attempting to explain and apply his work inevitably turn his theory into a set of beliefs. Thus theoretical terms coined by Derrida and other modern theorists – différance, trace, strategies of containment, interpretive communities – have suffered the same fate as older terms like 'ideology'.

Fish's anti-theoretical theory – that theory has no consequences – is not immune from this process. When it is applied to practice it too becomes belief, as Fish would no doubt admit, but he does not draw the more uncomfortable conclusion that like all belief it cannot be dissociated from political considerations. It can be argued, for example, that the application of his claim that theory has no consequences for practice leads to the maintenance of the status quo and undermines any attempt to argue that literary criticism can effect fundamental social and political change. Although Fish has attacked the hegemony of traditional criticism and supported interpretation from positions that most traditionalists would judge as inadmissible, he sees these new forms of interpretation as being incorporated in an ever-enlarging literary institution which, their exponents might claim, contains and domesticates them. The form of literary interpretation which has most powerfully challenged both the literary institution and the institutions of society in recent years is feminist criticism, many of whose advocates would reject any separation between theory and practice. Has feminist theory been able 'to guide and/or alter practice' or has it merely created another 'interpretive community' which has taken its place among others within the literary institution? The next chapter may help to suggest an answer to this question.

CHAPTER 8

Feminist interpretation

The emergence of feminist interpretation as a major force in literary criticism has been the most dramatic happening in literary studies since the war. The other critical innovations I have discussed can be related to a prior context of some kind but as recently as twenty-five years ago nothing resembling a feminist interpretative perspective even existed. The fact that it is now well-established and appears to constitute an alternative to other critical methods at the level of both theory and practice has been seen by many radicals as grounds for hope that revolutionary change is possible both within and beyond the literary institution. A contrary view is that it has been assimilated as another 'approach' and shows how the literary institution is able to contain and neutralise challenges.

The power of feminism within Western culture since the late 1960s has had a particularly powerful effect on literary criticism in Britain and America because of the fact that women constitute a large majority of the students in higher education who study literature. Student interest and demand have been responsible for feminist courses being offered in most literature departments, especially in America, and this has necessitated appointing those capable of teaching such courses. Thus more women have been given teaching posts, although literature departments still tend to be dominated by men. Publishers have not been slow to exploit the situation: feminist criticism has become one of the main growth areas in literary critical publication, with numerous authors and works being subject to a 'feminist reading'. Increased attention has also been devoted to women authors, both 'major' and 'minor', and attempts have been made to combine feminism with various innovations in critical theory.

Literary criticism, however, has not merely reflected the rise of interest in feminism; it has been partly responsible for generating that interest in the first place. Works of literary criticism were among the most influential feminist texts to appear during the late 1960s and early 1970s when feminism began to have a major social effect – works such as Mary Ellmann's *Thinking About Women* and Kate Millett's *Sexual Politics*. Millett's book had a particularly strong impact, but it raises a fundamental question: is it more important to change the world than to write criticism that is powerful purely in critical terms? Or if there is a conflict can it be resolved?

Sexual Politics studies the work of several male writers from a committed feminist angle. Their works are judged negatively if they are seen as expressing views or ideas which are anti-feminist. There is an obvious affinity with early Marxist ideological criticism, which assesses writers in relation to how far they and their works can be seen as sympathetic or unsympathetic to socialist ideas. Significantly, when Millett goes on to deal with literature after having discussed theoretical, historical and political questions, she entitles this section of her book, 'The literary reflection', recalling Marxist reflection theory. The kind of criticism she produces can only be described, at least from the standpoint of readers whose main interest is in literature and in an analytic criticism that attempts to do justice to it, as a relentlessly 'monological' form of interpretation.

Millett, like post-structuralists or new historicists, argues that there needs to be a break from formalist and traditional historical criticism:

> I have operated on the premise that there is room for a criticism which takes into account the larger cultural context in which literature is conceived and produced. Criticism which originates from literary history is too limited in scope to do this; criticism which originates in aesthetic considerations, 'New Criticism', never wished to do so.[1]

But what this leads to in practice is an attack on such novelists as Lawrence or Norman Mailer because the apparent content of their works is anti-feminist, with, for example, Lawrence being identified with his characters or his novels being seen as expressing in uncomplicated form the idea of masculine superiority:

> At the next erection, Connie and the author-narrator together inform us that the penis is 'overweening', 'towering', and 'terrible'. Most material of all, an erection provides the female with irrefutable evidence that male supremacy is founded upon the most real and incontrovert-

ible grounds. A diligent pupil, Connie supplies the catechist's dutiful
response, 'Now I know why men are so overbearing'. (*Sexual Politics
(SP)*, 239)

Lady Chatterley's Lover may not be Lawrence's most subtle novel,
but Millett seems determined to extract the most monologic reading
possible from the text, excluding any possible ambiguity from
Connie's remark by interpreting it simply as a 'dutiful response'.
Sons and Lovers receives similar treatment: 'Paul Morel is of course
Lawrence himself, treated with a self-regarding irony which is often
adulation' (*SP*, 246).

Millett's book had a much greater influence than Mary Ellmann's
earlier feminist study, *Thinking About Women*, which Toril Moi in
her book *Sexual/Textual Politics* sees as more interesting from a
literary critical angle, anticipating, for example, deconstruction:

> it is precisely through the use of satirical devices that Ellmann manages
> to demonstrate first that the very concepts of masculinity and femini-
> nity are social constructs which refer to no real essence in the world,
> and second that the feminine stereotypes she describes invariably
> deconstruct themselves'.[2]

As Moi points out, Ellmann's book was criticised by some feminists
as evasive. But from a feminist position one can argue that what the
times called for was not literary criticism that would appeal to
literary specialists but social and political change, and in that context
it was totally justifiable for Millett to produce interpretations of the
work of writers like Lawrence that may seem crude from a literary
critical point of view. It was more important that her interpretations
changed people's, particularly women's, attitudes.

Millett recognises a tension between her interpretative approach
and the question of aesthetics, when she admits that her attention is
directed at an author's ideas rather than at such matters as artistic
structure: 'It strikes me as better to make a radical investigation
which can demonstrate why Lawrence's analysis of a situation is
inadequate, or biased, or his influence pernicious, without ever
needing to imply that he is less than a great and original artist' (*SP*,
xii). This tension between the aesthetic and the moral or political
dimensions of texts has been central to the school of feminist
criticism that has been most strongly influenced by Millett: 'Images
of women' criticism, which is predominantly concerned with how
women characters are represented in literature, particularly in works

written by men. One of its main exponents, Josephine Donovan, argues that the first priority for feminist criticism must be to change the world, which recalls, of course, Marx's remark that before him philosophers had only interpreted the world, whereas the aim should be to change it. But Donovan directly confronts the fact that this creates a problem with regard to the aesthetic qualities of literary texts. Discussing Faulkner's *Light in August* she writes of the difficulty a feminist critic faces reading this novel:

> I have no difficulty appreciating the formal elements of the work. Structurally it is brilliant, and the style is magnificent. From the point of view of form I can appreciate the beauty of the work. This is an aesthetic judgment.
> However, the rank misogynism and racism that run through the moral text make it impossible for me as a feminist and a humanist to suspend disbelief and to accept the probabilities of Faulkner's fictional world.

She concludes that 'Where one cannot accept the ethics of the text, one cannot accept the aesthetics.'[3]

Donovan applies this philosophy in another essay in which she discusses works that have been regarded as central to Western civilisation: Homer's *Odyssey*, Dante's *Divine Comedy* and Goethe's *Faust*. She asserts that

> Women in literature written by men are for the most part seen as Other, as objects, of interest only insofar as they serve or detract from the goals of the male protagonist. Such literature is alien from a female point of view because it denies her essential selfhood.[4]

The feminist critic's role as interpreter is 'to determine the degree to which sexist ideology controls the text' ('Beyond the net' ('BN'), 42), which involves a refusal to accept any separation between aesthetics and morals. All works, even the most elevated, have to survive feminist scrutiny; some more or less survive. In *King Lear*, Goneril and Regan are 'irretrievably evil', but women are not unfairly singled out because Edmund is equally evil, although 'Feminists . . . may regret that Shakespeare did not allow Cordelia to survive . . . nevertheless, the denouement goes beyond sexist scapegoating' ('BN', 47). But other works, 'considered archetypal masterpieces of the Western tradition', are attacked for creating 'simplistic stereotypes of women' ('BN', 48). Homer's *Odyssey* provides the Western tradition with 'its archetypal sexist plot, depending as it does on a series of female stereotypes' ('BN', 48) (Donovan evidently is not persuaded by Samuel Butler's idea that it was written by a woman); Dante's *Divine Comedy* 'presents . . . one of the greatest elaborations of the ideal spiritual woman, who is nevertheless defined . . . in terms of her service to the male protagonist' ('BN', 49); and in Goethe's *Faust*, 'The unappealing philosophy underlying this work is that lesser people like Gretchen and most women are fuel for the great dynamic energy of the great male geniuses of history like Faust' ('BN', 50). Donovan admits that it may be possible to 'transcend one's sex in appreciating a literary work' ('BN', 50), but believes women should not do so:

> Such literature as treated in this article must remain alien. This does not mean that we should throw out or refuse to read these works, but that they should be read with perspective that recognizes the sexism inherent in their moral vision. ('BN', 51)

The goal of this form of feminist interpretation is political since its aim is to create a situation in which 'literature will no longer function as propaganda furthering sexist ideology' ('BN', 52). It undoubtedly possesses a refreshing directness which encourages one to see even the most familiar works in a new light. But it is fundamentally a reductive form of criticism that ignores many of the aspects of literary texts that from a strictly literary critical perspective would be judged as crucial, and the fact that this interpretative strategy can be defended on political grounds does not make it any the less reductive. Donovan's conception of the aesthetic is also extremely narrow, having much in common with late nineteenth-century aestheticism in that a work can be considered a masterpiece in terms of art even though what it is expressing may be totally objectionable. Leavis and the New Critics, with their denial that form can be separated from content, would of course reject the validity of this conception of aesthetics. A different problem is that this form of feminist criticism is open to the accusation of being essentialist – Donovan talks of women's 'essential selfhood' – and is vulnerable to a critique by those contemporary critics who accept Lacanian or neo-Marxist or deconstructionist theories in which the self is not given but constructed. It is therefore something of an embarrassment to more theoretically-minded feminists. However, 'Images of women' criticism is of major importance for establishing feminist interpretation as a powerful challenger to conventional approaches and for forcing both women and men to think of literature in different terms. Despite its limitations at the level of both practice and theory, it created the basis for later feminist criticism in its various manifestations.

One of the directions in which feminist criticism has moved has been towards the establishment of a specifically female tradition of writing. The major advocate of this has probably been Elaine Showalter, who has coined the term 'gynocritics' to categorise this form of feminist criticism. She sees 'gynocritics' as being concerned with woman as writer whereas the 'Images of women' approach, or what she calls 'feminist critique', focuses on woman as reader. She makes the following criticism of the latter:

> one of the problems of the feminist critique is that it is male-oriented. If we study stereotypes of women, the sexism of male critics, and the limited roles women play in literary history, we are not learning what women have felt and experienced, but only what men have thought women should be.[5]

Gynocritics, in contrast, directs its attention to female culture and consciousness. In her book, *A Literature of Their Own*, Showalter attempts to show that there is a distinct female tradition in the British novel, from the mid-nineteenth century up to the present. She sees this tradition as having three phases, which she calls 'feminine', 'feminist' and 'female'. Writers in the first group set out to emulate the achievements of male-centred culture, those in the second group protested about the situation of women and those in the third group aimed at creating a distinct female-centred fiction.

Showalter's book is undoubtedly more interesting to readers whose main concern is literary criticism than, say, Millett's, although it sacrifices in the process the latter's forcefulness and political edge. It does not adopt an innovative critical methodology but rather uses feminist interests as a means of understanding the problems that faced women writers during the period she focuses on and as the basis for thematic interpretation of novels written by women, revealing connections between both writers and novels that would otherwise be missed if they were not segregated from the world of male writing. George Eliot, for example, is seen interestingly as a counterproductive influence on women writers because 'they felt excluded from, and envious of, her world. Her very superiority depressed them', and *Jane Eyre* is interpreted as an attempt 'to depict a complete female identity'.[6] A problem with privileging feminist issues in looking at the work of women writers, however, is that there is a basic assumption that the female dimension of writers such as Charlotte Brontë or George Eliot is more important than, for example, the fact that they were part of a Victorian cultural context, that Christianity was central to both their lives, that they can be placed within a Romantic tradition of writing. Is their femaleness more significant than these or other determining forces? One could argue that the femaleness of these writers interacts with and thus rearticulates their relation to other cultural forces and also that there are grounds on the basis of 'reverse discrimination' for giving special emphasis to their femaleness since previous criticism has tended to ignore it, but this does not justify their femaleness being accorded priority in an intrinsic sense over other determinants.

Showalter does not provide a theoretical justification for the privileging of feminist interests in interpreting the work of these writers and she also tends to discuss feminist themes in isolation from wider cultural issues. The kind of thematic interpretation this produces is therefore vulnerable to the charge of essentialism since feminist concerns are seen in an abstract context. Discussing the ending of *Jane Eyre* she writes: 'Can we imagine an ending to *Jane Eyre* in which Jane and Bertha leave Rochester and go off together? Obviously such a solution would be unthinkable. Such possibilities and such solutions are beyond the boundaries of the feminine novel.'[7] The difficulty with this is that the 'feminine' novel cannot be seen in isolation from the Victorian novel in general and the kind of constraints within which Victorian writers had to work. Showalter suggests that the author of a 'feminine' novel could hardly have imagined the kind of ending she envisages for *Jane Eyre*. But how many Victorian novels end with a man and woman going off together to live in sin or with two men opting for homosexuality? Does this mean Victorian novelists could not conceive of such happenings? Because novelists like Charlotte Brontë and George Eliot do not show women rejecting men in general does not mean that they could not envisage such a thing or even that they might not try to represent it indirectly in their fiction. By ignoring the Victorian cultural context which contained – in both senses – the 'feminine' novel, Showalter presents an over-simplified account which closes off from the start certain interpretative possibilities.

In a later essay Showalter seems to admit that feminist critics need to relate the femaleness of women writers to other determining forces in the culture, although she still maintains there is a distinct female cultural dimension:

A cultural theory acknowledges that there are important differences between women as writers: class, race, nationality, and history are literary determinants as significant as gender. Nonetheless, women's culture forms a collective experience within the cultural whole, an experience which binds women writers to each other over time and space.[8]

The last sentence still leaves her open to the charge of essentialism.

Many of the women writers Showalter discusses in *A Literature of Their Own* would be regarded as minor in canonic terms, but virtually all of the novels she discusses would be accepted by the male-dominated literary institution as being worthy of critical consideration. Many feminist critics, however, have been troubled by the fact that so much writing by women is generally regarded as having no artistic merit. This has led to attempts to undermine the basis of the judgements that underlie the construction of the traditional canon and to efforts being made to create a critical discourse that can make such works interesting for the purposes of literary interpretation. This has involved undermining many of the assumptions of traditional aesthetically-based criticism.

Jane P. Tompkins has endeavoured to demonstrate that Harriet Beecher Stowe's *Uncle Tom's Cabin* is not merely an important cultural document because of its great influence but that both it and the 'sentimental novel' of which it is a part can stand up to critical scrutiny. She both attacks traditional literary criteria for being governed by male prejudice as to what is of artistic interest and argues that such novels cannot merely be dismissed as being without artistic merit on the grounds that they are sentimental:

> In contrast to male authors like Thoreau, Whitman, and Melville, who are celebrated as models of intellectual daring and honesty, these women are generally thought to have traded in false stereotypes, dishing out weak-minded pap to nourish the prejudices of an ill-educated and underemployed readership.[9]

Tompkins's opposed view is 'that the popular domestic novel of the nineteenth century represents a monumental effort to reorganize culture from the woman's point of view' ('Sentimental power' ('SP'), 83). Although she claims that she is not seeking to dethrone the likes of Hawthorne and Melville, she states:

> I will argue that the work of the sentimental writers is complex and significant in ways *other than* those that characterize the established masterpieces. I will ask the reader to set aside some familiar categories

for evaluating fiction – stylistic intricacy, psychological subtlety, epistemological complexity – and to see the sentimental novel, not as an artifice of eternity answerable to certain formal criteria and to certain psychological concerns, but as a political enterprise, halfway between sermon and social theory, that both codifies and attempts to mold the values of its time. ('SP', 84–5)

Of course, not only women have employed sentiment in fiction – one thinks of the sentimental novel in the eighteenth century, works such as Mackenzie's *The Man of Feeling,* and in the nineteenth century Dickens's *The Old Curiosity Shop* is an obvious example – but Tompkins does not seem interested in male sentimental writing, perhaps because it suits her purpose to separate the genre from 'high' literature and to confine it to women as far as possible.

Sentimental fiction's power to move its readers, Tompkins argues, using a reader-response approach, 'depends upon the audience's being in possession of the conceptual categories that constitute character and event', and

Once in possession of the system of beliefs that undergirds the patterns of sentimental fiction, it is possible for modern readers to see how its tearful episodes and frequent violations of probability were invested with a structure of meanings that fixed these works, for nineteenth-century readers, not in the realm of fairy tale or escapist fantasy, but in the very bedrock of reality. ('SP', 85)

On this basis she believes that one of the most derided features of sentimental novels can be artistically justified. Little Eva's death in *Uncle Tom's Cabin* and similar deaths intended to arouse sentimental response should be interpreted as having a philosophical and political function that can be compared with the death of Christ:

They enact, in short, a *theory* of power in which the ordinary or 'commonsense' view of what is efficacious and what is not (a view to which most modern critics are committed) is simply reversed, as the very possibility of social action is made dependent on the action taking place in individual hearts. ('SP', 85–6)

Uncle Tom's Cabin should not be read in the same way that one would read a realistic novel, claims Tompkins, but as a typological narrative that 'retells the culture's central religious myth, the story of the crucifixion, in terms of the nation's greatest political conflict – slavery – and of its most cherished social beliefs – the sanctity of motherhood and the family' ('SP', 91). Tompkins concludes, in stark contrast, for example, to Jauss's view that art achieves its liberating potential by challenging its audience at the level of both meaning and form, by arguing that

> Stowe's very conservatism – her reliance on established patterns of living and traditional beliefs – is precisely what gives the novel its revolutionary potential. By pushing these beliefs to an extreme and by insisting that they be applied universally . . . Stowe means to effect a radical transformation of her society. . . . Stowe relocates the center of power in American life, placing it . . . in the kitchen. And that means that the new society will not be controlled by men but by women. ('SP', 99–100)

The narrowness and parochialism which critics have found in sentimental novels reflect upon those who make such judgements, not on the works themselves or their authors.

Tompkins's position raises problems not so much because of any intrinsic weaknesses in her argument but rather because of its potential to generate *reductio ad absurdum* responses that may lead to feminist interpretation being attacked or dismissed by certain elements within the literary institution. If the kind of sentimental fiction that she discusses is artistically valid then what about romantic fiction? Could Barbara Cartland's novels not be defended as works that are wrongly judged by the stylistic, psychological and epistemological criteria normally employed to decide on artistic merit when they should be seen as embodying a radical critique of society from a Christian point of view? Are they not therefore as deserving of critical attention as the novels of Joyce or Lawrence? Is the poetry of Pam Ayres not more socially concerned and relevant to the experience of women than, say, that of Geoffrey Hill? Many male critics would accept that feminism has altered interpretative perspectives to such an extent that it is legitimate to question the established canon, but few would be likely to go as far as Tompkins in setting aside traditional aesthetic criteria. What should such criteria be replaced by? If it is felt that feminist criticism – and criticism from other previously 'marginalised' standpoints – undermines any basis for literary discrimination, then it will meet strong opposition not only from traditional forces within the literary institution, which are still powerful, but also from certain contemporary approaches which are reluctant to abandon the notion of literary value.

On pragmatic grounds, then, it seems likely that many feminist critics will be reluctant to go so far in attacking the canon as to argue that it should include those popular genres that have been most associated with women, such as sentimental and romantic fiction – what Jauss would no doubt categorise as *Unterhaltungskunst* or 'culinary' art. But the work of such critics as Tompkins cannot be easily dismissed since it subjects the concept of literary value to scrutiny and challenges those who unthinkingly accept the literary canon. One of the most powerful features of feminist criticism has been its ability to question in a more direct way than deconstruction and the new historicism whether the aesthetic and the ideological belong to different realms and thus to undermine the distinterested-ness of aesthetic judgements and values.

Feminist criticism in the 1980s

What is most striking about feminist criticism in the 1980s is its establishment as an accepted and secure part of the literary institu-tion, at least in America, and its development in a more theoretical direction through interacting with contemporary critical theory. Perhaps the critical work which has done most to make feminist interpretation accepted by the literary institution is Sandra M. Gilbert's and Susan Gubar's book, *The Madwoman in the Attic*, a massive study of women writers in the nineteenth century. It might perhaps be seen as a kind of feminist version of Leavis's *The Great Tradition*. The book has a theoretical power lacking in Showalter's *A Literature of Their Own*, even if Gilbert and Gubar do not confront contemporary critical theories, combined with more detailed and powerful interpretations of texts than can be found in Showalter's book or in the work of 'Images of women' critics. The texts they choose to analyse are also for the most part works by women writers that have been accepted as major by the literary critical establish-ment. The comprehensive interpretations they produce of works such as *Wuthering Heights*, *Jane Eyre* and *Middlemarch* fuse a feminist perspective with a New Critical mode of analysis to produce readings of these novels as persuasive as any in the later tradition of the New Criticism. Gilbert and Gubar have thus demonstrated that feminist literary interpretation can survive comparison with and find a place within the mainstream of literary interpretation. That their main aim has been to establish feminist interpretation as a central and accepted part of the literary institution is suggested by the fact that they have recently produced a Norton anthology of women's writing as a textbook for students that clearly aims to stand alongside the Norton anthologies that cover the rest of English and American literature.

Many contemporary feminist critics, however, believe that feminist criticism should reject absorption within the mainstream of the literary institution by aligning itself with contemporary theory. Toril Moi, a strong advocate of contemporary critical theory, claims that Gilbert and Gubar's work fails to make a radical break from patriarchal assumptions: 'some Anglo-American feminism – and Gilbert and Gubar are no exceptions – is still labouring under the traditional patriarchal values of New Criticism'.[10] There has been debate within feminist criticism as to which path it should follow. Critics such as Showalter and Annette Kolodny have expressed doubts about any alignment with contemporary theoretical criticism, Showalter, for example, arguing that feminist critics should be suspicious of structuralist and Marxist theories which 'claim to be sciences of literature, and repudiate the personal, fallible, interpretative reading'. These and other theories 'have offered literary critics the opportunity to demonstrate that the work they do is as manly and aggressive as nuclear physics – not intuitive, expressive and feminine, but strenuous, rigorous, impersonal and virile'.[11] But in her more recent essay, 'Feminist criticism in the wilderness', even Showalter turns against feminist criticism that is conventionally interpretative in favour of a more theoretical approach: 'in the free play of the interpretive field, the feminist critique can only compete with alternative readings, all of which have the built-in obsolescence of Buicks, cast away as newer readings take their place'. Disagreeing with Kolodny, who advocates pluralism, she writes:

> If we see our critical job as interpretation and reinterpretation, we must be content with pluralism as our critical stance. But if we wish to ask questions about the process and the contexts of writing . . . we cannot rule out the prospect of theoretical consensus at this early stage.[12]

Showalter is among those who believe that feminist criticism should not so much try to accommodate the work of 'male critical theory' but concentrate on the writings of feminist theorists. Thus a great deal of attention has been directed at French feminist theory, especially the work of Julia Kristeva, Hélène Cixous and Luce

Irigaray. But some feminist critics believe that certain male theorists whose work calls into question the fundamental basis of the dominant tradition of Western thinking, such as Lacan and Derrida, have an intrinsic affinity with feminism. Other powerful 'male theoretical' influences on recent feminist criticism have been Marxism, cultural materialism and the new historicism. The fact that many of the male critics associated with the latter are sympathetic to the political aspirations of feminism is an obvious reason why such materialist criticism has a strong appeal to feminist critics.

The emergence of a theorised feminist criticism has been one of the most interesting developments in contemporary critical interpretation. Elizabeth A. Meese has argued that feminist criticism needs to go in this direction in order to resist being neutralised politically by the pluralism of the literary institution, which will regard feminist interpretation as merely another 'approach'. She suggests that many critics have generally been content to accept Stanley Fish's idea of the literary institution as made up of 'interpretive communities' – which entails pluralism – because it appears to allow for freedom of interpretation without abandoning controls, yet such controls are benign since they are not asserted by force of authority. Meese claims that this situation is illusory for the 'interpretive community' is in fact the 'authoritative community': members of such communities 'control the admissibility of facts, texts, and evidence, as well as the norms constitutive of reasonableness in argumentation'. If feminist criticism is to resist the apparently benevolent but in fact oppressive embrace of the institution it must assert itself at the level of both politics and epistemology:

> Fish, in his notion of the interpretive (authoritative) community, proffers equality: literature is an open system, admitting any text (within reason); variations in interpretation are permitted (within reason); and persuasion is the means by which (reasonable) critics establish consensus. . . . But inherent in Fish's approach is the fact that the right to reason and the power of determination are located where power and reason have always rested in Western civilization – within the community of elite white men.

To counter this, feminist criticism must make its ideology explicit and 'seek to transform the structures of authority . . . and in doing so, unmask and expose them for all to see. . . . The future of feminist criticism rests on defying the oppositional logic currently fostering the very concept of privilege.'[13] Thus feminist criticism should seek to retain its radical force by making use of the work of French feminists such as Luce Irigaray and radical theorists like Foucault.

Feminist critical theory, like contemporary theory generally, is to a considerable extent divided between those sympathetic to purist forms of post-structuralist thinking – some, such as Hélène Cixous, even creating a feminist form of 'writerly' discourse or 'freeplay' – and those who favour a more contextualist approach that brings together theory, history, sociology and politics. An interpretation that belongs mainly in the former category – although written in relatively straightforward critical discourse – is an essay by Jacqueline Rose on *Hamlet*, entitled, '*Hamlet* – the *Mona Lisa* of literature', which makes considerable use of both deconstruction and psychoanalysis (the latter, especially in its Lacanian form, has had a significant influence on several modes of contemporary interpretation).

Focusing first of all on T. S. Eliot's essay, '*Hamlet* and his problems', Rose argues that the concept of the 'objective correlative', which Eliot had formulated both in order to express his dissatisfaction with that play and as a general aesthetic criterion, is integrally connected with the question of femininity. Eliot claimed that

> The only way of expressing emotion in the form of art is by finding an 'objective correlative'; in other words, a set of objects, a situation, a chain of events which shall be the formula of that *particular* emotion; such that when the external facts . . . are given, the emotion is immediately evoked.[14]

What made Hamlet's emotion, for Eliot, 'in *excess* of the facts as they appear', was that, as Rose puts it, 'Gertrude is not an adequate equivalent for the disgust which she evokes in Hamlet' ('*Hamlet* – the *Mona Lisa* of literature' ('HM'), 36). The problem is not that Gertrude's characterisation is artistically weak, but that 'a son's feelings towards a guilty mother . . . should be in excess of their objective cause' ('HM', 36). The difficulty is therefore one of representation. Since unconscious emotions are incapable of finding an objective outlet, they cannot be adequately represented in terms of an 'objective correlative', with the result that in *Hamlet* we find, as Eliot puts it, 'the "buffoonery" of an emotion which [Shakespeare] cannot express in art' ('HM', 37).

Rose points out that many of the terms Eliot uses in his discussion of the play have, since Freud, become identified with the very process of writing: 'buffoonery, ecstasy, the excessive and unknowable' ('HM', 37). In such a context, their connection with 'a woman who is seen as cause of the excess and deficiency in the play and again a woman who symbolises its aesthetic failure' ('HM', 37) repeats both the action of the play – which is concerned with the excess of Gertrude's sexuality as well as the horror of Hamlet's and the ghost's response to it – and

> a more fundamental drama of psychic experience itself as described by Freud, the drama of sexual difference in which the woman is seen as the cause of just such a failure in representation, as something deficient, lacking or threatening to the system and identities which are the precondition not only of integrated artistic form but also of so-called normal adult psychic and sexual life. ('HM', 37)

Eliot's choosing of a woman as the vehicle for elements in the play that are beyond expression 'ties the enigma of femininity to the problem of interpretation itself' ('HM', 38).

The identification of art with that which can be controlled or managed, Rose argues, necessitates the exclusion of the feminine, particularly female sexuality. She sees Eliot's conception of writing, in which the artist should identify with a tradition and thus 'avoid his own disordered subjectivity and transmute it into form' as the operation of a 'particularly harsh type of literary super-ego' ('HM', 39) which contemporary literary theory aims at undermining. The centrality of female sexuality in *Hamlet* is a problem for Eliot in terms of both the form and content of the play, since 'femininity . . . becomes the focus for a partly theorised recognition of the psychic and literary disintegration which can erupt at any moment into literary form' ('HM', 40).

Turning to the play itself and to the major themes of death and sexuality, Rose argues that it 'turns on mourning and marriage – the former the means whereby death is given its symbolic form and enters back into social life, the latter the means whereby sexuality is brought into the orbit of the law' ('HM', 41). The overstatement of these two 'regulators' at the beginning of the play leads to a troubling confusion between them which Eliot's essay connects with wider aesthetic issues: 'Eliot's essay on *Hamlet*, and his writing on literature in general, gives us a sense of how these matters, which he recognises in the play, underpin the space of aesthetic representation itself and how femininity figures crucially in that conceptualisation' ('HM', 41).

Rose goes on to discuss Ernest Jones's Freudian reading of the play which is also posited on the belief that 'there must be no aesthetic excess' ('HM', 42). Both Eliot and Jones use female images to express their sense of the play's inscrutability: the 'Mona Lisa' in Eliot's case and the Sphinx in Jones's. Jones's attempt at a straightforward Oedipal reading deconstructs itself by his categorisation of Hamlet as a hysteric and by the fact that he finds connections between Hamlet and the feminine: 'Femininity turns out to be lying behind the Oedipal drama, indicating its impasse or impossibility of resolution' ('HM', 44). After discussing other psychoanalytic readings by André Green and Lacan, Rose questions Green's view 'that Shakespeare saved his sanity by projecting this crazed repudiation of the feminine on to the stage, using his art to give it "an acceptable form" ' ('HM', 46–7). Rose asks to whom this form is acceptable: 'Or rather what does it mean to us that one of the most elevated and generally esteemed works of our Western literary tradition should enact such a negative representation of femininity, or even such a violent repudiation of the femininity in man?' ('HM', 47).

But unlike a critic such as Donovan, Rose does not urge that the play be rejected on moral grounds. Indeed, her essay has called into question the kind of distinction between the aesthetic and the moral that Donovan assumes. Her concern is rather to make apologists for the Western literary tradition aware of how a work central to that tradition 'encodes' an unacceptable image of the woman, and that the 'problem of femininity' is inescapable even by those like Eliot who appear to ignore it. She concludes that this is a 'reminder' to those who seek to uphold 'a cultural order in which the woman is given too much and too little of a place . . . of the precarious nature of the certainties on which that order rests' ('HM', 47).

It could be objected that a belief in the primacy of the feminine precedes and therefore compromises Rose's theoretical critique. Although Eliot and Jones may compare *Hamlet* to the 'Mona Lisa' and the Sphinx, it is arguable that Rose does not convincingly demonstrate that the 'excess' which is irreconcilable with these critics' idea of form in a work of art is necessarily to be solely identified with the feminine. It seems very likely that the underlying source of Eliot's concern with aesthetic form and that which cannot be accommodated by it in the *Hamlet* essay is Nietzsche's contrast between the Apollonian, identified with order and control, and the Dionysian, that which resists all limitation and destroys any form of order. In *The Birth of Tragedy* Nietzsche had argued that although both were necessary to art, the Apollonian must be dominant. Although the feminine can be included within the concept of the Dionysian – especially as Nietzsche sees artistic creation as motivated by a lack which brings into play psychoanalytic concern with the phallic and castration – it can clearly be only one aspect or manifestation of it. The association between Shakespeare and buffoonery, which Eliot mentions, also has a source in Nietzsche, who wrote in *Ecce Homo*: 'I know no more heart-rending reading than Shakespeare: what must a man have suffered to have such a need of being a buffoon!'[15]

Another difficulty raised by Rose's essay is that although she ably deconstructs 'misreadings' of the play by critics, it is not entirely clear whether the play should be held responsible for these 'misreadings'. How far is the play complicit with the attitudes to the feminine that Rose attributes to Eliot, or should one take the de Manian view that Rose's deconstruction of critics' interpretations has been anticipated and performed by the play itself? This is left ambiguous at the end of her essay. In some ways it is a crucial question for feminist criticism, for if works of art have only been appropriated illegitimately by the prevailing male culture then the possibility exists not only of their exposing the distortions and contradictions within that culture but also of their being reinterpreted positively by feminists. What would seem to be needed if one adopts this point of view is a positive feminist hermeneutics as an alternative to the negative hermeneutics practised by earlier feminist critics. One can imagine supporters of a more politically committed feminist criticism objecting to this because it suggests that works of art have somehow transcended ideology and history.

Catherine Belsey is a critic who has attempted to combine feminism with British post-structuralism and cultural materialism to create a politically relevant form of literary interpretation. For her, following Lacan, the subject is 'the site of contradiction' and 'perpetually in the process of construction', and the importance of the literary use of language is that it can be one of the most persuasive means of influencing how people 'grasp themselves and their relation to the real relations in which they live'. Consequently, since 'The interpellation of the reader in the literary text could be argued to have a role in reinforcing the concepts of the world and of subjectivity which ensure that people "work by themselves" in the social formation', criticism should 'challenge these concepts . . . call in question the particular complex of imaginary relations between individuals and the real conditions of their existence which helps to reproduce the present relations of class, race and gender'. In her form of deconstruction, the text, 'Composed of contradictions . . . is no longer restricted to a single, harmonious and authoritative reading. Instead it becomes *plural*, open to re-reading, no longer an object for passive consumption but an object of work by the reader to produce meaning'. The object of criticism is not a unified or coherent or comprehensive interpretation, as it was for the New Criticism: such a 'smoothing out' of contradictions makes criticism become

> the accomplice of ideology. Having created a canon of acceptable texts, criticism then provides them with acceptable interpretations, thus effectively censoring any elements in them which come into collision with the dominant ideology. To deconstruct the text, on the other hand, is to open it, to release the possible positions of its intelligibility, including those which reveal the partiality (in both senses) of the ideology inscribed in the text.[16]

In an essay on George Eliot's *Daniel Deronda* Belsey attacks Leavis's way of reading the novel in *The Great Tradition*, for manifesting 'a prior commitment in its reproduction of the values and strategies of the text it undertakes to judge', and also because 'it reduces in the process the plurality of the original novel'.[17] A 'more productive' way to read it is to see it 'as challenging the sexual power relations of its society in ways which have an identifiable bearing on our own' ('Re-reading the great tradition' ('RR'), 130). Although treating the novel as a feminist text may not be 'to take it on the terms the narrative voice proposes as its own', Belsey nevertheless claims that 'the interest in social relations as relations of domination and subordination is quite explicit and recurrent in the novel' ('RR', 130).

She regards Gwendolen Harleth's hysteria as being 'in excess of the immediate motivation: the letter from Lydia Glasher' ('RR', 132), but unlike Rose's interpretation of the 'excess' in *Hamlet* she reads Gwendolen's hysteria in much more direct terms as a rejection of patriarchy through a refusal to identify with her sexuality: 'No discourse, apart from hysteria itself, is available in the 1870s for resistance at the very core of patriarchy, and the narrative voice has in this instance no authoritative "explanation" to offer of

Gwendolen's outbursts of unaccountable and wordless horror' ('RR', 133-4). Belsey goes on to draw a parallel between Gwendolen's situation and that of Deronda's mother, whom she also sees as an instance of resistance to patriarchy and who by coming into the novel so late seems beyond the narrative control that a 'classic realist' novel would usually exert: 'Her history, unmotivated by narrative convention, but recounted with such intensity, constitutes a parallel vision of "a woman's life" ' ('RR', 134).

Belsey accepts that her interpretation of *Daniel Deronda* as 'a text which both breaks the limits of classic realism and challenges the evident laws of a natural (patriarchal) order' is, like Leavis's, 'partial', that is, 'it is a reading which is consciously and explicitly *produced* rather than "recognised" ' ('RR', 134). But she claims that it is less partial than Leavis's, for it is aware of its partiality and does not aspire to finality. What she is doing in her interpretation is 'bringing to bear on the raw material of the work itself discourses pertinent to the twentieth century' ('RR', 130).

An obvious difficulty raised by Belsey's interpretation is whether it is likely to be persuasive to a reader of the novel with a different set of interests and priorities, a Zionist, for example. Such a reader would almost certainly be reluctant to view Deronda's mother, a rebel against her Jewish upbringing who tries to cut her son off from his Jewish heritage, as a victim of patriarchy. Belsey leaves herself vulnerable to the charge of relativism in advocating a criticism that is governed by what is politically necessary within a particular social formation. A reading of the novel in terms of patriarchy is, she tells us, only an 'instance' of a 'more productive' reading; different political situations presumably would call forth 'productive' readings of a different political complexion. Belsey's approach to criticism can clearly produce interpretations which have something of the direct social impact of earlier forms of feminist criticism while exhibiting a thorough grasp of contemporary theory, but in refusing to allow the text itself to exert any power over its interpreter she runs the risk of depriving the text of otherness and therefore of undermining one of the fundamental interests of literary interpretation: the critical encounter with that otherness.

As with Marxist criticism, feminist interpretation needs to be seen in a wider context than the literary critical since the major priority of feminism is to promote social and political change. Certain of the objections I have made to some types of feminist criticism may therefore be judged as beside the point or trivial if seen in relation to that wider context. On the other hand, several feminist critics, notably Toril Moi, who are equally committed to the politics of feminism and to contemporary theory, have argued that feminist criticism must seek to reconcile the two even if this means subjecting previous forms of feminist criticism to a severe critique. Indeed, what is likely to keep feminist criticism at the forefront of literary interpretation is that it incorporates within itself and in a particularly powerful form conflicts and tensions that are central to contemporary literary interpretation in general and which may develop most interestingly and productively within a feminist context. For this reason it seems certain that feminism will have a powerful role to play in literary interpretation for the foreseeable future.

CHAPTER 9

Afterword

A re any of the theories of interpretation that have come to pro-minence since the hegemony of the later New Criticism was undermined likely to achieve a dominant position within the literary institution? Will New Critical and traditional historical inter-pretative methods outlast recent alternatives and recover their former power? At present it looks as if division and conflict are likely to increase rather than diminish. Elsewhere I have compared the current state of literary criticism to a hung parliament in which no single party is strong enough to gain control.[1] There are a number of groups or parties or 'interpretive communities' which are engaged in a continuing struggle to build up sufficient support to achieve a position of power but there is little sign that any one party is close to attaining a majority over all the others. Smaller parties are likely to combine to defeat any large minority party that looks as if it might have a chance of dominating the literary institution. Thus if the new historicism, which has made a strong impact in the last few years, threatens to attain such a degree of power it will probably have to confront an alliance, perhaps an unholy one, between conventional historicists, New Critics, deconstructionists and various smaller groups.

What this study has shown is that literary interpretation has undergone radical changes in the past twenty years or so. During the era in which the New Critical tradition was in the ascendancy, interpretation was governed by such concepts as organic unity, coherence, comprehensiveness, and the literary text was treated as a privileged object that should be considered predominantly in its own terms with contextual factors being assigned to a minor role. But if there is any common ground among the various theory-based modes of interpretation that have emerged to challenge the New Critical tradition it is that in different ways they interpret the text 'against the grain', by showing, for example, how a text's rhetoric is at odds with its thematic organisation, or how radical contextualising can reveal that the text does not transcend its time but is informed by the contradictions within the culture that produced it, or how literary production like any other form of production cannot be dissociated from the question of ideology, or how the subjective interests of the reader construct the text and therefore condition the way in which it is read and interpreted.

Obviously there are fundamental conflicts here that are perhaps beyond resolution. In the past interpretation tended to be seen as a search for truth or validity but in the current situation it is in effect a struggle for power. It is unlikely that any consensus will emerge, as happened in the 1950s, when a kind of compromise was effected between New Critical close textual analysis and scholarly and historical criticism. But rather than lamenting the breakdown of consensus, one should, I would argue, see conflict and division as productive since they have promoted debate about fundamental issues and problems which had previously been stifled. The last twenty years have surely been one of the liveliest periods ever in the history of literary criticism, even if they have been traumatic for those who are conservative by temperament or who regard stability as a value in itself.

What seems certain in the current situation is that interpretation will continue to develop in response to debate among the various parties. One factor that may affect such development is how the 'voter' will respond to current debates, since parliaments, to continue the analogy, usually have to take account, at some point, of the electorate. One major reason why the New Criticism rose to a position of power was that it could be easily taught – at least after the production of such critical books as Brooks's and Warren's *Understanding Poetry*, the most powerful text of the New Criticism in terms of its effect – and was thus accessible in some degree to students of literature at virtually every level. It might seem doubtful whether contemporary approaches to interpretation with their reliance, for example, on Derridean, Lacanian, Althusserian, Foucauldian, Kristevan theories, or combinations of them, will ever be within the intellectual grasp of the majority of students below graduate level or of that endangered species, the general reader. This could lead to an unsatisfactory situation in which traditional methods are adopted in teaching at undergraduate levels with theory-based forms of interpretation being confined to work done at postgraduate level or for publication. This would greatly increase the élitism that already exists in literary studies, and would contrast with the democratic spirit of the New Critical tradition in which everyone was equal, at least notionally, before the text and could conceivably make some contribution in interpreting it as no special historical knowledge or theoretical mastery, it seemed, was required. However, as I pointed out in the chapter on the New Criticism, the situation in practice was not nearly as simple as that.

As one sees from publishers' lists, efforts are being made to introduce and make accessible theory-based approaches to a wide student audience, this book, of course, being an example. It remains to be seen how far such efforts will succeed but it seems unlikely that traditional forms of interpretation will be seriously threatened unless new interpretative modes make an impact at all levels of the teaching of literature and criticism.

What may help new modes of interpretation to achieve such an impact is the determination of much contemporary criticism to move beyond a narrow preoccupation with literature to an engagement with wider cultural issues. This could increase the appeal of literary studies in spite of the fact that theory-based critical interpretation, with its use of concepts from other disciplines and of specialised terminology, is much more difficult than interpretation in the New Critical tradition. Gerald Graff and Reginald Gibbons write:

> The close, concrete reading of literary works, which remains one of the primary tasks of criticism, is not likely to recover the sense of mission that once informed it as long as it takes place in a vacuum – separated from historical, philosophical and social contexts.[2]

This widening of literary study has led to one of the most interesting recent developments in criticism: the application of interpretative techniques associated with literary criticism to the interpretation of non-literary phenomena, such as philosophical or psychoanalytical texts, historical writing, film and popular culture generally.

It could also be argued that contemporary criticism is not breaking fundamentally with earlier criticism in moving in this direction. Both Bakhtin and Kenneth Burke attempted to combine criticism with a more general cultural critique in the 1920s and 1930s and supply a precedent for much current critical interpretation. Even the presently unfashionable work of Leavis has some relevance here. Leavis's proposal that the study of the seventeenth century be central to literary studies, 'not merely in literature, but as a whole; the Seventeenth Century as a key phase, or passage in the history of civilization', has something in common with what new historicists and cultural materialists are advocating. Leavis went on to say that 'it would be a study in concrete terms of the relations between the economic, the political, the moral, the spiritual, religion, art and literature, and would involve a critical pondering of standards and key-concepts – order, community, culture, civilization and so on'.[3] However, for Leavis, as for the New Critics generally, the implicit assumption is that those texts that are considered of literary value are central and therefore privileged, whereas a feature of contemporary criticism, both textualist and contextualist, has been its questioning of the idea that literature is a privileged form of discourse.

One problematic aspect of the project to incorporate literature within cultural studies is the question of politics. Some critics – notably Marxists, feminists, cultural materialists, new historicists – go on from this to advocate a politically committed criticism. Jean E. Howard and Marion F. O'Connor write in a book on Shakespeare:

> One end of a political criticism . . . is to explore the ideological functions of texts at various historical junctures and in various cultural practices. A further aim of much political criticism, however, is not only to *describe*, but to *take a position on*, the political uses of texts: to challenge some critical, theatrical, or pedagogical practices involving Shakespeare and to encourage others. In short, it is a critical practice in which the critic acknowledges his or her own interested position within the social formation, rather than claiming an Olympian disinterested-ness.[4]

It is clear that many of these critics recognise no conflict between such political commitment and 'objectivity'. Indeed, the attraction of theory, they suggest, is that it can provide validation for a politically committed criticism: 'The vast majority of recent political writing on Shakespeare has sided with the victims of state power, class hierarchy, patriarchy, racism, and imperialism, a partisanship, it is worth asserting, not only compatible with but also necessary to objectivity in scholarship.'[5]

Such critics would claim that all criticism is implicitly political and that they are only rejecting the pretence that it is not, but the

possible consequence of this widely-held view is that it could result
in the various 'interpretive communities' that make up the literary
institution becoming divided along clearly defined political lines.
Whether this extension of the 'parliament' analogy would be a
welcome development is open to question, especially if political
divisions become so great that, as in certain real parliamentary
situations, debate or dialogue with opposed groups becomes meaningless. In practice this could lead to critics merely dismissing
without consideration the interpretations produced by a different
'interpretive community' from their own. Clearly this happens to a
considerable extent at the moment but the politicisation of literary
criticism could split the literary institution to such an extent that
there ceased even to be conflict between opposed groups: they
merely ignored each other. This does not mean that political
interpretation should be rejected but in my view it must strive to
retain contact with critique if it is to avoid dogmatism and engage in
productive debate. There seems little future at the present time for
any form of literary criticism that does not continually subject its
aims and methods to theoretical critique.

The recent work of J. Hillis Miller indicates that interpretation
continues to be central to contemporary literary criticism and that
conflict between different modes of interpretation furthers productive debate about fundamental issues of theory and practice. Miller
has expressed his commitment to what he calls an 'ethics of reading':
the recognition that there is a power invested in the words of the text
which the reader must direct his or her attention to:

> In any ethical moment there is an imperative, some 'I must' . . . . If the
> response is not one of necessity, grounded in some 'must', if it is a
> freedom to do what one likes, for example to make a literary text mean
> what one likes, then it is not ethical, as when we say, 'That isn't
> ethical'.[6]

Miller rejects the commonsense view that reading is one thing and
that interpretation is merely an additional extra that is not essential.
For him the kind of textual scrutiny and exploration characteristic of
deconstruction should be seen as inseparable from any authentic
form of reading. Interpretation is thus integral to the reading
process. Literary critics have an ethical imperative to read in this
sense. He also argues that such an ethics of reading has little to do
with 'freeplay' as popularly understood and commits critics to the
belief that their interpretations are right. Discussing the fact that his

own interpretations of particular works have changed, he writes:

> This by no means indicates that I do not think I am right in the interpretations here. I believe all right-thinking readers will come to agree with what I say if they go on thinking about my poems long enough. I do mean, however, that there is always more to say about a given poem, as one moves along the line, track, or bridge of critical interpretation, or as 'in the lowest deep a lower deep still opens'. Each new reading builds on the old, even one's own old readings. 'It can never be satisfied, the mind, never.' The word *finis* can never be written to the work of interpretation.[7]

Miller claims that the various forms of contextualist interpretation which have tended to dominate literary criticism in the 1980s offend against such an ethics of reading. As he puts it, the 'common, in fact almost universal, topic of literary studies these days, [is] investigations of the political, historical, and social connections of literature'. Miller attacks such criticism from his 'ethics of reading' standpoint by asserting that the language of the literary text has priority over its context, which in any case does not exist independently of language:

> The notion of context hovers uneasily between metonymy in the sense of mere contingent adjacency and synecdoche, part for whole, with an assumption that the part is some way genuinely like the whole. . . . This is another way of saying that the study of literature, even the study of the historical and social relations or determinants of literature, remains within the study of language.

If the contextualists are right, claims Miller,

> The study of literature would then be no more than the study of a symptom or superstructure of something else more real and more important, and literature would be no more than a minor by-product of history, not something that in any way makes history.[8]

Here one sees deconstructive or rhetorical criticism revealing its continuity with the New Criticism and its advocacy of the priority of the words on the page. It is doubtful whether many of the critics Miller is attacking would accept that they set out to make a text mean whatever they want it to mean. Even Catherine Belsey, whose 'productive' interpretative approach I discussed in the previous chapter, seeks to establish a textual basis for her interpretations. It is more plausible to assume that critics believe in their interpretations at the moment of producing them even if they go on to produce different readings at some later date. Few contextualist critics are likely to accept, therefore, that their interpretations are less bound up with necessity and therefore less 'ethical' than Miller's. However, even if Miller's attempt to ground deconstructive criticism in an ethical imperative that competing forms of interpretation lack – a ground that is itself surely vulnerable to deconstruction – is open to question, it seems to me important that textualist and contextualist critics engage in debate rather than merely ignoring each other. Such a debate is also likely to influence the direction in which the theory and practice of interpretation could take in the future. Miller writes: 'Nothing is more urgently needed these days in humanistic study than the incorporation of the rhetorical study of literature into the study of the historical, social, and ideological dimensions of literature.'[9]

What Miller's attack on contextualist criticism shows is that although pluralism may be inevitable in literary interpretation for the simple reason that critics are virtually certain to have incompatible beliefs that will lead them to develop different interpretative approaches, such pluralism need not result in an easy acceptance of relativism. Rather, it promotes debate about the purpose and value of literary criticism and interpretation and thus forces both critics and students of literature to confront critical, philosophical and ideological questions. This should enliven literary teaching. If relativism prevailed, such debate would have little point. What is striking about criticism of the last twenty years is the fact that many important critics have changed their critical perspectives significantly and even fundamentally as a result of being involved in critical conflict and debate. Thus Hillis Miller's current deconstructionism is a major break from his earlier phenomenological criticism, Terry Eagleton's Marxist criticism of the 1980s is very different from his earlier work and has clearly been shaped by his confronting the challenge presented by post-structuralism, and there are numerous other examples one could cite. In ten years' time the dominant modes of interpretation may be significantly different from those that exist today. Despite the disorientation such change can create, it is fundamentally healthy, for if interpretative theory and method remain static they eventually become formulaic and predictable. This happened to the New Criticism and one has seen it happen to deconstruction and the new historicism in recent years. The continual development of the theory and practice of interpretation should therefore be welcomed.

Notes

Chapter 1: Introduction: interpretation and literary criticism

1. Jonathan Culler, *The Pursuit of Signs*, p. 16.
2. John M. Ellis, *The Theory of Literary Criticism*, p. 202.
3. Samuel Johnson, *The Lives of the English Poets*, p. 136.
4. See Joseph Anthony Mazzeo, *Varieties of Interpretation*, pp. 52–5.
5. Robert Snukal, *High Talk: The Philosophical Poetry of W. B. Yeats*, p. 223.
6. Matthew Arnold, *Essays in Criticism: Second Series*, pp. 37–8.
7. *Ibid.*, pp. 39, 40.
8. See T. S. Eliot, 'The metaphysical poets', in *Selected Essays*, p. 288.
9. *Hamlet*, ed. J. Dover Wilson, p. 151.
10. Fredson Bowers, *Textual and Literary Criticism*, p. 7.
11. *Hamlet*, ed. Harold Jenkins, pp. 436–7.
12. *Hamlet*, ed. G. R. Hibbard, pp. 383–4.
13. Christopher Norris, 'Post-structuralist Shakespeare: Text and ideology', p. 56.

Chapter 2: The New Criticism and the rise of interpretation

1. Hugh Trevor-Roper, 'Sir Walter Scott and history', pp. 226, 227.
2. I. A. Richards, *Practical Criticism*, p. 5.
3. I. A. Richards, 'Poetry and belief', in *Poetries and Science*, p. 58.
4. See W. K. Wimsatt, Jr, *The Verbal Icon*.
5. Matthew Arnold, *Essays in Criticism: Second Series*, pp. 1, 2.
6. Quoted in *Modern Literary Theory*, eds Ann Jefferson and David Robey, p. 28.

7. Victor Shklovsky, 'Art as technique', in *Russian Formalist Criticism*, ed. and trans. Lee T. Lemon and Marion J. Reis, p. 15.
8. Cleanth Brooks, 'The formalist critic', in *The Modern Critical Spectrum*, eds G. J. and N. M. Goldberg, pp. 1, 3, 6.
9. See Joseph Frank, 'Spatial form in modern literature'.
10. T. S. Eliot, 'The metaphysical poets', in *Selected Essays*, pp. 286, 287.
11. I. A. Richards, *Principles of Literary Criticism*, p. 250.
12. Cleanth Brooks, *The Well Wrought Urn*, pp. 178-9.
13. Samuel Johnson, *The Lives of the English Poets*, p. 31.
14. See Caroline F. E. Spurgeon, *Shakespeare's Imagery and What It Tells Us* (Cambridge: Cambridge University Press, 1935).
15. Oscar James Campbell, 'Shakespeare and the "New" critics', in *Macbeth*, ed. Sylvan Barnet, pp. 227, 228.
16. R. S. Crane, *The Idea of the Humanities and Other Essays Critical and Historical*, vol. 2, pp. 37, 40.
17. See R. S. Crane, 'The critical monism of Cleanth Brooks', in *Critics and Criticism: Ancient and Modern*, ed. R. S. Crane, pp. 83-107.
18. Stanley Fish, *Is There a Text in This Class?*, p. 163.
19. See Geoffrey H. Hartman, *Criticism in the Wilderness*.
20. John M. Ellis, *The Theory of Literary Criticism*, pp. 206-7.
21. Stein Haugom Olsen, *The Structure of Literary Understanding*, p. 146.
22. See W. K. Wimsatt and Monroe Beardsley, 'The intentional fallacy', in Wimsatt, *The Verbal Icon*, pp. 3-18.
23. F. R. Leavis, *Revaluation*, pp. 228-9.
24. John Crowe Ransom, *The New Criticism*, p. 102.
25. Cleanth Brooks, 'Empson's criticism', p. 209.
26. John Crowe Ransom, 'Mr Empson's muddles', pp. 331, 336.
27. Brooks, 'Empson's criticism', pp. 212, 213.
28. F. R. Leavis, *Education and the University*, quoted in 'The literary discipline and liberal education', pp. 596-7.
29. Stanley Edgar Hyman, *The Armed Vision*, p. 247.
30. Kenneth Burke, *Language As Symbolic Action*, p. 498.
31. Kenneth Burke, *The Philosophy of Literary Form*, p. 3.
32. *Ibid.*, pp. 21, 23.
33. Kenneth Burke, *'A Grammar of Motives' and 'A Rhetoric of Motives'*, p. 447.
34. René Wellek, *A History of Modern Criticism: 1750-1950: American Criticism, 1900-50*, p. 239.
35. René Wellek, *A History of Modern Criticism: 1750-1950: English Criticism, 1900-50*, p. 276.
36. For example, Murray Krieger writes in 'An apology for poetics', p. 90:
    Though I may be persuaded about language as the marshalling of arbitrary and differentiated signifiers, I would hold out for the possibility that a single verbal structure can convert its elements so that we read them under the aegis of metaphorical identity with its claim to presence. It is this hold-out claim to what the poem can persuade us its language is doing which ties me

still to the New-Critical tradition despite my concessions to Structuralist theory.

Chapter 3: Hermeneutics

1. *The Hermeneutics Reader*, ed. Kurt Mueller-Vollmer, pp. 86, 90, 95, 96.
2. *Ibid.*, p. 161.
3. E. D. Hirsch, Jr, 'Three dimensions of hermeneutics', p. 247.
4. E. D. Hirsch, Jr. *Validity in Interpretation*, p. 1.
5. Hans-Georg Gadamer, 'The eminent text', pp. 3, 6.
6. Hirsch, 'Three dimensions of hermeneutics', p. 252.
7. *Ibid.*, p. 259. Italics in original.
8. P. D. Juhl, *Interpretation*, pp. 71-2.
9. Steven Knapp and Walter Benn Michaels, 'Against theory', p. 728.
10. *Ibid.*, p. 732.
11. See W. K. Wimsatt, Jr, *The Verbal Icon*, pp. 3-18.
12. T. S. Eliot, *The Sacred Wood*, pp. 49, 50.
13. Juhl, *op. cit.*, p. 148.
14. Paul Ricoeur, *Freud and Philosophy*, pp. 27, 32.
15. *Ibid.*, p. 35.
16. Jürgen Habermas, 'A review of Gadamer's *Truth and Method*', p. 361. Italics in original.
17. For Gadamer's response to Habermas's critique, see his *Philosophical Hermeneutics*, pp. 26-38.

Chapter 4: Against interpretation

1. Susan Sontag, *Against Interpretation and Other Essays*, pp. 7-8.
2. The role of criticism in the institution is discussed in *Criticism in the University*, eds Gerald Graff and Reginald Gibbons.
3. Richard Levin, *New Readings vs Old Plays*, p. 196.
4. Graff and Gibbons, *op. cit.*, p. 71.
5. Stanley Fish, 'Professional anti-professionalism', p. 1363. See also Fish's essay, 'Profession despise thyself: Fear and loathing in literary studies'.
6. Tzvetan Todorov, 'Definition of poetics' in *Introduction to Poetics*, p. 3.
7. Gérard Genette, 'Structuralism and literary criticism', in *Figures of Literary Discourse*, p. 4.
8. Jonathan Culler, 'Beyond interpretation: The prospects of contemporary criticism', p. 246.
9. Jonathan Culler, *On Deconstruction*, pp. 20, 220, 260.
10. Jonathan Culler, *The Pursuit of Signs*, p. 39.
11. Julia Kristeva, 'The system and the speaking subject'.

Chapter 5: Post-structuralism and the question of interpretation

1. Northrop Frye, *Anatomy of Criticism*, pp. 136, 140.
2. Fredric Jameson, *The Political Unconscious*, p. 21.
3. See the discussion of Culler in the previous chapter.
4. David Lodge, 'Deconstruction', p. 25.
5. Jacques Derrida, 'Structure, sign, and play in the discourse of the human sciences', pp. 264–5.
6. M. H. Abrams, 'The deconstructive angel', p. 429.
7. Shoshana Felman, 'Turning the screw of interpretation', p. 185.
8. Jonathan Culler, 'Issues in contemporary American critical debate', p. 3.
9. Paul de Man, *Blindness and Insight*, p. 108.
10. Derrida does not accept de Man's criticism. See his *Mémoires for Paul de Man*, pp. 125ff.
11. Roland Barthes, *Criticism and Truth*, p. 73.
12. Roland Barthes, *S/Z*, p. 3.
13. Barbara Johnson, *The Critical Difference*, p. 5.
14. J. Hillis Miller, *Fiction and Repetition*, p. 1.
15. J. Hillis Miller, 'Stevens' rock and criticism as cure, II', p. 341.
16. *The Structuralist Controversy*, p. 248.
17. Rodolphe Gasché, 'Deconstruction as criticism', p. 207.
18. Christopher Norris, *The Deconstructive Turn*, p. 168.
19. J. Hillis Miller, 'Tradition and difference', pp. 11, 12.
20. Miller is perhaps close to this position. He writes of his own approach to interpretation: 'My enterprise too is a search to locate a ground beyond language for the linguistic patterns present in my poems. Who would not wish to escape the prison house of language and stand where one could see it from the outside?' See J. Hillis Miller, *The Linguistic Moment*, p. xvii.
21. Harold Bloom et al., *Deconstruction and Criticism*, p. ix.
22. Geoffrey H. Hartman, *Criticism in the Wilderness*, pp. 167, 213, 196.
23. Harold Bloom, *The Anxiety of Influence*, pp. 12–13.
24. Harold Bloom, *Poetry and Repression*, pp. 3, 2.
25. Harold Bloom, *A Map of Misreading*, p. 3.
26. Stein Haugom Olsen, *The End of Literary Theory*, pp. 110–18.
27. Vincent B. Leitch, 'Derrida's assault on the institution of style', pp. 23–4.
28. For example, Gerald Graff writes of Derrida's essay in the *Deconstruction and Criticism* volume: 'Though I did focus my eyes on every word of this essay, I cannot deny that my attention was frequently defeated. Derrida's sentences . . . double back on themselves in grotesquely self-consuming contortions.' 'Deconstruction as dogma, or, "Come back to the raft ag'n, Strether honey" ', p. 417. And David Lodge has written: 'Derrida's own late work has become increasingly whimsical, fictive and difficult to methodise.' 'Deconstruction', p. 25.

29. Paul de Man, 'The resistance to theory', p. 7.
20. *Ibid.*, p. 11.
31. See Knapp and Michael's discussion of de Man in 'Against theory', pp. 734–5.
32. Paul de Man, *The Rhetoric of Romanticism*, p. 16.
33. Anne K. Mellor, 'On romantic irony, symbolism and allegory', p. 229. See Jacques Derrida, 'Like the sound of the sea deep within a shell: Paul de Man's war', for further discussion of the relation between de Man's early and later writing.
34. Miller, *The Linguistic Moment*, p. xviii.
35. William V. Spanos, 'Breaking the circle: Hermeneutics as dis-closure', p. 448.
36. William V. Spanos, 'Heidegger, Kierkegaard, and the hermeneutic circle', p. 117.
37. William V. Spanos, 'The detective and the boundary', pp. 150, 154, 155.
38. William V. Spanos, 'The un-naming of the beast: The postmoderning of Sartre's *La Nausée*', p. 231.
39. Spanos, 'The detective and the boundary', p. 164.
40. J. Hillis Miller, 'Deconstructing the deconstructers', p. 31.
41. Joseph N. Riddel. 'A Miller's tale', pp. 61, 63.
42. See *Diacritics*, 6 (1976), pp. 2–7.
43. Edward W. Said, *The World, the Text, the Critic*, p. 4.

Chapter 6: Marxist criticism, cultural materialism, the new historicism

1. Christopher Caudwell, *Illusion and Reality*, pp. 114–15.
2. Pierre Macherey, *A Theory of Literary Production*, p. 7.
3. Stanley Fish, *Is There a Text in This Class?*, p. 355.
4. Terry Eagleton, *Criticism and Ideology*, p. 83.
5. Fredric Jameson, *The Political Unconscious*, p. 58.
6. See Jameson's foreword to Jean-François Lyotard's *The Postmodern Condition*, p. xii.
7. See Louis Althusser, *Lenin and Philosophy and Other Essays*.
8. See 'An interview with Pierre Macherey', *Red Letters*, 5 (1977), pp. 3–9.
9. Terry Eagleton, *Literary Theory: An Introduction*, pp. 200, 205.
10. Terry Eagleton, *William Shakespeare*, pp. ix, 7, 101.
11. Raymond Williams, *Keywords*, p. 28.
12. Raymond Williams, 'Marxism, structuralism and literary analysis', pp. 64–5.
13. Raymond Williams, *Problems in Materialism and Culture*, p. 34.
14. Raymond Williams, *The Country and the City*, p. 113.
15. Jonathan Dollimore, *Radical Tragedy*, pp. 201, 202.

16. Richard Rorty, *Consequences of Pragmatism*, p. 162.
17. Christopher Norris, *The Contest of Faculties*, p. 25. Norris provides a useful account of the foundationalism–anti-foundationalism debate in chapters 1 and 6.
18. Jonathan Dollimore and Alan Sinfield, *Political Shakespeare*, p. viii.
19. Dollimore, *op. cit.*, p. 197.
20. See Stephen Greenblatt, 'Invisible bullets'.
21. Stephen Greenblatt, *Renaissance Self-Fashioning*, pp. 3–4.
22. Stephen Greenblatt, 'Towards a poetics of culture', pp. 13, 14. See also his book *Shakespearean Negotiations*.

Chapter 7: Reception theory and reader-response criticism

1. Hans Robert Jauss, *Toward an Aesthetic of Reception*, p. 11.
2. See Hans Robert Jauss, *Aesthetic Experience and Literary Hermeneutics*.
3. Rein T. Segers, 'An interview with Hans Robert Jauss', p. 84.
4. *Ibid.*, p. 85.
5. Paul de Man, 'Introduction' to *Toward an Aesthetic of Reception*, pp. xvii, xxiii.
6. Wolfgang Iser, 'Indeterminacy and the reader's response in prose fiction', pp. 2, 3, 4.
7. Wolfgang Iser, *The Act of Reading*, p. 18.
8. See 'The mode of existence of a literary work of art', in René Wellek and Austin Warren, *Theory of Literature*, pp. 142–57.
9. Terry Eagleton, *Literary Theory*, p. 79.
10. *Ibid.*, p. 83.
11. Wolfgang Iser, *The Implied Reader*, p. xii.
12. Wolfgang Iser, 'Interview', p. 59.
13. Norman N. Holland, 'Re-covering "The purloined letter" ', p. 356.
14. Norman N. Holland, 'Reading and Identity', pp. 8, 9.
15. Norman N. Holland, 'The miller's wife and the professors', pp. 436, 442.
16. See W. K. Wimsatt and Monroe Beardsley, 'The affective fallacy', in Wimsatt, *The Verbal Icon*, pp. 21–39.
17. Stanley Fish, *Is There a Text in This Class?*, p. 2.
18. Stanley Fish, 'Why no one's afraid of Wolfgang Iser', p. 7.
19. *Ibid.*
20. Stanley Fish, *The Living Temple*, p. 35.
21. Stanley Fish, 'Consequences', p. 437.

Chapter 8: Feminist interpretation

1. Kate Millett, *Sexual Politics*, p. xii.
2. Toril Moi, *Sexual/Textual Politics*, p. 36.
3. Josephine Donovan, 'Feminism and aesthetics', pp. 607, 608.
4. Josephine Donovan, 'Beyond the net: Feminist criticism as a moral criticism', p. 41.
5. Elaine Showalter, 'Towards a feminist poetics', in *Women's Writing and Writing about Women*, ed. Mary Jacobus, p. 27.
6. Elaine Showalter, *A Literature of Their Own*, pp. 107, 112.
7. *Ibid.*, p. 124.
8. Elaine Showalter, 'Feminist criticism in the wilderness', in *The New Feminist Criticism*, ed. Elaine Showalter, p. 260.
9. Jane P. Tompkins, 'Sentimental power: *Uncle Tom's Cabin* and the politics of literary history', in *The New Feminist Criticism*, ed. Elaine Showalter, pp. 82-3.
10. Moi, *op. cit.*, p. 67.
11. Showalter, 'Towards a feminist poetics', p. 38.
12. Showalter, 'Feminist criticism in the wilderness', p. 246.
13. Elizabeth A. Meese, 'Sexual politics and critical judgment', pp. 92, 99, 100.
14. Quoted in Jacqueline Rose, '*Hamlet* – the *Mona Lisa* of literature', p. 36.
15. *Basic Writings of Nietzsche*, p. 702.
16. Catherine Belsey, 'Constructing the subject: Deconstructing the text', pp. 50, 51, 54, 56-7.
17. Catherine Belsey, 'Re-reading the great tradition', p. 122.

Chapter 9: Afterword

1. *Twentieth-Century Literary Theory*, ed. K. M. Newton, pp. 16-17.
2. *Criticism in the University*, pp. 10-11.
3. F. R. Leavis, 'The literary discipline and liberal education', pp. 601, 602, 603, 604.
4. *Shakespeare Reproduced*, eds Jean E. Howard and Marion F. O'Connor, p. 4.
5. Walter Cohen, 'Political criticism of Shakespeare', in *Shakespeare Reproduced*, p. 20.
6. J. Hillis Miller, *The Ethics of Reading*, p. 4.
7. J. Hillis Miller, *The Linguistic Moment*, p. xx.
8. Miller, *The Ethics of Reading*, pp. 4, 6-7, 8.
9. *Ibid.*, p. 7.

Bibliography

Abrams, M. H., *Natural Supernaturalism: Tradition and revolution in Romantic literature* (New York: W. W. Norton, 1973).

Abrams, M. H., 'The deconstructive angel', *Critical Inquiry*, 3 (1977), pp. 425–38.

Althusser, Louis, *Lenin and Philosophy and Other Essays*, trans. Ben Brewster (London: New Left Books, 1971).

Arnold, Matthew, *Essays in Criticism: Second series*, ed. S. R. Littlewood (London: Macmillan, 1960).

Auerbach, Erich, *Mimesis: The representation of reality in western literature*, trans. Willard R. Trask (Princeton: Princeton University Press, 1953).

Barthes, Roland, *S/Z*, trans. Richard Miller (London: Jonathan Cape, 1975).

Barthes, Roland, *Criticism and Truth*, trans. and ed. K. P. Keuneman (London: Athlone Press, 1987).

Belsey, Catherine, 'Re-reading the great tradition', in Peter Widdowson (ed.), *Re-Reading English* (London: Methuen, 1982).

Belsey, Catherine, 'Constructing the subject: Deconstructing the text', in Judith Newton and Deborah Rosenfelt (eds), *Feminist Criticism and Social Change* (New York: Methuen, 1985).

Bloom, Harold, *The Anxiety of Influence* (New York: Oxford University Press, 1973).

Bloom, Harold, *A Map of Misreading* (New York: Oxford University Press, 1975).

Bloom, Harold, *Poetry and Repression* (New Haven: Yale University Press, 1976).

Bloom, Harold, Jacques Derrida, Geoffrey H. Hartman and J. Hillis Miller, *Deconstruction and Criticism* (London: Routledge and Kegan Paul, 1979).

Bowers, Fredson, *Textual and Literary Criticism* (Cambridge: Cambridge University Press, 1959).

Brooks, Cleanth, 'Empson's criticism', *Accent*, 4 (1944), pp. 208–16.

Brooks, Cleanth, *The Well Wrought Urn: Studies in the structure of poetry*, (London: Dennis Dobson, 1949).

Brooks, Cleanth, 'The formalist critic', in G. J. and N. M. Goldberg (eds), *The Modern Critical Spectrum*, (Englewood Cliffs, NJ: Prentice Hall, 1962).

Burke, Kenneth, *The Philosophy of Literary Form: Studies in symbolic action* (New York: Vintage Books, 1957).

Burke, Kenneth, *'A Grammar of Motives'* and *'A Rhetoric of Motives'* (Cleveland: Meridian Books, 1962).

Burke, Kenneth, *Language As Symbolic Action: Essays on life, literature, and method* (Berkeley: University of California Press, 1973).

Campbell, Oscar James, 'Shakespeare and the "new" critics', in Sylvan Barnet (ed.), *Macbeth* (New York: The New American Library, 1963).

Caudwell, Christopher, *Illusion and Reality* (London: Lawrence and Wishart, 1946).

Crane, R. S. 'The critical monism of Cleanth Brooks', in R. S. Crane, (ed.), *Critics and Criticism: Ancient and modern* (Chicago: University of Chicago Press, 1952).

Crane, R. S., *The Idea of the Humanities and Other Essays Critical and Historical*, 2 vols (Chicago: University of Chicago Press, 1967).

Culler, Jonathan, *Structuralist Poetics: Structuralism, linguistics and the study of literature* (London: Routledge and Kegan Paul, 1975).

Culler, Jonathan, 'Beyond interpretation: The prospects of contemporary criticism', *Comparative Literature*, 28 (1976), pp. 244-56.

Culler, Jonathan, 'Issues in contemporary American critical debate', in Ira Konigsberg (ed.), *American Criticism in the Post-Structuralist Age*, Studies in the Humanities (Ann Arbor: University of Michigan, 1981).

Culler, Jonathan, *The Pursuit of Signs: Semiotics, literature, deconstruction* (London: Routledge and Kegan Paul, 1981).

Culler, Jonathan, *On Deconstruction: Theory and criticism after structuralism* (London: Routledge and Kegan Paul, 1983).

de Man, Paul, *Blindness and Insight: Essays in the rhetoric of contemporary criticism* (New York: Oxford University Press, 1971).

de Man, Paul, *Allegories of Reading: Figural language in Rousseau, Nietzsche, Rilke and Proust* (New Haven: Yale University Press, 1979).

de Man, Paul, 'Introduction' to Hans Robert Jauss, *Toward an Aesthetic of Reception*, trans. Timothy Bahti (Brighton: Harvester Press, 1982).

de Man, Paul, 'The resistance to theory', *Yale French Studies*, 63 (1982), pp. 3-20.

de Man, Paul, *The Rhetoric of Romanticism* (New York: Columbia University Press, 1984).

Deleuze, Gilles and Felix Guattari, *Anti-Oedipus: Capitalism and schizophrenia*, trans. Robert Hurley, Mark Seem and Helen R. Lane (New York: Viking Press, 1977).

Derrida, Jacques, 'Structure, sign, and play in the discourse of the human sciences', in Richard Macksey and Eugenio Donato (eds), *The Structuralist Controversy: The languages of criticism and the science of man* (Baltimore: Johns Hopkins University Press, 1972).

Derrida, Jacques, *Of Grammatology*, trans. Gayatri C. Spivak (Baltimore: Johns Hopkins University Press, 1976).

Derrida, Jacques, *Mémoires for Paul de Man*, trans. Cecile Lindsay, Jonathan Culler and Eduardo Cadava (New York: Columbia University Press, 1986).

Derrida, Jacques, 'Like the sound of the sea deep within a shell: Paul de Man's war', *Critical Inquiry*, 14 (1988), pp. 590-652.

Dollimore, Jonathan, *Radical Tragedy: Religion, ideology and power in the drama of Shakespeare and his contemporaries* (Brighton: Harvester Press, 1984).

Dollimore, Jonathan and Alan Sinfield (eds), *Political Shakespeare: New essays in cultural materialism* (Manchester: Manchester University Press, 1985).

Donovan, Josephine, 'Feminism and aesthetics', *Critical Inquiry*, 3 (1977), pp. 605-8.

Donovan, Josephine, 'Beyond the net: Feminist criticism as a moral criticism', *Denver Quarterly*, 17 (1983), pp. 40-57.

Eagleton, Terry, *Criticism and Ideology: A study in marxist literary theory* (London: New Left Books, 1976).

Eagleton, Terry, *Walter Benjamin or Towards a Revolutionary Criticism* (London: Verso and New Left Books, 1981).

Eagleton, Terry, *Literary Theory: An introduction* (Oxford: Basil Blackwell, 1983).

Eagleton, Terry, *William Shakespeare* (Oxford: Basil Blackwell, 1986).

Eliot, T. S., *The Sacred Wood: Essays on poetry and criticism* (London: Methuen, 1960).

Eliot, T. S., *Selected Essays* (London: Faber and Faber, 1976).

Ellis, John M., *The Theory of Literary Criticism: A logical analysis* (Berkeley: University of California Press, 1974).

Felman, Shoshana, 'Turning the screw of interpretation', *Yale French Studies*, 55/56 (1977), pp. 94-207.

Fish, Stanley, *The Living Temple: George Herbert and catechizing* (Berkeley: University of California Press, 1978).

Fish, Stanley, *Is There a Text in This Class? The authority of interpretive communities* (Cambridge, Mass.: Harvard University Press, 1980).

Fish, Stanley, 'Why no one's afraid of Wolfgang Iser?' *Diacritics*, 11 (1981), pp. 2-13.

Fish, Stanley, 'Professional anti-professionalism', *Times Literary Supplement*, 10 December 1982, p. 1363.

Fish, Stanley, 'Profession despise thyself: Fear and loathing in literary studies', *Critical Inquiry*, 10 (1983), pp. 349-64.

Fish, Stanley, 'Consequences', *Critical Inquiry*, 11 (1985), pp. 433-58.

Frank, Joseph, 'Spatial form in modern literature', *Sewanee Review*, 53 (1945), pp. 221-40, 433-45, 643-65.

Frye, Northrop, *Anatomy of Criticism: Four essays* (Princeton: Princeton University Press, 1957).

Gadamer, Hans-Georg, *Philosophical Hermeneutics*, trans. and ed. David E. Linge (Berkeley: University of California Press, 1976).

Gadamer, Hans-Georg, *Truth and Method*, trans. William Glen-Doepel (London: Sheed and Ward, 1979).

Gadamer, Hans-Georg, 'The eminent text', *Bulletin of the Midwest Language Association*, 13 (1980), pp. 3-10.

Gasché, Rodolphe, 'Deconstruction as criticism', *Glyph*, 6 (1979), pp. 177–216.

Genette, Gérard, *Figures of Literary Discourse*, trans. Alan Sheridan (Oxford: Basil Blackwell, 1982).

Gilbert, Sandra M. and Susan Gubar, *The Madwoman in the Attic: The woman writer and the nineteenth-century literary imagination* (New Haven: Yale University Press, 1979).

Graff, Gerald, 'Deconstruction as dogma, or, "come back to the raft ag'n, Strether honey" ', *Georgia Review*, 34 (1980), pp. 404–21.

Graff, Gerald and Reginald Gibbons (eds), *Criticism in the University* (Evanston: Northwestern University Press, 1985).

Greenblatt, Stephen, *Renaissance Self-Fashioning: From More to Shakespeare* (Chicago: University of Chicago Press, 1980).

Greenblatt, Stephen, 'Invisible bullets: Renaissance authority and its subversion', *Glyph*, 8 (1981), pp. 40–61.

Greenblatt, Stephen, 'Towards a poetics of culture', *Southern Review*, 20 (1987), pp. 3–15.

Greenblatt, Stephen, *Shakespearean Negotiations: The circulation of social energy in renaissance England* (Oxford: Clarendon Press, 1988).

Habermas, Jürgen, 'A review of Gadamer's *Truth and Method*', in Fred R. Dallmayr and Thomas McCarthy (eds), *Understanding and Social Inquiry* (Notre Dame: University of Notre Dame Press, 1977).

Hartman, Geoffrey H., *Criticism in the Wilderness: The study of literature today* (New Haven: Yale University Press, 1980).

Hartman, Geoffrey H., *Saving the Text: Literature, Derrida, philosophy* (Baltimore: Johns Hopkins University Press, 1981).

Hirsch, E. D., Jr, *Validity in Interpretation* (New Haven: Yale University Press, 1967).

Hirsch, E. D., Jr, 'Three dimensions of hermeneutics', *New Literary History*, 3 (1971–2), pp. 245–61.

Holland, Norman N., 'Reading and identity: A psychoanalytic revolution', *Academy Forum* (American Academy of Psychoanalysis) 23 (1979), pp. 7–9.

Holland, Norman N., 'Re-covering "The purloined letter": Reading as a personal transaction', in Susan R. Suleiman and Inge Crosman (eds), *The Reader in the Text: Essays on audience and interpretation* (Princeton: Princeton University Press, 1980).

Holland, Norman N., 'The miller's wife and the professors: Questions about the transactive theory of reading', *New Literary History*, 17 (1986), pp. 423–47.

Howard, Jean E. and Marion F. O'Connor (eds), *Shakespeare Reproduced: The text in history and ideology* (New York and London: Methuen, 1987).

Hyman, Stanley Edgar, *The Armed Vision: A study in the methods of modern literary criticism* (New York: Vintage Books, 1955).

Iser, Wolfgang, 'Indeterminacy and the reader's response in prose fiction', in J. Hillis Miller (ed.), *Aspects of Narrative: Selected papers from the English institute* (New York: Columbia University Press, 1971).

Iser, Wolfgang, *The Act of Reading: A theory of aesthetic response* (London:

Routledge and Kegan Paul, 1978).

Iser, Wolfgang, *The Implied Reader: Patterns of communication in prose fiction from Bunyan to Beckett* (Baltimore: Johns Hopkins University Press, 1980).

Iser, Wolfgang, 'Interview', *Diacritics*, 10 (1980), pp. 57–74.

Jacobus, Mary (ed.), *Women's Writing and Writing About Women* (London: Croom Helm, 1979).

Jameson, Fredric, *The Political Unconscious: Narrative as a socially symbolic act* (London: Methuen, 1981).

Jameson, Fredric, 'Foreword' to Jean-François Lyotard, *The Postmodern Condition: A report on knowledge*, trans. Geoff Bennington and Brian Massumi (Manchester: Manchester University Press, 1984).

Jauss, Hans Robert, *Aesthetic Experience and Literary Hermeneutics*, trans. Michael Shaw (Minneapolis: University of Minnesota Press, 1982).

Jauss, Hans Robert, *Toward an Aesthetic of Reception*, trans. Timothy Bahti (Brighton: Harvester Press, 1982).

Jefferson, Ann and David Robey (eds), *Modern Literary Theory: A comparative introduction* (London: Batsford, 1986).

Johnson, Barbara, *The Critical Difference: Essays in the contemporary rhetoric of reading* (Baltimore: Johns Hopkins University Press, 1980).

Johnson, Samuel, *The Lives of the English Poets* (Glasgow: Collins, 1963).

Juhl, P. D., *Interpretation: An essay in the philosophy of literary criticism* (Princeton: Princeton University Press, 1980).

Knapp, Steven and Walter Benn Michaels, 'Against theory', *Critical Inquiry*, 8 (1982), pp. 723–42.

Krieger, Murray, 'An apology for poetics', in Ira Konigsberg (ed.), *American Criticism in the Post-Structuralist Age*, Michigan Studies in the Humanities (Ann Arbor: University of Michigan, 1981).

Kristeva, Julia, 'The system and the speaking subject', *Times Literary Supplement*, 12 October 1973, pp. 1249–50.

Leavis, F. R., 'The literary discipline and liberal education', *Sewanee Review*, 55 (1947), pp. 586–609.

Leavis, F. R., *Revaluation: Tradition and development in English poetry* (Harmondsworth: Penguin, 1972).

Leitch, Vincent B., 'Derrida's assault on the institution of style', *Bucknell Review*, 29 (1985), pp. 17–31.

Lemon, Lee T. and Marion J. Reis (eds), *Russian Formalist Criticism: Four essays* (Lincoln: University of Nebraska Press, 1965).

Levin, Richard, *New Readings vs Old Plays: Recent trends in the interpretation of English renaissance drama* (Chicago: University of Chicago Press, 1979).

Lodge, David, 'Deconstruction', *The Guardian*, 8 April, 1988, p. 25.

Macherey, Pierre, 'An interview with Pierre Macherey', trans. and ed. Colin Mercer and Jean Radford, *Red Letters*, 5 (1977), pp. 3–9.

Macherey, Pierre, *A Theory of Literary Production*, trans. Geoffrey Wall (London: Routledge and Kegan Paul, 1978).

Mazzeo, Joseph Anthony, *Varieties of Interpretation* (Notre Dame: University of Notre Dame Press, 1978).

Meese, Elizabeth A., 'Sexual politics and critical judgment', in Gregory S.

Jay and David L. Miller (eds), *After Strange Texts: The role of theory in the study of literature* (Alabama: University of Alabama Press, 1985).

Mellor, Anne K., 'On romantic irony, symbolism and allegory', *Criticism*, 21 (1979), pp. 217–29.

Miller, J. Hillis, 'Tradition and difference', *Diacritics*, 2 (1972), pp. 6–13.

Miller, J. Hillis, 'Deconstructing the deconstructers', *Diacritics*, 5 (1975), pp. 24–31.

Miller, J. Hillis, 'Stevens' rock and criticism as cure, II', *Georgia Review*, 30 (1976), pp. 330–48.

Miller, J. Hillis, *Fiction and Repetition: Seven English novels* (Oxford: Basil Blackwell, 1982).

Miller, J. Hillis, *The Linguistic Moment: From Wordsworth to Stevens* (Princeton: Princeton University Press, 1985).

Miller, J. Hillis, *The Ethics of Reading: Kant, de Man, Eliot, Trollope, James and Benjamin* (New York: Columbia University Press, 1987).

Millett, Kate, *Sexual Politics* (London: Sphere Books, 1972).

Moi, Toril, *Sexual/Textual Politics: Feminist literary theory* (London: Methuen, 1985).

Mueller-Vollmer, Kurt (ed.), *The Hermeneutics Reader: Texts of the German tradition from the enlightenment to the present*, (Oxford: Basil Blackwell, 1986).

Newton, K. M., *In Defence of Literary Interpretation: Theory and practice* (London: Macmillan, 1986).

Newton, K. M. (ed.), *Twentieth-Century Literary Theory: A reader* (Basingstoke: Macmillan, 1988).

Nietzsche, Friedrich, *Basic Writings of Nietzsche*, trans. Walter Kaufmann (New York: The Modern Library, 1968).

Norris, Christopher, *The Deconstructive Turn: Essays in the rhetoric of philosophy* (London: Methuen, 1983).

Norris, Christopher, *The Contest of Faculties: Philosophy and theory after deconstruction* (London: Methuen, 1985).

Norris, Christopher, 'Post-structuralist Shakespeare: Text and ideology', in John Drakakis (ed.), *Alternative Shakespeares* (London: Methuen, 1985).

Olsen, Stein Haugom, *The Structure of Literary Understanding* (Cambridge: Cambridge University Press, 1978).

Olsen, Stein Haugom, *The End of Literary Theory* (Cambridge: Cambridge University Press, 1987).

Ransom, John Crowe, 'Mr Empson's muddles', *Southern Review*, 4 (1938–9), pp. 322–39.

Ransom, John Crowe, *The New Criticism* (Norfolk, Conn.: New Directions, 1941).

Ricoeur, Paul, *Freud and Philosophy: An essay on interpretation* (New Haven: Yale University Press, 1978).

Richards, I. A., *Practical Criticism: A study of literary judgment* (London: Routledge and Kegan Paul, 1964).

Richards, I. A., *Poetries and Science: A reissue of 'Science and Poetry' (1926, 1935) with commentary* (London: Routledge and Kegan Paul, 1970).

Richards, I. A., *Principles of Literary Criticism* (London: Routledge and

Kegan Paul, n.d).

Riddel, Joseph N., 'A Miller's tale', *Diacritics*, 5 (1975), pp. 56–65.

Rorty, Richard, *Consequences of Pragmatism: Essays: 1972–1980* (Brighton: Harvester Press, 1982).

Rose, Jacqueline, '*Hamlet* – the *Mona Lisa* of Literature', *Critical Quarterly*, 28, nos 1 and 2 (1986), pp. 35–49.

Said, Edward W., *Beginnings: Intention and method* (Baltimore: Johns Hopkins University Press, 1975).

Said, Edward W., *Orientalism* (London: Routledge and Kegan Paul, 1978).

Said, Edward W., *The World, the Text, the Critic* (London: Faber and Faber, 1984).

Segers, Rein T., 'An interview with Hans Robert Jauss', trans. Timothy Bahti, *New Literary History*, 11 (1979), pp. 83–95.

Shakespeare, William, *Hamlet*, ed. J. Dover-Wilson (Cambridge: Cambridge University Press, 1964).

Shakespeare, William, *Hamlet*, ed. Harold Jenkins (London: Methuen, 1982).

Shakespeare, William, *Hamlet*, ed. G. R. Hibbard (Oxford: Oxford University Press, 1987).

Showalter, Elaine, *A Literature of Their Own: British women novelists from Brontë to Lessing* (Princeton: Princeton University Press, 1977).

Showalter, Elaine (ed.) *The New Feminist Criticism: Essays on women, literature, and theory* (London: Virago, 1986).

Snukal, Robert, *High Talk: The philosophical poetry of W. B. Yeats* (Cambridge: Cambridge University Press, 1973).

Sontag, Susan, *Against Interpretation and Other Essays* (London: Eyre and Spottiswoode, 1967).

Spanos, William V., 'The detective and the boundary: Some notes on the postmodern literary imagination', *boundary 2*, 1 (1972), pp. 147–68.

Spanos, William V., 'Heidegger, Kierkegaard, and the hermeneutic circle', *boundary 2*, 4 (1976), pp. 115–48.

Spanos, William V., 'Breaking the circle: Hermeneutics as dis-closure', *boundary 2*, 5 (1977), pp. 421–57.

Spanos, William V., 'The un-naming of the beasts: The postmodernity of Sartre's *La Nausée*', *Criticism*, 20 (1978), pp. 223–80.

Todorov, Tzvetan, *Introduction to Poetics*, trans. Richard Howard (Brighton: Harvester Press, 1981).

Trevor-Roper, Hugh, 'Sir Walter Scott and history', *The Listener*, 19 August 1971, pp. 225–32.

Wellek, René, *A History of Modern Criticism: 1750–1950: American criticism, 1900–1950* (London: Jonathan Cape, 1986).

Wellek, René, *A History of Modern Criticism: 1750–1950: English criticism, 1900–1950* (London: Jonathan Cape, 1986).

Wellek, René and Austin Warren, *Theory of Literature* (Harmondsworth: Penguin, 1966).

Williams, Raymond, *The Country and the City* (London: Chatto and Windus, 1973).

Williams, Raymond, *Marxism and Literature* (Oxford: Oxford University

Press, 1977).

Williams, Raymond, *Keywords: A vocabulary of culture and society* (Glasgow: Fontana/Croom Helm, 1979).

Williams, Raymond, *Problems in Materialism and Culture: Selected essays* (London: Verso and New Left Books, 1980).

Williams, Raymond, 'Marxism, structuralism and literary analysis', *New Left Review*, 129 (1981), pp. 51–66.

Wimsatt, W. K. Jr, *The Verbal Icon: Studies in the meaning of poetry* (New York: Noonday Press, 1964).

Index